D0113826

21-5

BIOGRAPHY AS AN ART

Selected Criticism 1560-1960

BIOGRAPHY AS AN ART

Selected Criticism 1560-1960

Edited by James L. Clifford

A Galaxy Book

New York OXFORD UNIVERSITY PRESS 1962

Barry College Library
Miami, Florida

©Oxford University Press, 1962

First published as a Galaxy Book, 1962

PRINTED IN THE UNITED STATES OF AMERICA

82945

-55

CONTENTS

INTRODUCTION

Unlike poetry, fiction, and the drama, biography has never been the subject of intense critical study. Even today, when the climate of opinion is favourable, the number of books and articles devoted to the problems involved in writing a life is slight when compared to the thousands which concentrate on the other genres. A customary explanation is that literary criticism has to do largely with the process of creation, and that biography is essentially not creative. Yet today any such claim is sure to be followed by an immediate denial.

What, really, is a biographer? Is he merely a superior kind of journalist, or must he be an artist? Is writing a life a narrow branch of history or a form of literature? Or may it be something in between, a strange amalgam of science and art? The difference between a craftsman and an artist is obvious. The one knows exactly what his product will be. He works with specific materials and uses traditional techniques. His skill comes as a result of serious study and long practice. The other works intuitively, evolving each move that he makes, and not certain until the end just what his work will be. Originality and genius are more important than practice. Is the life-writer one or the other, or both?

Because of this uncertainty as to the very nature of biography there has been a tendency to ignore it as a major division of literature. Critics have shied away from what seemed to them the province of the historian, and historians have been more interested in broader problems. Little thought has been given to the proper requirements for writing a life, that is, in addition to industry and skill in composition. Often in the past it was assumed that little more was involved than finding all the available evidence, deciding what was suitable to print, and then fitting it into an agreeable narrative.

Today, with a wide stirring of curiosity about human motives and an increasing interest in the ways and means by which they may be exemplified, literary critics are at last devoting more attention to biography. To be sure, it would be going too far to say that only in the twentieth century has there been much significant criticism of this genre. At various periods of the past there has been an intense interest in the writing of lives and some curiosity about the difficulties faced by the author. But not until our day has there been any widespread discussion of the complex psychological and artistic problems involved in the re-creation of character. It is surely significant that almost half of the present collection is made up of selections from the past forty years. Moreover, for the modern section a mass of interesting material could have been added, though the editor would have found it difficult to discover other observations of equal importance during the preceding four centuries. At the risk of obvious oversimplification, it is still possible to say that biography, as a literary genre, is a relatively modern topic.

The earliest biographers in England had little curiosity about the nature of their art. They knew what they had to do, and did it. Their purpose was edification. Their justification was the glory of God, through the praise of His saints. Describing a truly holy person, their works would succeed or fail to the extent to which they taught Christian virtue and strengthened wavering faith. They had no conceivable desire to create rounded characters. Indeed, such an ideal would have horrified any self-respecting hagiographer. A saint or a king was obviously set apart from ordinary folk, and it was the duty and the prerogative of the writer to emphasize these differences.

It was well understood also that a hagiographer need not be bound by the tyranny of fact. In the middle of the ninth century Agnellus, Bishop of Ravenna, when completing a series of lives of his predecessors in that see, openly confessed that when he had been unable to obtain any detailed information concerning them—either from oral tradition, records, or any authentic source—'In order that there might not be a break in the series, I have composed the life myself, with the help of God and the prayers of the brethren.'[1] Divine revelation could fill in where historical records were scarce.

That these biographers conformed to well-established patterns is evident. Most important for each work was a list of the saint's miraculous powers, together with a rapturous account of his many memorable deeds. Personal appearance, family relationships, his inner thoughts or occasional doubts, naturally had no place in the picture. The saint's value as a model depended on his aloofness from human weakness and frailty. The result was generalized biography, albeit often literature of a very high quality.

[1] G. G. Coulton, *Medieval Panorama* (1938), 439.

All this can be deduced from the many lives of the saints which have survived. If the individual hagiographers ever thought deeply about their problems, or ever speculated concerning the nature of their profession, they did not set their musings down, and it is difficult to find anywhere a significant contemporary analysis of their craft. Where there is little difference of opinion as to aims and techniques, there is unlikely to be any searching criticism.

Similarly, the value of praising great men was an accepted fact. If one wanted instruction as to how to do it well, the rhetoricians were there with good advice. For example, Thomas Wilson in the sixteenth century lists the precise steps to be taken, and from the tone of his remarks there is almost an implied guarantee of success to the careful imitator. The desire for generalized characterization found support in the Theophrastian character. Again, it is not clear how much the character-writers theorized about their methods. With admired classical models easily available, why worry further? For them it was enough to imitate what had venerable authority.

Until the seventeenth century, then, there was not much critical interest in the problems of life-writing, and even then most biographers —even the admirable Izaak Walton—were content to hold to the old accepted traditions. But gradually with the increasing stress on the individual which accompanied the Reformation, and with the rise of scientific empiricism, there was more curiosity about the mainsprings of human character. Not that there was any sudden revolution of taste, or any exciting emergence of psychological portraiture. But at least new questions began to be asked. What ethical justification is there for printing a man's private correspondence? Should his sins and chief weaknesses be revealed? Can there be any excuse for including little homely details in a formal biography? Is the life of a simple, common man worth describing? And what are the pressures which force a biographer into devious trails of suppression and lying?

With Sprat and Aubrey, Burnet and Dryden, Toland and Addison, the main problems, finally, began to be faced, though no one, not even Dryden, the father of modern literary criticism, was moved to write at length on the nature of biography. Perhaps even if he had been so inclined he would have done nothing about it, for there was little public interest. It is now clear that one practising biographer in the early eighteenth century did think deeply about his craft, and did write a long analysis of the problems involved. This man was Roger

North. Yet, although his lively accounts of his three brothers were published shortly after his death, his ruminations on the art of life-writing, intended as an Introduction, have never been published. Indeed, until very recently they were not even known to exist. For that reason some details concerning their history may not be out of place.

Among the great mass of surviving manuscripts of Roger North now in the British Museum there are various versions of the lives of his brothers, used by his son Montagu North when preparing the rigorously edited first editions in 1742 and 1744. But an earlier manuscript of the life of the Lord Keeper had been separated from the rest, and finally came to rest in the Library of St. John's College, Cambridge. Prefixed to this are two versions of what was called a 'General Preface'. Just when these were written cannot with certainty be established, but the probability is that it was sometime during the second or third decade of the eighteenth century. North himself died in 1734.

By any standards the Preface is a remarkable document, but considering the state of biographical criticism at the time, it is outstanding. Perhaps most astonishing of all is North's anticipation of the later work of Johnson and Boswell (there is no evidence that the manuscript was ever seen by either). Many of the points which Johnson was to make in his *Rambler* and *Idler* essays were made by North in his private jottings over thirty years earlier. And most of his requirements for the perfect biographer were to be fulfilled by James Boswell.

Like Johnson, Roger North preferred the lives of ordinary individuals to general history, and argued that any man's life, no matter how unexciting on the surface, could be made interesting. He stressed the importance of the fullest coverage of private concerns. And throughout he insisted on the necessity for truth and impartiality. Like Johnson, too, he was oppressed by the deficiencies of his contemporaries who claimed to be writing biography. His criterion of judgement, to be sure, was not revolutionary. It was moral instruction he looked for, as well as entertainment. 'What signifies it to us,' North wrote, 'how many battles Alexander fought. It were more to the purpose to say how often he was drunk, and then we might from the ill consequences to him incline to be sober.' His comments throughout are as fresh and entertaining as on the day they were written.

Unfortunately North had no influence on later criticism whatsoever, and it is perhaps ironic to remember that the manuscript over which he slaved so carefully was to lie unnoticed for over two centuries, while the kind of writing he longed to see was slowly becoming popular. It was Samuel Johnson, instead, and his disciple James Boswell who came to be thought of as the progenitors of modern biography. And rightly so, for Boswell's superiority over all his predecessors and rivals was so great that he set a pattern which remained supreme for well over a century.

Not that Boswell invented any new techniques. Rather, he showed triumphantly what could be done by skilfully adapting what had been indifferently used by his predecessors—the inclusion of personal letters, of anecdotes and actual conversations—and he proved the value, when fashioning the living image of a great man, of combining assiduity, candour, and a keen dramatic sense. That he was a conscious artist, his surviving manuscripts leave no doubt. Always with the reader in mind, he was continually striving to achieve specific effects. To be sure, his was the empirical method, based upon a slow accumulation of evidence, with only occasional flashes of interpretation. Yet his account was made unforgettable by his colourful reporting of actual scenes in which his subject participated.

The very nature of Boswell's success created major problems for those who followed. It was as a recorder of conversation that he excelled, and it was this part of his formula which became the despair of those who tried to imitate him. Without his genius and determination, and, for the most part, lacking a similarly quotable subject, how could they produce comparable effects? Repeated failures gradually led to a sceptical attitude as to the possibility of re-creating accurately the talk of another person. Thus Lockhart went so far as to reject, in effect, the whole Boswellizing process. Moreover, the general shift of sensibility which resulted in what we call the Romantic Movement, while it brought an increased emphasis on human character (it was, so Coleridge insisted, 'the age of personality'), brought also fundamental changes which ran counter to the Boswellian assumptions. From an emphasis on complete factual truth, there was more stress on emotions and feelings. With poetry looking inward to the soul, there was more of a tendency to think of the biographer as an artist, rather than as an unemotional historian. Yet counter to this was the gradual development of a more straight-laced, prudish attitude towards sex and passion, which meant an increasing fear of indecent probing into personal actions and motives. Sympathy was desired, not frankness. With complete sympathy, of course, came hero-worship, and the natural result was a succession of unrevealing eulogies and ponderous tomes, totally lacking in any intention to tell the whole truth.

All these conflicting pressures are apparent in the arguments of the early nineteenth-century critics—in Wordsworth's caution about the biographer's breaking through 'many pre-existing delicacies' and his doubts about the publication of private correspondence—in Coleridge's attack on 'the cravings of worthless curiosity'—in James Stanfield's warning about the indiscriminate acceptance of particulars. Biography had obviously become a threat as well as a wholesome entertainment. On the one hand, it was welcomed because it concentrated on human affairs, and on the other, it was deprecated because it tended to invade the realms of personal privacy.

Criticism, at last, had found problems in biography not easy to solve. Even for the most ardent admirers of Boswell it was obvious that one could not in the nineteenth century merely imitate his technique. Some modification was necessary. But what? Here there was ample room for argument. In 1813 James Field Stanfield, a former actor and traveller, published the first full-scale book on biography, some 360 pages in all. Produced at Sunderland, instead of by one of the usual London publishers, his *An Essay on the Study and Composition of Biography* caused little stir at the time, and is now something of a rarity. Yet despite a deadening, monotonous style, it is historically an important work—the earliest critical study of the subject, in which the qualities of a good biographer are considered and the difficulties he faces thoroughly discussed. It is easy to emphasize its defects. As a contemporary, John Foster, pointed out, Stanfield overplayed the magnitude of his task, was ostentatious in throwing out philosophic generalizations, and in the latter part of the book, in which he developed an extensive plan for the writing of biography, was much too arbitrary and mechanical. Still, under the mass of words and the pomposity, one can see that Stanfield did face most of the important problems, and face them intelligently.

While Stanfield was the most pretentious of the early nineteenth-century critics of biography, there were others who were seriously concerned with the topic. In 1810 Coleridge discussed it in his periodical *The Friend*, and in 1818 J. L. Adolphus printed a prize essay on biography delivered at Oxford. Carlyle, Lockhart, Allan Cunningham,

Croker, and others had significant comments to add. With lives all 'the rage', so Tom Moore scornfully remarked, criticism haltingly followed in their train.

For later nineteenth-century critics the dominant concerns were ethical. How much should a biographer reveal of his subject's private life? Should he tell all he knew? Or should he draw a veil over moral lapses and foolish actions? In other words, what rights did the dead have? Doubtless Margaret Oliphant and Charles Whibley represented the opinion of most observers that some reticence was necessary, but there was by no means wholehearted agreement. In theory, at least, the doctrine that truth counted more than injured feelings had stubborn adherents, and with the turn of the century they became more vociferous. Edmund Gosse, indeed, may be taken as the leader of the movement towards a freer attitude. But it was not until the first world war, and the advent of Lytton Strachey, that the modern world of biography made its appearance.

If Boswell's is the name always to be reckoned with by nineteenth-century critics, Strachey's is the one which dominates the first half of the twentieth. Although Gamaliel Bradford, with his 'psychographs', had anticipated some revolutionary approaches, it was the ironic brilliance of Strachey which tended to set the new tone. His *Eminent Victorians* in 1918 came as a shock and a tremendous impetus. In the tide of disillusionment of the 1920s, with a spirit of irreverence and idol-breaking in the air, Strachey provided an irresistible model.

It is easy today to insist that he should not be held wholly to blame for the scandalous excesses perpetrated by those who called him master. But he cannot be wholly absolved, for there can be no doubt of the historical importance of his short preface to the volume of devastating Victorian portraits—with its insistence on brevity, on careful selection of colourful details, on emancipation from reverence, and on the use of ironic wit. In all subsequent arguments about the defects and merits of the 'New Biography' Strachey became the crucial symbol of modernism. For sober historians he was the obvious whipping-boy, since it was not difficult to show, through laboured accumulation of detail, how his selective method tended to distort the whole truth. Indeed, even such a close friend as Virginia Woolf was not oblivious to certain limitations in his technique. On the other hand, the overwhelming brilliance of his style and the bland certainty of his characterizations were difficult to resist. Hundreds who lacked his rigorous discipline and his conception of art dashed off raucous 'debunking' lives which were as false to life as had been the pious eulogies of their grandfathers.

It was not Strachey, however, who was the leader in the new criticism of biography. He served more as an example than as an analytical commentator. It remained for others to formulate the Rules. Practising biographers, notably André Maurois, Emil Ludwig, Sir Harold Nicolson, Virginia Woolf, and Lord David Cecil, thought deeply about their problems and published perceptive comments. In belligerent opposition were the research historians; and the outraged blast by Bernard DeVoto, included later in this volume, is merely a sample of the complete difference of opinion which split readers and critics during this period.

In this historic debate of the 1920s and 1930s the chief argument centred on the question of whether biography was intrinsically an art or a craft. Not that this was a new theme. All through the preceding century there had been talk about the biographer as artist—witness the enlightened remarks of an anonymous writer in the *Southern Literary Messenger*, published in Richmond, Virginia, in 1856. But for Victorian critics there was no thought of giving the artist complete freedom. Even the most adventurous theorizers agreed that the biographer was subject to obvious rigid restrictions, as well as reticences.

There was a much sharper division of opinion among the writers of the post-war generation. For Strachey, for Ludwig and Maurois, no reservations were possible: biography was a delicate art, demanding of its practitioners creative gifts of the same sort as those of the novelist and poet. For DeVoto, the biographer was essentially 'a harassed man who sweats his life out in libraries, court-houses, record offices, vaults, newspaper morgues, and family attics'. Others apparently vacillated, or tried to find an intermediate position. In 1927 Virginia Woolf called the modern biographer an artist, yet twelve years later regretfully concluded that he was essentially a craftsman, though obviously a valuable one. Biography is a juggler's art, so James Flexner insisted, based upon one's skill in combining things seemingly irreconcilable—fact and imagination, scholarship and dramatic skill—keeping the bright balls circling around one's head without colliding or falling to the floor.

On and on go the arguments, ranging from the flamboyant claim of Frank Harris that biography is the supreme art of all, since it can do what no other can do, portray the whole spirit of man, to the feeling of George Santayana that the less we know about the life of an author, the better. If nothing ever was settled, at least the differences were brought into the open. In the hands of some of the ablest writers of the time biographical criticism reached full stature [for a list of the more important books and essays published since 1900 see Appendix].

In the sharp debate of the third and fourth decades of the twentieth century there was often the implied conviction that art and pure history were irreconcilable. If I read the signs aright, the emphasis during the 1940s and 1950s has slowly changed. As one may see in the remarks of C. V. Wedgwood and others, there is more talk about the art of history, and less about scientific objectivity, perhaps from a clearer understanding of human motivation and new definitions of objectivity. And on the other side there is more realization of the dangers of uncontrolled creativity. The opponents appear to be coming together.

Among practising biographers there is increasing discussion of the problems of evaluating evidence, with obviously less certainty that factual truth can be easily discovered. Take, for example, the analysis by Marchette Chute of the details of Sir Philip Sidney's death, or Jacques Barzun's insistence on the dangers of using isolated facts without properly relating them to the nature of genius, or the discussion by the Marchesa Iris Origo of Mrs. Carlyle and the silk dress. Details must always be related to larger patterns.

Most of us now accept the fact that all biographies need not conform to a single set of standards, that quite legitimately there are different kinds of life-writing, each with its own possibilities and rules. There will always be the traditional scholarly compilations and the completely fictionalized lives, but between these two extremes we now have a variety of modulations. There is the bibliographical approach, so excellently described by Boswell's modern editor, Frederick A. Pottle; and there are brief psychographs and expertly fashioned ironical profiles. Moreover, we have developed a new kind of study made up almost entirely of background, in the manner of Marchette Chute, and smooth-flowing accounts like those of Catherine Drinker Bowen, which, while based on exhaustive research, attempt to fuse the evidence into a straight-forward narrative.

But what may be the most significant recent trend is what may simply be called the domestication of psychology. In the earlier part of the century Freudian complexes were like new mechanical gadgets —displayed crassly for their own sake, with little thought for the whole effect. Although at times they are still used insensitively, there is a growing tendency among sound scholars to search for what is valuable in the psychological techniques and to use them with caution. The modern biographer is expected to be fully grounded in psychiatric theory, but not to parade his knowledge through the use of technical jargon.

Perhaps the most subtle influence of the new psychology appears far below the surface in an increased awareness of the complex relationship of the biographer and his subject. The old terms, disciple or debunker, are much too simple. Today it would be unlikely for a writer to hate his subject without being aware of some of the sources of his dislike which are embedded in his own character and background. And conversely he is apt to be suspicious of any overweening adoration of his hero. The result is that he is increasingly reluctant to take an extreme position, and we are getting fewer examples of pure eulogy or violent hate. Instead of making his subject fit some preconceived pattern of nobility or villainy, the scrupulous modern biographer carefully studies his own motives at the same time as he is describing the other's. Rather than ignore qualities which seem out of place, or which he dislikes, he now attempts to present them in such a manner that the reader, too, will be able to judge of their significance. No longer is he willing to censor, or to excuse, or consciously to rationalize. Although he may suggest patterns and unifying themes, he is careful to let the reader see what he is doing. The picture he presents may sometimes be more ambiguous than those of his predecessors, but this increase of caution is a sign of maturity in the art. Certainly, a biographer's constant awareness of the intricate paradoxes not only in his subject, but also in himself, tends to produce more satisfying three-dimensional lives.

Moreover, if Leon Edel may be taken as characteristic of the newer type of critic of biography, the next decades should see a broadening of the whole genre. Still the old questions will be asked—on ethics, on the rights of the dead, on the nature of truth, on the proper evaluation of evidence, on the relation of life-writing to fiction—but there will be new queries having to do with the reasons behind the biographer's selection of material. As we grow more and more aware that every choice of a passage to be quoted involves a personal decision which is motivated by all the psychological factors which have formed the biographer's own personality and opinions, the complexities involved in the whole process of writing a life become more apparent. And with awareness should come deeper understanding and appreciation.

When this collection was first conceived, the plan was to group selections according to themes, emphasizing the major problems, which, as we have seen, have dominated critical discussions for three centuries. In theory excellent, the plan proved impossible to execute. How could one classify an essay in which all the major themes were touched upon? To split literary masterpieces into small snippets was unthinkable, and besides, bewildering to the reader. Furthermore, the chronological method does have one distinct advantage: its use makes clear the slow development of attitudes and theories, and permits an earlier writer to be evaluated as part of a well-recognized general sensibility. Since a critic often changes his mind about individual books, as well as his overall point of view, it would be palpably unfair to quote from an early work as if it represented his mature verdict. Furthermore, to put it in its proper place, along with other contemporary pieces, emphasizes the fact that certain cleavages have always been with us. The ethical problem of the biographer, faced with the decision of what he may decently tell, was as difficult to solve in the seventeenth century as in the twentieth. But today, with the rise of Freudian psychology, it is even more complicated.

No one can deny that a rigorously chronological arrangement has defects, since it precludes the grouping of analogous approaches, and compels the reader to make his own classification of themes. Granted, too, that this method is apt to result in annoying repetition of ideas. Nevertheless, the orderly historical sequence does seem preferable. In the following pages the selections are thus roughly arranged either by strict order of publication, or, when works were not in print until long after they were written, by order of apparent composition. Works by the same author, however, appear together under the earliest date.

Ideally, an editor should present each piece of evidence complete and uncensored. But for such a survey as this, covering many centuries, some principle of condensation and selection is essential. To include everything intact would require an entire shelf of volumes. Therefore, at the risk of vehement denunciations by irate reviewers, many essays are here represented merely by short excerpts; others have lengthy passages omitted. Where there are omissions inside longer works, the excisions are indicated by the usual symbols.[1] Even with much cutting, it has been impossible to avoid repetition. Yet there may be a kind of morbid fascination in watching different authors struggle with the same problems, phrasing and rephrasing the same basic ideas.

Despite numerous obligations to scholars and friends in Great Britain and the United States who have generously helped with advice and encouragement, the editor must finally take sole responsibility for each individual choice and omission. Why, one may ask, include so-and-so, and not what's-his-name? The latter is much more significant, and by far the better writer. Why leave out the very best passages in John Doe's essay? Why omit discussions of autobiography altogether? There can be only one answer. At one time or another, the choice seemed legitimate and necessary. Another editor, faced with the same body of material, would undoubtedly produce an entirely different volume. At least it is hoped that from the following selections a reader in the latter half of the twentieth century will be able to achieve some understanding of the slow rise, and the gradual maturing, of the criticism of biography.

[1] Four dots are used to indicate omissions ranging from a sentence to a number of paragraphs. Except in a few instances, capitalization and spelling have been normalized to modern practice. Easy reading has been stressed rather than strict conformity to original eccentricities of typography and printing styles.

ACKNOWLEDGEMENTS

In addition to those whose essays are included in this volume, I am indebted to various friends and colleagues who have given timely suggestions. It is obviously impossible to name all who have responded to queries and requests, but I should like at least to express deep appreciation for the help of the following: Herman Ausubel, John R. B. Brett-Smith, Donald J. Greene, Frances L. Hanson, Francis R. Hart, Allen T. Hazen, Joseph H. Iglehart, R. W. Ketton-Cremer, William Nelson, Eleanor Louise Nicholes, Joseph Reed, and Edward Ruhe. Special thanks are due to Richard D. Altick, who has throughout given valuable aid, and to my wife, who has assisted at every stage.

BIOGRAPHY AS AN ART

Selected Criticism 1560 - 1960

Before 1700

Thomas Wilson

* Now in praising a noble personage, and in setting forth at large his worthiness: Qintilian giveth warning, to use this threefold order.

To observe things. { Before this life. / In his life. / After his death. }

Before a man's life, are considered these places.

{ The realm.
The shire.
The town.
The parents.
The ancestors. }

In a man's life, praise must be parted threefold. That is to say, into the gifts of good things of the mind, the body, and of fortune. Now the gifts of the body and of fortune, are not praiseworthy of their own nature: but even as they are used, either to or fro, so they are either praised, or dispraised. Gifts of the mind deserve the whole tromp and sound commendation above all other, wherein we may use the rehearsal of virtues, as they are in order, and beginning at his infancy, tell all his doings till his last age.

* From *The Art of Rhetoric* (1560); reprinted, ed. G. H. Mair (1909), pp. 11–14, 178–9.

The places whereof are these

The birth, and infancy.		Whether the person be a man, or a woman.
The childhood.		The bringing up, the nurturing, and the behaviour of his life.
The stripling age, or spring-tide.	Whereunto are referred these.	To what study he taketh himself unto, what company he useth, how he liveth.
The man's state.		Prowess done, either abroad, or at home.
The old age.		His policies and witty devices, in behalf of the public weal.
The time of his departure, or death.		Things that have happened about his death.

Now to open all these places more largely, as well those that are before a man's life, as such as are in his life, and after his death, that the reader may further see the profit will I do the best I can.

The house whereof a noble personage came, declares the state and natures of his ancestors, his alliance, and his kinfolk. So that such worthy feats as they have heretofore done, and all such honours as they have had for such their good service, redounds wholly to the increase and amplifying of his honour, that is now living.

The realm declares the nature of the people. So that some country bringeth more honour with it, than an other doth. To be a French man, descending there of a noble house, is more honour than to be an Irish man: To be an English man born, is much more honour than to be a Scot, because that by these men, worthy prowesses have been done, and greater affairs by them attempted, than have been done by any other.

The shire or town helpeth somewhat, towards the increase of honour: as it is much better to be born in Paris, than in Picardy: in London than in Lincoln. For that both the air is better, the people more civil, and the wealth much greater, and the men for the most part more wise.

To be born a manchild, declares a courage, gravity, and constancy. To be born a woman, declares weakness of spirit, neshness of body, and fickleness of mind.

Now, for the bringing up of a noble personage, his nurse must be considered, his play fellows observed, his teacher and other his servants called in remembrances. How every one of these lived then, with whom they have lived afterwards, and how they live now.

By knowing what he taketh himself unto, and wherein he most delighteth, I may commend him for his learning, for his skill in the French, or in the Italian, for his knowledge in cosmography: for his skill in the laws, in the histories of all countries, and for his gift of enditing. Again, I may commend him for playing at weapons, for running upon a great horse, for charging his staff at the tilt, for vaulting, for playing upon instruments, yea, and for painting, or drawing of a plat, as in old time noble princes much delighted therein.

Prowess done, declare his service to the King, and his country, either in withstanding the outward enemy, or else in aswaging the rage of his own countrymen at home.

His wise counsel, and good advice given, sets forth the goodness of his wit.

At the time of his departing, his sufferance of all sickness, may much commend his worthiness. As his strong heart, and cheerful patience even to the end, cannot want great praise. The love of all men towards him, and the lamenting generally for his lack, help well most highly to set forth his honour.

After man's death, are considered his tomb, his coat armour set up, and all such honours as are used in funerals.

If any one list to put these precepts in practice, he may do as him liketh best. And surely I do think, that nothing so much furthereth knowledge as daily exercise, and enuring our selves to do that in deed, which we know in word. . . .

[Diversity of natures]

And not only are matters set out by description, but men are painted out in their colours, yea, buildings are set forth, kingdoms and realms are portured, places and times are described. The Englishman for feeding and changing for apparel. The Dutchman for drinking. The Frenchman for pride and inconstance. The Spaniard for nimbleness of body, and much disdain: the Italian for great wit and policy: the Scots for boldness, and the Boeme for stubbornness.

Many people are described by their degree, as a man of good years, is counted sober, wise, and circumspect: a young man wild and careless: a woman babbling, inconstant, and ready to believe all that is told her.

By vocation of life, a soldier is counted a great bragger, and a vaunter of himself: a scholar simple: a russet coat, sad, and sometimes crafty: a courtier, flattering: a citizen, gentle.

In describing of persons, there ought always a comeliness to be used, so that nothing be spoken, which may be thought is not in them. As if one shall describe Henry the sixth, he might call him gentle, mild of nature, led by persuasion, and ready to forgive, careless for wealth, suspecting none, merciful to all, fearful in adversity, and without forecast to espy his misfortune. Again, for Richard the third, I might bring him in, cruel of heart, ambitious by nature, envious of mind, a deep dissembler, a close man for weighty matters, hardy to revenge, and fearful to lose his high estate, trusty to none, liberal for a purpose, casting still the worst, and hoping ever the best. By this figure also we imagine a talk, for some one to speak, and according to his person, we frame the oration. As if one should bring in noble Henry the eight, of most famous memory to inveigh against rebels, thus he might order his oration. What if Henry the eight were alive, and saw such rebellion in his realm, would not he say thus, and thus? Yea, me thinks I hear him speak even now. And so set forth such words, as we would have him to say.

Francis Bacon

* Just history is of three kinds, with regard to the three objects it designs to represent; which are either a portion of time, a memorable person, or an illustrious action. The first kind we call writing annals or chronicles; the second, lives; and the third, narratives or relations. Chronicles share the greatest esteem and reputation, but lives excel in advantage and use, as relations do in truth and sincerity. For chronicles represent only grand public actions, and external shows and appearances to the people, and drop the smaller passages and motions of men and things. But as the divine artificer hangs the greatest weight upon the smallest strings, so such histories rather show the pomp of affairs, than their true and inward springs. And though it intersperses counsel, yet delighting in grandeur, it attributes more gravity and prudence to human actions, than really appears in them; so that satire might be a truer picture of human life, than certain histories of this kind: whereas lives, if wrote with care and judgement, proposing to represent a person, in whom actions, both great and small, public and private, are blended together, must of necessity give a more genuine, native, and lively representation, and such as is fitter for imitation. . . .

With regard to lives, we cannot but wonder that our own times have so little value for what they enjoy, as not more frequently to write the lives of eminent men. For, though kings, princes, and great personages are few, yet there are many other excellent men who

* From *De Augmentis Scientiarum* (1623), Book II, Chapter 7, translated by Peter Shaw, revised by Joseph Devey.

deserve better than vague reports, and barren eulogies. Here the fancy of a late poet, who has improved an ancient fiction, is not inapplicable. He feigns that at the end of the thread of every man's life, there hung a medal, on which the name of the deceased is stamped; and that Time, waiting upon the shears of the fatal sister, as soon as the thread was cut, caught the medals, and threw them out of his bosom into the river Lethe. He also represented many birds flying over its banks, who caught the medals in their beaks, and after carrying them about for a certain time, allowed them to fall in the river. Among these birds were a few swans, who used, if they caught a medal, to carry it to a certain temple consecrated to immortality. Such swans, however, are rare in our age. . . . So in that laudable way of speaking of the dead, 'of happy memory! of pious memory!' etc., we seem to acknowledge, with Cicero and Demosthenes, 'that a good name is the proper inheritance of the deceased'; which inheritance is lying waste in our time, and deserves to be noticed as a deficiency.

Thomas Fuller

* England may not unfitly be compared to a house, not very great, but convenient; and the several shires may properly be resembled to the *rooms* thereof. Now, as learned Master Camden and painful Master Speed, with others, have described the rooms themselves, so it is our intention, God willing, to describe the *furniture* of these rooms; such eminent commodities which every county doth produce, with the persons of quality bred therein, and some other observables coincident with the same subject.

Cato, that great and grave philosopher, did commonly demand, when any new project was propounded unto him, 'Cui bono?' what good would ensue, in case the same was effected? A question more fit to be asked than facile to be answered in all undertakings, especially in the setting forth of new books, insomuch that they themselves, who complain that they are too many already, help daily to make them more.

Know then, I propound five ends to myself in this book: first, to gain some glory to God: secondly, to preserve the memories of the dead: thirdly, to present examples to the living: fourthly, to entertain the reader with delight: and lastly (which I am not ashamed publicly to profess), to procure some honest profit to myself. If not so happy to obtain all, I will be joyful to attain some; yea, contented and thankful too, if gaining any (especially the first) of these ends, the motives of my endeavours.

* From *The History of the Worthies of England* (1662), Chapter I.

First, glory to God, which ought to be the aim of all our actions; though too often our bow starts, our hand shakes, and so our arrow misseth the mark. Yet I hope that our describing so good a land, with the various fruits and fruitful varieties therein, will engage both writer and reader in gratitude to that God who hath been so bountiful to our nation. In order whereunto, I have not only always taken, but often sought occasions to exhort to thankfulness, hoping the same will be interpreted no straggling from my subject, but a closing with my calling.

Secondly, to preserve the memories of the dead. A good name is an ointment poured out, smelt where it is not seen. It hath been the lawful desire of men in all ages to perpetuate their memories, thereby in some sort revenging themselves of mortality, though few have found out effectual means to perform it. For monuments made of wood are subject to be burnt; of glass, to be broken; of soft stone, to moulder; of marble and metal, (if escaping the teeth of time) to be demolished by the hand of covetousness; so that, in my apprehension, the safest way to secure a memory from oblivion is (next his own virtues) by committing the same in writing to posterity.

Thirdly, to present examples to the living, having here precedents of all sorts and sizes; of men famous for valour, wealth, wisdom, learning, religion, and bounty to the public, on which last we most largely insist. The scholar, being taxed by his writing master for idleness in his absence, made a fair defence, when pleading that his master had neither left him paper whereon or copy whereby to write. But rich men will be without excuse, if not expressing their bounty in some proportion, God having provided them paper enough ('the poor you have always with you') and set them signal examples, as in our ensuing work will plainly appear.

Fourthly, to entertain the reader with delight. I confess, the subject is but dull in itself, to tell the time and place of men's birth, and deaths, their names, with the names and number of their books; and therefore this bare skeleton of time, place, and person, must be fleshed with some pleasant passages. To this intent I have purposely interlaced (not as meat, but as condiment) many delightful stories, that so the reader, if he do not arise (which I hope and desire) *religiosior* or *doctior*, with more piety or learning, at least he may depart *jucundior*, with more pleasure and lawful delight.

Lastly, to procure moderate profit to myself in compensation of my pains. It was a proper question which plain-dealing Jacob pertinently propounded to Laban his father-in-law: 'And now when shall I provide for mine house also?' Hitherto no stationer hath lost by me; hereafter it will be high time for me (all things considered) to save for myself.

Thomas Sprat

* This familiar way of verse puts me in mind of one kind of prose wherein Mr. Cowley was excellent; and that is his letters to his private friends. In these he always expressed the native tenderness, and innocent gaiety of his mind. I think, Sir, you and I have the greatest collection of this sort. But I know you agree with me, that nothing of this nature should be published. . . . The truth is, the letters that pass between particular friends, if they are written as they ought to be, can scarce ever be fit to see the light. They should not consist of fulsome compliments, or tedious polities, or elaborate elegancies, or general fancies. But they should have a native clearness and shortness, a domestical plainness, and a peculiar kind of familiarity; which can only affect the humour of those to whom they were intended. The very same passages, which make writings of this nature delightful amongst friends, will lose all manner of taste, when they come to be read by those that are indifferent. In such letters the souls of men should appear undressed: and in that negligent habit, they may be fit to be seen by one or two in a chamber, but not to go abroad into the streets. . . .

* From 'An Account of the Life and Writings of Mr. Abraham Cowley', in *Works* (1668). Addressed to Martin Clifford.

Gilbert Burnet

* For the lives of great persons, though it might have been expected that after the many excellent patterns Plutarch had left the world, those should have been generally well written; yet there is no sort of history worse done, they being so full of gross partiality and flattery, and often swelled with trifling and impertinent things, so that it is no great wonder if this kind of writing be much decried and neglected.

* * *

† No part of history is more instructive and delighting than the lives of great and worthy men. The shortness of them invites many readers, and there are such little and yet remarkable passages in them, too inconsiderable to be put in a general history of the age in which they lived; that all people are very desirous to know them. This makes Plutarch's Lives to be more generally read than any of all the books which the ancient Greeks or Romans writ.

But the lives of heroes and princes, are commonly filled with accounts of the great things done by them, which do rather belong to a general than a particular history; and do rather amuse the reader's fancy with a splendid show of greatness than offer him what is really so useful to himself; and indeed the lives of princes are either writ with so much flattery, by those who intended to merit by it at their

* From *Memoirs of the Lives and Actions of James and William, Dukes of Hamilton and Castleherald* (1677), Preface.

† From *The Life and Death of Sir Matthew Hale, Kt.* (1682), Preface.

own hands, or others concerned with them: or with so much spite, by those who being ill used by them, have revenged themselves on their memory, that there is not too much to be built on them: and though the ill nature of many makes what is satirically writ to be generally more read and believed, than when the flattery is visible and coarse, yet certainly resentment may make the writer corrupt the truth of history, as much as interest: and since all men have their blind sides, commit errors, he that will industriously lay there together, leaving out, or but slightly touching what should be set against them, to balance them, may make a very good man appear in very bad colours: so upon the whole matter, there is not that reason to expect either much truth or great instruction, from what is written concerning heroes or princes for few have been able to imitate the patterns Suetonius set the world in writing of the lives [of] the Roman Emperors with the same freedom that they led them: but the lives of private men, though they seldom entertain the reader with such a variety of passages as the other do; yet certainly they offer him things that are more imitable, and do present wisdom and virtue to him, not only in a fair *Idea*; which is often looked on as a piece of the invention or fancy of the writer, but in such plain and familiar instances, as do both direct him better and persuade him more; and there are not such temptations to bias those who write them, so that we may generally depend more on the truth of such relations as are given in them.

John Aubrey

* Sir!

I have, according to your desire, put in writing these minutes of lives tumultuarily, as they occurred to my thoughts or as occasionally I had information of them. They may easily be reduced into order at your leisure by numbering them with red figures, according to time and place, &c. 'Tis a task that I never thought to have undertaken till you imposed it upon me, saying that I was fit for it by reason of my general acquaintance, having now not only lived above half a century of years in the world, but have also been much tumbled up and down in it, which hath made me much known; besides the modern advantage of coffee-houses in this great city, before which men knew not how to be acquainted, but with their own relations, or societies. I might add that I come of a longaevous race, by which means I have imped some feathers of the wings of time, for several generations; which does reach high. When I first began, I did not think I could have drawn it out to so long a thread.

I here lay-down to you (out of the conjunct friendship between us) the truth, and, as near as I can and that religiously as a penitent to his confessor, nothing but the truth: the naked and plain truth, which is here exposed so bare that the very *pudenda* are not covered, and affords many passages that would raise a blush in a young virgin's cheek. So that after your perusal, I must desire you to make a castration (as Raderus to Martial) and to sew-on some fig-leaves—i.e. to be my *Index expurgatorius*.

* From letter to Anthony à Wood, 15 June 1680; included in *Aubrey's Brief Lives*, ed. Andrew Clark (1898), I, pp. 10–11.

What uncertainty do we find in printed histories? they either treading too near on the heels of truth that they dare not speak plain, or else for want of intelligence (things being antiquated) become too obscure and dark! I do not here repeat any thing already published (to the best of my remembrance) and I fancy my self all along discoursing with you; alleging those of my relations and acquaintance (as either you knew or have heard of) *ad faciendam fidem*: so that you make me to renew my acquaintance with my old and deceased friends, and to *rejuvenescere* (as it were) which is the pleasure of old men. 'Tis pity that such minutes had not been taken 100 years since or more: for want wherof many worthy men's names and notions are swallowed-up in oblivion; as much of these also would [have been], had it not been through your instigation: and perhaps this is one of the usefullest pieces that I have scribbled.

John Dryden

* History is principally divided into three species. Commentaries or annals; history properly so called; and biographia, or the lives of particular men. . . .

Biographia, or the history of particular men's lives, comes next to be considered; which in dignity is inferior to the other two; as being more confined in action, and treating of wars, and counsels, and all other public affairs of nations, only as they relate to him, whose life is written, or as his fortunes have a particular dependence on them, or connexion to them: all things here are circumscribed, and driven to a point, so as to terminate in one: consequently if the action, or counsel were managed by colleagues some part of it must be either lame or wanting; except it be supplied by the excursion of the writer: herein likewise must be less of variety for the same reason; because the fortunes and actions of one man are related, not those of many. Thus the actions and atchievements of Sylla, Lucullus, and Pompey are all of them but successive parts of the Mithridatic War: of which we could have no perfect image, if the same hand had not given us the whole, though at several views, in their particular lives.

Yet though we allow, for the reasons above alleged that this kind of writing is in dignity inferior to history and annals, in pleasure and instruction it equals, or even excels both of them. 'Tis not only commended by ancient practice, to celebrate the memory of great and worthy men, as the best thanks which posterity can pay them;

* From 'The Life of Plutarch', prefixed to *Plutarch's Lives, Translated from the Greek by Several Hands* (1683–6), Volume I.

but also the examples of virtue are of more vigour, when they are thus contracted into individuals. As the sun beams, united in a burning-glass to a point, have greater force than if they were darted from a plain superficies; so the virtues and actions of one man, drawn together into a single story, strike upon our minds a stronger and more lively impression, than the scattered relations of many men, and many actions; and by the same means that they give us pleasure they afford us profit too. For when the understanding is intent and fixed on a single thing, it carries closer to the mark, every part of the object sinks into it, and the soul receives it unmixed and whole. For this reason Aristotle commends the unity of action in a poem; because the mind is not capable of digesting many things at once, nor of conceiving fully any more than one idea at a time. Whatsoever distracts the pleasure, lessens it: and as the reader is more concerned with one man's fortune, than those of many; so likewise the writer is more capable of making a perfect work, if he confine himself to this narrow compass. The lineaments, features, and colourings of a single picture may be hit exactly; but in a history-piece of many figures, the general design, the ordinance or disposition of it, the relation of one figure to another, the diversity of the posture, habits, shadowings, and all the other graces conspiring to an uniformity, are of so difficult performance, that neither is the resemblance of particular persons often perfect, nor the beauty of the piece complete. For any considerable error in the parts, renders the whole disagreeable and lame. Thus then the perfection of the work, and the benefit arising from it are both more absolute in biography than in history. . . .

Biographia, or the histories of particular lives, though circumscribed in the subject, is yet more extensive in the style than the other two: for it not only comprehends them both, but has something super-added, which neither of them have. The style of it is various, according to the occasion. There are proper places in it, for the plainness and nakedness, of narration, which is ascribed to annals; there is also room reserved for the loftiness and gravity of general history, when the actions related shall require that manner of expression. But there is withal, a descent into minute circumstances, and trivial passages of life, which are natural to this way of writing, and which the dignity of the other two will not admit. There you are conducted only into the rooms of state; here you are led into the private lodgings of the hero: you see him in his undress, and are made familiar with his most private actions and conversations. You may behold a Scipio and a Lelius gathering cockle-shells on the shore, Augustus playing at bounding stones with boys; and Agesilaus riding on a hobby-horse among his children. The pageantry of life is taken away; you see the poor reasonable animal, as naked as ever nature made him; are made acquainted with his passions and his follies, and find the Demy-God a man.

Anonymous

* To write the lives of single persons is then a commendable undertaking, when by it some moral benefit is designed to mankind. He who has that in aim, will not employ his time or pen, to record the history of bad men, how successful or great soever they may have been; unless by relating their tragical ends (which, through the just judgement of the Almighty, most commonly overtakes them) or by discriminating, with a due note of infamy, whatever is criminal in their actions, he warn the reader to flee their example.

But to celebrate, whether the gifts or graces, the natural endowments, or acquired laudable habits of persons eminent in their generations, while it gives glory to God, the bestower of all good things, and (by furnishing a model) tends to the edification of our brethren, is little less than the duty of every Christian: which seems acknowledged by the late supervisors of our Common Prayer; when they added to the Collect for the Church militant, a clause commemorating the *Saints and Servants of God departed this life in his Fear*. . . .

* From a life of John Milton [Bodleian Library MS. Wood, D 4], included in *The Early Lives of Milton*, ed. Helen Darbishire (1932), p. 17.

John Toland

* Observing in this performance the rules of a faithful historian, being neither provoked by malice, nor bribed by favour, and as well daring to say all that is true, as scorning to write any falsehood, I shall not conceal what may be thought against my author's honour, nor add the least word for his reputation: but three things I would have you specially observe. First, I shall not be too minute in relating the ordinary circumstances of his life, and which are common to him with all other men. Writings of this nature should in my opinion be designed to recommend virtue, and to expose vice; or to illustrate history, and to preserve the memory of extraordinary things. That a man, for example, was sick at such a time, or well at another, should never be mentioned; except in the causes or effects, cure or continuance, there happens something remarkable, and for the benefit of mankind to know. I had not therefore related *Milton's* headaches in his youth, were it not for the influence which this indisposition had afterwards on his eyes, and that his blindness was rashly imputed by his enemies to the avenging judgement of God. Secondly, in the characters of sects and parties, books or opinions, I shall produce his own words, as I find them in his works; that those who approve his reasons, may owe all the obligation to himself, and that I may escape the blame of such as may dislike what he says. For it is commonly seen, that historians are suspected rather to make their hero what they would have him be, than such as he really was; and that, as they are prompted by

* From *The Life of John Milton* (1698), reprinted in *The Early Lives of Milton*, ed. Helen Darbishire (1932), pp. 83–85.

different passions, they put those words in his mouth which they might not speak themselves without incurring some danger, and being accused perhaps of flattery or injustice: but I am neither writing a satyr, nor a panegyric upon *Milton*, but publishing the true history of his actions, works, and opinions. In the third place, I would not have it expected that when I quote a few verses or passages in a different language, I should always pretend to translate them, when the whole turn or fancy absolutely depends upon the force of the original words; for the ignorant could be nothing the wiser, and the best translation would spoil their beauty to the learned. But this happens so rarely, and almost only during his travels abroad, that it scarce deserved an advertisement. The amplest part of my materials I had from his own books, where, constrained by the defamations of his enemies, he often gives an account of himself. I learnt some particulars from a person that had been once his amanuensis, which were confirmed to me by his daughter now dwelling in London, and by a letter written to one at my desire from his last wife, who is still alive. I perused the papers of one of his nephews, learnt what I could in discourse with the other; and lastly consulted such of his acquaintance, as, after the best inquiry, I was able to discover. . . .

The Eighteenth Century

Joseph Addison

* There is a race of men lately sprung up among this sort of writers, whom one cannot reflect upon without indignation as well as contempt. These are Grub-street biographers, who watch for the death of a great man, like so many undertakers, on purpose to make a penny of him. He is no sooner laid in his grave, but he falls into the hands of an historian; who, to swell a volume, ascribes to him works which he never wrote, and actions which he never performed; celebrates virtues which he was never famous for, and excuses faults which he was never guilty of. They fetch their only authentic records out of Doctors' Commons; and when they have got a copy of his last will and testament, they fancy themselves furnished with sufficient materials for his history. This might, indeed, enable them in some measure, to write the history of his death; but what can we expect from an author that undertakes to write the life of a great man, who is furnished with no other matters of fact besides legacies; and instead of being able to tell us what he did, can only tell us what he bequeathed? This manner of exposing the private concerns of families, and sacrificing the secrets of the dead to the curiosity of the living, is one of those licentious practices which might well deserve the animadversion of our government, when it has time to contrive expedients for remedying the many crying abuses of the press. In the mean while, what a poor idea must strangers conceive of those persons who have been famous among us in their generation, should they form their notions of them from the writings of these our historiographers! What

* From *The Freeholder*, No. 35, 20 April 1716.

would our posterity think of their illustrious forefathers, should they only see them in such weak and disadvantageous lights! But, to our comfort, works of this nature are so short-lived, that they cannot possibly diminish the memory of those patriots which they are not able to preserve.

The truth of it is, as the lives of great men cannot be written with any tolerable degree of elegance or exactness, within a short space after their decease; so neither is it fit that the history of a person, who has acted among us in a public character, should appear, till envy and friendship are laid asleep, and the prejudice both of his antagonists and adherents be, in some degree, softened and subdued. There is no question but there are several eminent persons in each party, however they may represent one another at present, who will have the same admirers among posterity, and be equally celebrated by those whose minds will not be distempered by interest, passion, or partiality. It were happy for us, could we prevail upon ourselves to imagine, that one who differs from us in opinion, may possibly be an honest man; and that we might do the same justice to one another, which will be done us hereafter by those who shall make their appearance in the world, when this generation is no more. But in our present miserable and divided condition, how just soever a man's pretensions may be to a great or blameless reputation, he must expect his share of obloquy and reproach; and, even with regard to his posthumous character, content himself with such a kind of consideration, as induced the famous Sir Francis Bacon, after having bequeathed his soul to God, and his body to the earth, to leave his fame to foreign nations, and, after some years, to his own country.

Roger North

1. *History of private lives more profitable than state history*

* The history of private lives adapted to the perusal of common men, is more beneficial (generally) than the most solemn registers of ages, and nations, or the acts and monuments of famed governors, statesmen, prelates, or generals of armies. The gross reason is, because the latter contain little if any thing, comparate or applicable to instruct a private economy, or tending to make a man either wiser or more cautelous [*sic*], in his own proper concerns. But on the contrary where strength of mind or judgement is wanting, it may happen that great actions and events superior to a man's own condition made familiar by reading shall induce a positive inconvenience as was feigned of Quixote. For the amusements of state policy, and private economy will not indifferently serve the public and private capacities; and happening to work cross in men's minds often makes horrible blunders in their reasoning. Ministers of state may argue low and private men high of themselves and both very improperly and prejudicial to their several interests. I shall a little more enlarge this subject afterwards, but at present (with salvo to what is already observed) declare that I do not intend to depreciate general histories,

* From 'General Preface' to 'Life of the Lord Keeper North'—hitherto unpublished (St. John's College, Cambridge, MS. James, No. 613). Now printed through the kind permission of the Master and Fellows of St. John's College. Contractions have been expanded, and spelling and capitalization largely normalized. Some old spellings, where significant, have been retained. What appear here as numbered paragraph headings are marginal glosses in the manuscript.

however lofty the subject may be, but join in recognizing all the great and good that in authority or common place is usually ascribed to them. But always referring to a proper application.

2. *Readers of general history distinguished antiquaries, menders, corrupters*

And thereupon I must distinguish readers of histories; of whom two sorts are to be noted. 1. the curiosos who are richer in time than employment, and hunting after amusements and pleasure only often find enough in literature of most kinds to answer their ends, especially history. I may subjoin as the perfection of this kind such men as criticize and improve history and spend their time in perusing memorials of antiquity collating authorities, discovering of omissions, contradictions, and partialities of authors, or in a word, antiquaries who render the argument of history more limpid and authoritative; these are to be honoured as public benefactors although without a peculiar pleasure they never could persevere as some do. There have been some who with no regard to truth, but with wonderful industry and application; and all for false and ambitious purposes have corrupted the histories of antiquity and modern times; these are the Jesuits, and as the good antiquaries merit all the honours posterity can ascribe, so these deserve also to be remembered, but with extreme detestation and infamy.

2 (continued). *Politicians, ambitious, public spirit*

Then, 2nd the politicians of whom there are also 2 sorts, first the ambitious. . . .

8. *Objection, low history, contemptible*

All this to the understanding of a good man is best confirmed by histories. I mean such as are of the behaviour and successes of private persons in fortune and condition like himself, and not out of histories of states and empires, with which he has no reason to concern himself. But some will say that low history is contemptible, it is of kings and mighty things that reading advances, and all the actors and events must be of the first magnitude, to rouse the attention, and compensate the time, and to this tune most of our critics chime. They will scarce muster the relations of petit states and republics, and on this account divers of our lesser Italian histories such as Guazzo and Capriata suffer, nothing but invicible art and eloquence could have saved Thucydides, because the Peloponesian war was but a strife of two cities for the mastery, and did not influence the revolution of vaster powers, and make such a clutter in the world as the actions of Xerxes, Alexander and Caesar did. What regard then say they is to be had to histories of private men, whose conduct never touched the public? Let their own descendants entertain themselves therewith as citizens with the stories of their own corporation; persons more refined will drop such impertinents, whatever pretended useful surprising incidents may be found in them. . . .

11. *Objection, dullness, is the author's fault*

But now to resume an objection touched before, and to consider it more fully, some will say what pleasure can there be in reading the account of a private man's economy, how he was educated, matched, governed his family, conducted his affairs, or passed his time? However pliant and lively the descriptions may be, yet there wants a spur to engage one to go through with them; and admitting them pregnant of good council and example, yet the entertainment compared with the haut-goût of state will be jejune. For as men are apt to court greatness itself, so the relation of great things pleaseth, and consequently engageth to all which I answer that (pleasing) is not so much contended for, as (profit) for the sake of which, the other is courted, and with good reason, too, for (if I may so use the word) temptation may be unto good as well as evil purposes, and then it's pity it should be wanted on the right side. But as to pleasing, the best histories to aiery people are dull, and the more so, as the subject is great, and solemn: a young man had rather read the life of a tinker, than a Caesar or Pompey; Apollo was in the right to punish a tautologist with reading of Guicciardine [*sic*] which saving the use and authority of it, is to a reasonable creature, but a leaden diversion. After all a dullness is never to be charged on a subject but on the author, who should find spirit enough in himself to give relish to every thing he writes, whether of low, or of lofty matters. An Italian found means to raise up an heroic poem upon a village quarrel about a water bucket, and a Frenchman upon the lazy friar's contest about the reading desk, not forgetting Rabelais' bloody war about a plum cake. It is objected that the beauties of those species are owing to the fiction, which no history allows of. I answer that the same ingredients that are usually brought to adorn fiction may come forward, and be as well applied to the setting forth of truths; that is choice of words, charming periods, invention of figures, interspersion of sentences, and facetious expressions. We see in many ordinary instances the power of words and composition, as of the most filthy obscenity, which may be so couched in figurate terms as not to be fulsome, or so much as indecent, but rather acceptable. For words are like dressing that covers the indecorums of nature, which all persons know, but none will endure to observe, in the very nudity.

12. *Plain truth without impertinence never properly dull*

The parallel is here taken in the extreme, but holds in all mediocrities, of which Thucidides may be an instance, who (as was said) by dint of language and judgement, hath turned the paltry squabbles of the Greek towns, into a stately history of human affairs. But it seems that fiction however deliciously dressed, hath not those advantages to improve as history hath, for that it is not true is a cooling reflection. And what force can any moral arguments or sentences have that are derived upon feigned events? Nothing can invigorate eloquence like truth. . . . There is great art, as well as felicity, in making a good description of plain facts, and it is not affected amusements but justice and integrity of sense, and significancy of language that sets it off. . . .

14. *Romances preferred to pompous histories and the reasons*

. . . [about romances, etc.] I only confirm, viz. that histories of men, and things of common condition, neatly parallel to the state of most men's circumstances, and in which no handles are held out for uplifting vain humours and whereof the whole subject falls within ordinary understanding, done with spirit and judgement, would be incomparably more preferable to the community of men than the pompous histories of governments, and great changes happening in the world. . . .

15. *Private life history rare for they commonly are wrote to serve turns*

And as this sort of history is most diffusively useful, so is it rare, for in all our bibliotheques, we scarce find a book writ of lives, but what is done chiefly to introduce the history of the time, or for some other special byend or purpose. And if any pages are spent upon the person or his ordinary behaviour it is perfunctory, as beside the grand design, and introduced only to make the relation more formal. And for this reason it is that biographers have selected certain lives of the first magnitude, and having saluted the place of their nativity, and noted the time, hurry into intrigues of state, and lofty ministrations. [He comments on Diogenes Laertius, Plutarch, etc.]. . . .

17. *Some errors in life writing with instances of some good*

But as to the rarity of private life-writing it may be opposed that authors of that kind have not wholly obliged for the characters, and economy of their subjects, but have touched much as well as their public behaviour: and instances are given from Plutarch; I grant there is somewhat, and if we are so pleased we may think it all, because we know not what is wanting; if we did I guess it would appear little enough, nor doth the manner of that writing promise much; and how should Plutarch or any one gather the privacies of so many men remote in time, and place from him, but from loose fame, which is but a poor instruction. How, and where we may expect it to be tolerably done I shall touch afterwards. As for the many sketches or profiles of great men's lives, pretended to be synoptical or multum in parvo, we are sure there is nothing we look for in them. One may walk in a gallery, and extract as fair an account from the air of their countenances or the cut of their whiskers. What signifies it to us, how many battles Alexander fought. It were more to the purpose to say how often he was drunk, and then we might from the ill consequences to him incline to be sober. Some have wrote lives purely for favour to certain theses, opinions, or facts; and then all is in an hurry to come at them. We have many of this sort, but none more infamous (not excepting the Popish legends) than the late piece called Baxter's life, which is no better than an harrangue for presbytery and nonconformity. I do not quarrel with all, but allow many to be very well wrote, as those of the German reformers by Melchior Adam. . . .

18. *How few have given just account of private examples of good and evil, and the use of such as do*

I do not pretend to catalogue or censure more of these authors, although I have many at the pen's point. But I must own that amongst them all I have scarce found a person taken up and sat down again in a private capacity. I should gladly meet with an author that in the course of a written life delineates to us in lively examples the precipitous steps, and dangerous meanders of youth, the difficulties of riper years, and the fondnesses of old age, and where one may see distinctly the early application of some persons to proper employments, with the eventual prosperities attending them. As by what small beginnings they advanced to great estates, with the methods, and true causes of it stated. And on the other side the devious courses, and errours of persons vicious and idle, who from plentiful fortunes, and fair reputations, fell to want, and more than balanced the account of their luxury and folly, by substantial misery and infamy. These cases appearing in a strong historical light, must needs touch the very vitals of a person who reads, and inspire a satisfaction in the consciences of those, who find they have done well, and a sensible reflection in others, who may there see the precipice before them; and thereby many persons undetermined, may be engaged to choose for the best. But besides these moralities, with the proper effects as to good and evil, most fit to be depicted in the strongest colours, there is also a copious harvest of discretion, and wisdom in common dealing, and disposing the affairs of a family, and making fit provisions for it, and also for the education and settlement of children, and other emergent concerns of human life, to be gathered from the patterns of private men, who have at their great risk proved divers ways of living, and it may be have found out the best at last, and possibly suffered by their mistakes. Therefore nothing can be more profitably instructive to private men, than relations of other men's proceedings in like condition. . . .

25. *The style should be adequate and promise justice rather than partiality*

The rigour held over all historical undertakings, requires not only strict truth, and the whole, but all the tokens of veracity, and none of partiality or suppression. So far is it from being reasonable to affect, as many do, to tell strange stories. Some people's style runs all in superlatives, as most wonderful, prodigious, excessive, and the like, and what is worse, often on both sides alike, for good one way and similar the other. It is a very difficult task to adjust terms to things, for as they may not seem greater or less, better or worse than the truth of them warrants; but the endeavour ought to be for it, the rather because if in any one instance there appears a pidling disposition, it casts disparagement upon the whole. And this rigour of truth doth extend not solely to facts, and existencies but to characters and moralities, and some are so squeamish that to avoid seeming partial, they do justice to nothing and there lies the greatest difficulty, for truths may be so touchy, that a plain telling them, with a proper and due reflection, will be termed partiality of which afterwards, but it ought always to appear, that the writer is in his own mind and intent rigidly sincere. . . . [An historical writer ought to interpose his own sentiments and censures of wisdom and folly.]

33. *Life writing harder to do well than state history with the reasons*

To proceed therefore, I must remember that although I am here induced to say much of history in general, I am not out of my way towards that kind, which I mentioned at first, and am now about more directly to profess viz. private biography. For all fitting qualifications belong to every species of history; and as that of private men's lives is more rarely found good than that of nations (as hath already been noted) so is it much more difficult to compose, as it ought to be done, than the other kind is. For state history hath the assistance of public registers, records, pamphlets, gazettes, and often the memoirs of private persons, which are the most serviceable to truth of any. . . . But where should one go to be informed of the course of any one man's life? How many excellent men, as well as vile debauchees go off, and no person left behind capable, or willing to represent their characters and successes, in a just history? I question whether there is now in the world extant the history of any one man's life so full as it ought to be, and since we have nothing to judge by, but what is left us, such as it is, who can say whether any one account is full and just or no? That which is remembered may be of the slightest kind, and the most momentous passages, not touched; and the design may be apparently invective, or panegyric, such as Burnet's lives of the Lord Rochester, and Judge Hales, the persons of whom none ever knew, but must also know, that those written lives of them are mere froth, whipped up to serve a turn. I must grant that not only accounts of lives, but histories of nations owe much to the ignorance of such, as they are made to inform; for they knowing no better, must take what they find; therefore historical controversy is the most useful thing in the world; for that lets the readers into a capacity of setting themselves right, without being carried away with prejudice of good or ill opinions, of men and things, contrary to justice and truth. For such controversies interpret enigmas, correct partial informations, supply defects, fill up blanks and omissions, and what is most of all, expose the knavery of writers, which is a disease that in the folio volumes of our time calls for a cure. But a life may be ill wrote, and none of these checks come forward to correct it, and of that kind people are very prone to take for truth all that is well writ; in short all history of one form or other is like painting, never exactly true; that which comes nearest is best, and however discrepant, there may be some use or other that makes it reasonable, not to slight, but to preserve it.

Barry College Library
Miami, Florida

34. *The many defects and imperfections in the way of good life history*

No man at large, who is not expressly qualified, can fairly take upon him to write the life of any other man; they may make gatherings and excerpts out of letters, books, or reports concerning him, but those are memorials, or rather bundles of uncemented materials, but not the life, and it is obnoxious to this shrewd failing, that all these gatherings, and the conjectures built upon them, are of course taken as positive truths, of which much, or the greatest part most commonly are utter mistakes, and without a due check make a strange history. Therefore a life-writer in education, friendship, conversation, and all commerce of life, ought to be the nearest of any allied to his subject, and not a contingent gatherer, or compiler, only as I said before, for such are but sowers of errors, either to the prejudice, or for undue favour of the person wrote of. And what further qualifications are requisite, I intend to touch afterwards. But it's no wonder so few lives are tolerably wrote, when it is considered that men often change their residence, company, and manner of living; and there is seldom or never any one person what can answer for the whole life, and actions of any man, but however friendly and intimate they were, there is remaining absence, employment, or somewhat that hinders a continual notice of his actions, determinations, and occurrences. But supposing a Pilades and Orestes, never asunder, do such use to keep pocket books, to use for journal memorandums of each other? Or amongst all the friendships in the world, how many think, or dream of giving an account of a friend's life before he is dead and gone? And then for want of notes, as to all that may be recollected there is nothing but frail memory to trust to; which must needs be very imperfect both as to times and matter transacted? But admit a good memory, how few have a felicity of style, and method, in their own opinion at least, proper for such an undertaking? And men that do not very much exercise the pen, will soon find the want of those requisites, such as should invite them to do justice to a friend or the public, in that manner. Nay most people are so averse to that exercise, they will not do right to themselves, whom they may best account for.

35. *The very great use of a life journal by a man of himself*

Whoever hath a mind either his family, or the public should profit by his example, and would be known to posterity truly as he was, ought to keep a journal of all the incidents that may afford useful remarks upon the course of his life; for the aid and encouragement of such a journal would engage a good pen to work fairly upon it, and draw his picture well, which otherwise could not be reasonably attempted. This practice would be useful to a man in many respects, he might retrospect his actions, and seeing his errours, and failings, endeavour to mend them; it would also be a check upon all his exorbitancies, and considering, that being set down, they would stain his reputation; nay the very pleasure of looking back upon past occurrences, would amply compensate the pains, and I may well say that would be done, by the very exercitation of daily penning, and writing, the profit of which those may consider who want it, as many do, who had rather carry gutts to the bears, than write a letter.

36. *Diverse examples of such journalists, and a caution against partiality towards self or friends*

There are many examples of this kind of idiography. The famous, or rather infamous Cardan wrote de vitâ propriâ: and doth himself more right, than all the friends or enemies he had in the world, could have done, for he owns himself a very knave, and a cheat, and proves it by diverse immane cruelties, and impostures. Bassompier wrote the journal of his own life which (besides his first design) is printed, and there his true character appears, a very soldier, and a rake, imprisoned by Richelieu, because he was afraid of his merits, there's his vanity, though in some sort true; the petit journal of Ed. 6. even a youth, may be a pattern for the greatest men. But above all the great and good Archbishop Laud's journal had a sublime effect by vindicating his integrity against the foul aspersions of his adversaries, which without that record had struck more of calumny upon his fame than since that appeared by all their wicked means, they have been able to do. These registers are of greatest use in biography, but allowance must be made for self, which cannot but be partial. Some will say, that all life writing is obnoxious to the like infirmity, because ordinarily it is done by relations, or intimate friends, whose very design is praise. And it is easy to panegyrize, when there are no means, either to prove or to disprove the facts, and invention can bestow characters ad libitum, and there are instances of criminals to the laws, who on account of pure party, have been dubbed heroes, or martyrs; writers for faction will illuminate the reputations of their departed friends, to cast a lustre, upon their living partisans. All that may be answered to this is, that it is too often so, and there is reason for more jealousy of a life-writer, than of any author whatsoever. But yet there may be a veracity, even in praises, and certain symptoms will discover a writer's partiality (I mean such partiality, as betrays him to falsify) and on the other side vouchers of his integrity may be produced, in some degree at least, by which and the ordinary critical processes against authors, his proceeding whether just or unjust will be accordingly approved or condemned as I may in course demonstrate.

37. *The writer of a life must be qualified, and first by a confirmed character of honesty*

These considerations have made me recollect as well as I may, what kind of authority or warrant a lifewriter may hope for, to credit his history, of the life and behaviour of any private person, and more especially the moral character he gives him. And all that I can think of to that purpose is reducible to two heads. 1. The character, and circumstances of the writer. 2. The remains of the person, to be described, whether by the real monuments of his egregious actions, or by his writings. 1. The writer ought to be of good fame, and as to truth and honesty untainted; and so far the case is often notorious, for about the moral characters of men, common fame is seldom or never a liar, though as to particular facts seldom true. And 2nd he must be out of all roads towards preferment, or gain, for those lead to all the abuses of history; the present age groans under such heavier and more mortifying than ever was known, in any age or country: what is to be expected from an history, that comes with a flattering preface, and there's 300 guineas for that, or articled with a bookseller to contain —— sheets, for £100, besides dignities in the sequel, to encourage the family of corrupters; nay the very lure of selling a copy, is a corrupt interest, that taints an historical work, for the sale of the book must not be spoiled, by the dampness of overmuch truth, but rather be made vivacious, and complete by overmuch lying. But of all the authors these I am treating of chiefly require a clear character, because less confutable directly than others are; for that most of the facts lean on the author's peculiar authority. But 3dly, besides all this, it must appear their course of life was such, as rendered them capable of the undertaking, and that is by having been in almost continual conversation, or commerce with the subjects, and so attached to the very persons, that little of importance in their whole lives could escape their notice. Such friendships often happen between persons, who live almost at bed, and board together, and communicate to each other their most recondite thoughts and designs and profit each other by mutual council; such as these are so far qualified to be authors of lives. But where this intimacy is not found, men (as I said) may gather and compile what is called a life, but is in truth any thing else rather than that of which it bears the name.

38. *The remains of the subject, as all monumental actions or writings*

2. All these advantages granted, a man's character is not, and scarce can be, justly represented, by mere words in the way of history, without some specimens derived from himself, either of his writing, or some speaking testimony of things remaining, and referred to. Friends may, but things will not prevaricate, or falsify; and no description can come up to the force and expression of them. These 2 criteria (1) the qualifications of the writer, and (2) the monuments of the subject joined together promise a good life history, but either apart are defective, and want the reciprocal interpretation that the one gives the other. If an author commends a man for being a good poet, and produceth none, but silly verses; if for a good orator and makes him speak obscurely or nonsense; if for a good soldier, and yet tells that for the most part he is beaten and the like, I doubt both author and subject will suffer contempt alike: as on the one side all the eulogies in the world will not sustain a character against the real testimony of fact, so the fact may be flagrant, and get the better of all the prejudice and malice of times, abetted by powers, and then a written character will less suffer by the imbecility of the pen, in case a weak brother undertakes the vindication of it.

39. *An account of the undertaking the lives of the Lord Keeper North, Dudley North and John North*

But now it is more than time to check this course of essaying about historiography (a subject of infinit copia, as well as commonplace in authors) and advance to a declaration of what is here hoped for by it, and that is chiefly some apology for an officious I might say unqualified undertaking to be a lifewriter and as such to dress up my remembrances of 3 honourable brothers and friends. . . .

Conyers Middleton

* There is no part of history which seems capable of yielding either more instruction or entertainment, than that which offers to us the *select lives* of great and virtuous men who have made an eminent figure on the public stage of the world. In these we see at one view what the annals of a whole age can afford that is worthy of notice; and in the wide field of universal history, skipping as it were over the barren places, gather all its flowers, and possess ourselves at once of everything that is good in it.

But there is one great fault which is commonly observed in the writers of *particular lives*, that they are apt to be partial and prejudiced in favour of their subject, and to give us a panegyric, instead of a history. They work up their characters as painters do their portraits; taking the praise of their art to consist, not in copying, but in adorning nature; not in drawing a just resemblance, but giving a fine picture; or exalting the man into a hero: and this indeed seems to flow from the nature of the thing itself, where the very inclination to write is generally grounded on prepossession, and an affection already contracted for the person whose history we are attempting; and when we sit down to it with the disposition of a friend, it is natural for us to cast a shade over his failings, to give the strongest colouring to his virtues; and, out of a good character, to endeavour to draw a perfect one.

I am sensible that this is the common prejudice of *biographers*, and have endeavoured therefore to divest myself of it as far as I was

* From the Preface to *The Life and Letters of Marcus Tullius Cicero* (1741).

able. . . . I have taken care always to leave the facts to speak for themselves, and to affirm nothing of any moment without an authentic testimony to support it; which yet, if consulted in the original at its full length, will commonly add more light and strength to what is advanced, than the fragments quoted in the text and the brevity of notes would admit. . . .

My first business therefore, after I had undertaken this task, was to read over Cicero's works, with no other view than to extract from them all the passages that seemed to have any relation to my design: where the tediousness of collecting an infinite number of testimonies scattered through many different volumes; of sorting them into their classes, and ranging them in proper order; the necessity of overlooking many in the first search, and the trouble of retrieving them in a second or third; and the final omission of several through forgetfulness or inadvertency; have helped to abate that wonder which had often occurred to me, why no man had ever attempted the same work before me, or at least in this enlarged and comprehensive form in which it is now offered to the public.

In my use of these materials, I have chosen to insert as many of them as I could into the body of my work; imagining that it would give both a lustre and authority to a sentiment, to deliver it in the person and the very words of Cicero; especially if they could be managed so as not to appear to be *sewed on*, like *splendid patches*, but woven originally into the text as the genuine parts of it. With this view I have taken occasion to introduce several of his letters, with large extracts from such of his orations as gave any particular light into the facts, or customs, or characters described in the history, or which seemed on any other account to be curious and entertaining.

Samuel Johnson

*All joy or sorrow for the happiness or calamities of others is produced by an act of the imagination, that realizes the event however fictitious, or approximates it however remote, by placing us, for a time, in the condition of him whose fortune we contemplate; so that we feel, while the deception lasts, whatever motions would be excited by the same good or evil happening to ourselves.

Our passions are therefore more strongly moved, in proportion as we can more readily adopt the pains or pleasure proposed to our minds, by recognizing them as once our own, or considering them as naturally incident to our state of life. It is not easy for the most artful writer to give us an interest in happiness or misery, which we think ourselves never likely to feel, and with which we have never yet been made acquainted. Histories of the downfall of kingdoms, and revolutions of empires, are read with great tranquillity; the imperial tragedy pleases common auditors only by its pomp of ornament, and grandeur of ideas; and the man whose faculties have been engrossed by business, and whose heart never fluttered but at the rise or fall of stocks, wonders how the attention can be seized, or the affection agitated by a tale of love.

Those parallel circumstances, and kindred images, to which we readily conform our minds, are, above all other writings, to be found in narratives of the lives of particular persons; and therefore no species of writing seems more worthy of cultivation than biography, since none can be more delightful or more useful, none can more certainly

* *The Rambler*, No. 60, Saturday, 13 October 1750.

enchain the heart by irresistible interest, or more widely diffuse instruction to every diversity of condition.

The general and rapid narratives of history, which involve a thousand fortunes in the business of a day, and complicate innumerable incidents in one great transaction, afford few lessons applicable to private life, which derives its comforts and its wretchedness from the right or wrong management of things which nothing but their frequency makes considerable, *Parva, si non fiunt quotidie*, says Pliny, and which can have no place in those relations which never descend below the consultation of senates, the motions of armies, and the schemes of conspirators.

I have often thought that there has rarely passed a life of which a judicious and faithful narrative would not be useful. For, not only every man has, in the mighty mass of the world, great numbers in the same condition with himself, to whom his mistakes and miscarriages, escapes and expedients, would be of immediate and apparent use; but there is such an uniformity in the state of man, considered apart from adventitious and separable decorations and disguises, that there is scarce any possibility of good or ill, but is common to human kind. A great part of the time of those who are placed at the greatest distance by fortune, or by temper, must unavoidably pass in the same manner; and though, when the claims of nature are satisfied, caprice, and vanity, and accident, begin to produce discriminations and peculiarities, yet the eye is not very heedful, or quick, which cannot discover the same causes still terminating their influence in the same effects, though sometimes accelerated, sometimes retarded, or perplexed by multiplied combinations. We are all prompted by the same motives, all deceived by the same fallacies, all animated by hope, obstructed by dangers, entangled by desire, and seduced by pleasure.

It is frequently objected to relations of particular lives, that they are not distinguished by any striking or wonderful vicissitudes. The scholar who passed his life among his books, the merchant who conducted only his own affairs, the priest, whose sphere of action was not extended beyond that of his duty, are considered as no proper objects of public regard, however they might have excelled in their several stations, whatever might have been their learning, integrity, and piety. But this notion arises from false measures of excellence and dignity, and must be eradicated by considering, that in the esteem of uncorrupted reason, what is of most use is of most value.

It is, indeed, not improper to take honest advantages of prejudice, and to gain attention by a celebrated name; but the business of the biographer is often to pass slightly over those performances and incidents, which produce vulgar greatness, to lead the thoughts into domestic privacies, and display the minute details of daily life, where exterior appendages are cast aside, and men excel each other only by prudence and by virtue. The account of Thuanus is, with great propriety, said by its author to have been written, that it might lay open to posterity the private and familiar character of that man, *cujus ingenium et candorem ex ipsius scriptis sunt olim semper miraturi*, whose candour and genius will to the end of time be by his writings preserved in admiration.

There are many invisible circumstances which, whether we read as inquirers after natural or moral knowledge, whether we intend to enlarge our science, or increase our virtue, are more important than public occurrences. Thus Salust, the great master of nature, has not forgot, in his account of Catiline, to remark that *his walk was now quick, and again slow*, as an indication of a mind revolving something with violent commotion. Thus the story of Melancthon affords a striking lecture on the value of time, by informing us, that when he made an appointment, he expected not only the hour, but the minute to be fixed, that the day might not run out in the idleness of suspense; and all the plans and enterprises of De Witt are now of less importance to the world, than that part of his personal character which represents him as *careful of his health, and negligent of his life*.

But biography has often been allotted to writers who seem very little acquainted with the nature of their task, or very negligent about the performance. They rarely afford any other account than might be collected from public papers, but imagine themselves writing a life when they exhibit a chronological series of actions or preferments; and so little regard the manners or behaviour of their heroes, that more knowledge may be gained of a man's real character, by a short conversation with one of his servants, than from a formal and studied narrative, begun with his pedigree, and ended with his funeral.

If now and then they condescend to inform the world of particular facts, they are not always so happy as to select the most important. I know not well what advantage posterity can receive from the only circumstance by which Tickell has distinguished Addison from the rest of mankind, *the irregularity of his pulse*: nor can I think myself overpaid for the time spent in reading the life of Malherb, by being enabled to relate, after the learned biographer, that Malherb had two predominant opinions; one, that the looseness of a single woman might destroy all her boast of ancient descent; the other, that the French beggars made use very improperly and barbarously of the phrase *noble Gentleman*, because either word included the sense of both.

There are, indeed, some natural reasons why these narratives are often written by such as were not likely to give much instruction or delight, and why most accounts of particular persons are barren and useless. If a life be delayed till interest and envy are at an end, we may hope for impartiality, but must expect little intelligence; for the incidents which give excellence to biography are of a volatile and evanescent kind, such as soon escape the memory, and are rarely transmitted by tradition. We know how few can portray a living acquaintance, except by his most prominent and observable particularities, and the grosser features of his mind; and it may be easily imagined how much of this little knowledge may be lost in imparting it, and how soon a succession of copies will lose all resemblance of the original.

If the biographer writes from personal knowledge, and makes haste to gratify the public curiosity, there is danger lest his interest, his fear, his gratitude, or his tenderness, overpower his fidelity, and tempt him to conceal, if not to invent. There are many who think it an act of piety to hide the faults or failings of their friends, even when they can no longer suffer by their detection; we therefore see whole ranks of characters adorned with uniform panegyric, and not to be known from one another, but by extrinsic and casual circumstances. 'Let me remember,' says Hale, 'when I find myself inclined to pity a criminal, that there is likewise a pity due to the country.' If we owe regard to the memory of the dead, there is yet more respect to be paid to knowledge, to virtue, and to truth.

* * *

* Biography is, of the various kinds of narrative writing, that which is most eagerly read, and most easily applied to the purposes of life.

In romances, when the wide field of possibility lies open to invention, the incidents may easily be made more numerous, the vicissitudes

* *Idler*, No. 84, 24 November 1759.

more sudden, and the events more wonderful; but from the time of life when fancy begins to be overruled by reason and corrected by experience, the most artful tale raises little curiosity when it is known to be false; though it may, perhaps, be sometimes read as a model of a neat or elegant style, not for the sake of knowing what it contains, but how it is written; or those that are weary of themselves, may have recourse to it as a pleasing dream, of which, when they awake, they voluntarily dismiss the images from their minds.

The examples and events of history press, indeed, upon the mind with the weight of truth; but when they are reposited in the memory, they are oftener employed for show than use, and rather diversify conversation than regulate life. Few are engaged in such scenes as give them opportunities of growing wiser by the downfall of statesmen or the defeat of generals. The stratagems of war, and the intrigues of courts, are read by far the greater part of mankind with the same indifference as the adventures of fabled heroes, or the revolutions of a fairy region. Between falsehood and useless truth there is little difference. As gold which he cannot spend will make no man rich, so knowledge which he cannot apply will make no man wise.

The mischievous consequences of vice and folly, of irregular desires and predominant passions, are best discovered by those relations which are levelled with the general surface of life, which tell not how any man became great, but how he was made happy; not how he lost the favour of his prince, but how he became discontented with himself.

Those relations are, therefore, commonly of most value in which the writer tells his own story. He that recounts the life of another, commonly dwells most upon conspicuous events, lessens the familiarity of his tale to increase its dignity, shows his favourite at a distance, decorated and magnified like the ancient actors in their tragic dress, and endeavours to hide the man that he may produce a hero.

But if it be true, which was said by a French prince, 'that no man was a hero to the servants of his chamber', it is equally true, that every man is yet less a hero to himself. He that is most elevated above the crowd by the importance of his employments, or the reputation of his genius, feels himself affected by fame or business but as they influence his domestic life. The high and low, as they have the same faculties and the same senses, have no less similitude in their pains and pleasures. The sensations are the same in all, though produced by very different occasions. The prince feels the same pain when an invader seizes a province, as the farmer when a thief drives away his cow. Men thus equal in themselves will appear equal in honest and impartial biography; and those whom fortune or nature places at the greatest distance may afford instruction to each other.

The writer of his own life has, at least, the first qualification of an historian, the knowledge of the truth; and though it may be plausibly objected that his temptations to disguise it are equal to his opportunities of knowing it, yet I cannot but think that impartiality may be expected with equal confidence from him that relates the passages of his own life, as from him that delivers the transactions of another.

Certainty of knowledge not only excludes mistake, but fortifies veracity. What we collect by conjecture, and by conjecture only can one man judge of another's motives or sentiments, is easily modified by fancy or by desire; as objects imperfectly discerned take forms from the hope or fear of the beholder. But that which is fully known cannot be falsified but with reluctance of understanding, and alarm of conscience: of understanding, the lover of truth; of conscience, the sentinel of virtue.

He that writes the life of another is either his friend or his enemy, and wishes either to exalt his praise or aggravate his infamy: many temptations to falsehood will occur in the disguise of passions, too specious to fear much resistance. Love of virtue will animate panegyric, and hatred of wickedness embitter censure. The zeal of gratitude, the ardour of patriotism, fondness for an opinion, or fidelity to a party, may easily overpower the vigilance of a mind habitually well disposed, and prevail over unassisted and unfriended veracity.

But he that speaks of himself has no motive to falsehood or partiality except self-love, by which all have so often been betrayed, that all are on the watch against its artifices. He that writes an apology for a single action, to confute an accusation, to recommend himself to favour, is, indeed, always to be suspected of favouring his own cause; but he that sits down calmly and voluntarily to review his life for the admonition of posterity, or to amuse himself, and leaves this account unpublished, may be commonly presumed to tell truth, since falsehood cannot appease his own mind, and fame will not be heard beneath the tomb.

* * *

Lives of the Poets [Addison], 1781 [Hill edition (1905), II, 116]

The necessity of complying with times and of sparing persons is the great impediment of biography. History may be formed from permanent monuments and records; but lives can only be written from personal knowledge, which is growing every day less, and in a short time is lost for ever. What is known can seldom be immediately told, and when it might be told it is no longer known. The delicate features of the mind, the nice discriminations of character, and the minute peculiarities of conduct are soon obliterated; and it is surely better that caprice, obstinacy, frolic, and folly, however they might delight in the description, should be silently forgotten than that by wanton merriment and unseasonable detection a pang should be given to a widow, a daughter, a brother, or a friend. As the process of these narratives is now bringing me among my contemporaries I begin to feel myself, 'walking upon ashes under which the fire is not extinguished', and coming to the time of which it will be proper rather to say 'nothing that is false, than all that is true'.

[From records of his conversation]

Boswell's *Life of Johnson*, 14 July 1763 [ed. Hill-Powell, I, 433]

He recommended to me to keep a journal of my life, full and unreserved. He said it would be a very good exercise, and would yield me great satisfaction when the particulars were faded from my remembrance. . . . I mentioned that I was afraid I put into my journal too many little incidents. JOHNSON. 'There is nothing, Sir, too little for so little a creature as man. It is by studying little things that we attain the great art of having as little misery and as much happiness as possible.'

Life, 10 May 1766 (letter to Langton) [II, 17]

I hope you make what enquiries you can, and write down what is told you. The little things which distinguish domestic characters are soon forgotten: if you delay to enquire, you will have no information; if you neglect to write, information will be vain.

Life, 31 March 1772 [II, 166]

He said, 'Goldsmith's Life of Parnell is poor; not that it is poorly written, but that he had poor materials; for nobody can write the life of a man, but those who have eat and drunk and lived in social intercourse with him.' I said, that if it was not troublesome and presuming too much, I would request him to tell me all the little circumstances of his life; what schools he attended, when he came to Oxford, when he came to London, &c. &c. He did not disapprove of my curiosity as to these particulars; but said, 'They'll come out by degrees as we talk together.'

Tour to the Hebrides, 21 August 1773 [V, 79–80]

MONBODDO. 'The history of manners is the most valuable. I never set a high value on any other history.' JOHNSON. 'Nor I; and therefore I esteem biography, as giving us what comes near to ourselves, what we can turn to use.' BOSWELL. 'But in the course of general history, we find manners. In wars, we see the dispositions of people, their degrees of humanity, and other particulars.' JOHNSON. 'Yes; but then you must take all the facts to get this; and it is but a little you get.' MONBODDO. 'And it is that little which makes history valuable.' Bravo! thought I; they agree like two brothers.

Tour to the Hebrides, 22 September 1773 [V, 240]

Talking of biography, he said, he did not think that the life of any literary man in England had been well written. Beside the common incidents of life, it should tell us his studies, his mode of living, the means by which he attained to excellence, and his opinion of his own works. He told us, he had sent Derrick to Dryden's relations, to gather materials for his Life; and he believed Derrick had got all that he himself should have got; but it was nothing.

Life, 20 March 1776 [II, 446]

We talked of biography. JOHNSON. 'It is rarely well executed. They only who live with a man can write his life with any genuine exactness and discrimination; and few people who have lived with a man know what to remark about him. The chaplain of a late Bishop, whom I was to assist in writing some memoirs of his Lordship, could tell me scarcely any thing.'

Life, 15 May 1776 [III, 71–72]

Talking of the great difficulty of obtaining authentic information for biography, Johnson told us, 'When I was a young fellow I wanted to write the "Life of Dryden", and in order to get materials, I applied to the only two persons then alive who had seen him; these were old Swinney, and old Cibber. Swinney's information was no more than this, "That at Will's coffee-house Dryden had a particular chair for himself, which was set by the fire in winter, and was then called his winter-chair; and that it was carried out for him to the balcony in summer, and was then called his summer-chair." Cibber could tell no more but "That he remembered him a decent old man, arbiter of critical disputes at Will's." You are to consider that Cibber was then at a great distance from Dryden, had perhaps one leg only in the room, and durst not draw in the other.'

Life, 17 September 1777 [III, 154–55]

Talking of biography, I said, in writing a life, a man's peculiarities should be mentioned, because they mark his character. JOHNSON. 'Sir, there is no doubt as to peculiarities: the question is, whether a man's vices should be mentioned; for instance, whether it should be mentioned that Addison and Parnell drank too freely; for people will probably more easily indulge in drinking from knowing this; so that more ill may be done by the example, than good by telling the whole truth.' Here was an instance of his varying from himself in talk; for when Lord Hailes and he sat one morning calmly conversing in my house at Edinburgh, I well remember that Dr. Johnson maintained, that 'If a man is to write *A Panegyric*, he may keep vices out of sight; but if he professes to write *A Life*, he must represent it really as it was': and when I objected to the danger of telling that Parnell drank to excess, he said, that 'it would produce an instructive caution to avoid drinking, when it was seen, that even the learning and genius of Parnell could be debased by it.' And in the Hebrides he maintained, as appears from my 'Journal', that a man's intimate friend should mention his faults, if he writes his life.

Life, 1781 [letter from Edmond Malone, 15 March 1782, referring to attacks on Johnson's 'Life of Addison'] [IV, 53]

If nothing but the bright side of characters should be shown, we would sit down in despondency, and think it utterly impossible to imitate them in *any thing*. The sacred writers [he observed] related the vicious as well as the virtuous actions of men; which had this moral effect, that it kept mankind from *despair*, into which otherwise they would naturally fall, were they not supported by the recollection that others had offended like themselves, and by penitence and amendment of life had been restored to the favour of Heaven.

Johnsonian Miscellanies [II, 417] [from William Weller Pepys]

Johnson [defending his life of Lyttelton] observed 'that it was the *duty* of a biographer to state *all* the failings of a respectable character.'

Johnsonian Miscellanies [II, 3] [from Hawkins' edition, Vol. XI]

The business of such a one [an exact biographer], said he, is to give a complete account of the person whose life he is writing, and to discriminate him from all other persons by any peculiarities of character or sentiment he may happen to have.

James Boswell

* The great lines of characters may be put down. But I doubt much if it be possible to preserve in words the peculiar features of mind which distinguish individuals as certainly as the features of different countenances. The art of portrait painting fixes the last; and musical sounds with all their nice gradations can also be fixed. Perhaps language may be improved to such a degree as to picture the varieties of mind minutely. In the meantime we must be content to enjoy the recollection of characters in our own breasts. . . . I cannot portray Commissioner Cochrane as he exists in my mind.

* * *

† This delusive propensity to imitate the vices of eminent men, makes it a question of some difficulty in biography, whether their faults should be recorded. We have indeed the high example of holy writ, where we find the errors and crimes even of saints and martyrs fairly and freely related. But we ought not to assimilate ordinary human compositions to what carries a reverential awe. And notwithstanding that, it is to be feared that there have been too many instances of people offending under the mistaken sanction of scriptural history. At the same time, truth is sacred, and real characters should be known. I am

* From his journal, 19 October 1775. *The Private Papers of James Boswell from Malahide Castle*, ed. Geoffrey Scott (1929). Vol. VI, p. 17.

† From 'The Hypochondriack', No. 35, *London Magazine*, August 1780; reprinted in *The Hypochondriack*, ed. Margery Bailey. Stanford University Press, 1928, II, pp. 13–14.

therefore of opinion, that a biographer should tell even the imperfections and faults of those whose lives he writes, provided that he takes a conscientious care not to blend them with the general lustre of excellence, but to distinguish and separate them, and impress upon his readers a just sense of the evil, so that they may regret its being found in such a man, and be anxiously disposed to avoid what hurts even the most exalted characters, but would utterly sink men of ordinary merit.

* * *

* But it is a work of very great labour and difficulty to keep a journal of life, occupied in various pursuits, mingled with concomitant speculations and reflections, in so much, that I do not think it possible to do it unless one has a peculiar talent for abridging. I have tried it in that way, when it has been my good fortune to live in a multiplicity of instructive and entertaining scenes, and I have thought my notes like portable soup, of which a little bit by being dissolved in water will make a good large dish; for their substance by being expanded in words would fill a volume. Sometimes it has occurred to me that a man should not live more than he can record, as a farmer should not have a larger crop than he can gather in. And I have regretted that there is no invention for getting an immediate and exact transcript of the mind, like that instrument by which a copy of a letter is at once taken off.

* * *

[From correspondence]

Boswell to Thomas Percy, 9 February 1788

I am ashamed that I have yet seven years to write of his life. I do it chronologically, giving year by year his publications, if there were any; his letters, his conversations, and every thing else that I can collect. It appears to me that mine is the best plan of biography that can be conceived; for my readers will as near as may be accompany Johnson in his progress, and, as it were, see each scene as it happened.

Boswell to William Temple, 25 February 1788

Mason's *Life of Gray* is excellent, because it is interspersed with letters which show us the *man*. His *Life of Whitehead* is not a life at all;

* From 'The Hypochondriack', No. 66, *London Magazine*, March 1783. Bailey, *op. cit.*, II, p. 259.

for there is neither a letter nor a saying from first to last. I am absolutely certain that *my* mode of biography, which gives not only a *history* of Johnson's *visible* progress through the world, and of his publications, but a *view* of his mind, in his letters and conversations is the most perfect that can be conceived, and will be *more* of a *Life* than any work that has ever yet appeared.

* * *

* The labour and anxious attention with which I have collected and arranged the materials of which these volumes are composed, will hardly be conceived by those who read them with careless facility. The stretch of mind and prompt assiduity by which so many conversations were preserved, I myself, at some distance of time, contemplate with wonder; and I must be allowed to suggest, that the nature of the work, in other respects, as it consists of innumerable detached particulars, all which, even the most minute, I have spared no pains to ascertain with a scrupulous authenticity, has occasioned a degree of trouble far beyond that of any other species of composition. Were I to detail the books which I have consulted, and the inquiries which I have found it necessary to make by various channels, I should probably be thought ridiculously ostentatious. Let me only observe, as a specimen of my trouble, that I have sometimes been obliged to run half over London, in order to fix a date correctly; which, when I had accomplished, I well knew would obtain me no praise, though a failure would have been to my discredit. And after all, perhaps, hard as it may be, I shall not be surprised if omissions or mistakes be pointed out with invidious severity. I have also been extremely careful as to the exactness of my quotations; holding that there is a respect due to the public, which should oblige every author to attend to this, and never to presume to introduce them with,—'I think I have read';—or—'If I remember right'; when the originals may be examined.

* * *

† Instead of melting down my materials into one mass, and constantly speaking in my own person, by which I might have appeared to have more merit in the execution of the work, I have resolved to adopt and

* From Advertisement to the first edition of the *Life of Samuel Johnson* (1791) [Hill-Powell edition, I, 5–7].

† From *Life of Samuel Johnson* (1791) [Hill-Powell edition, I, 29–33].

enlarge upon the excellent plan of Mr. Mason, in his Memoirs of Gray. Wherever narrative is necessary to explain, connect, and supply, I furnish it to the best of my abilities; but in the chronological series of Johnson's life, which I trace as distinctly as I can, year by year, I produce, wherever it is in my power, his own minutes, letters, or conversation, being convinced that this mode is more lively, and will make my readers better acquainted with him, than even most of those were who actually knew him, but could know him only partially; whereas there is here an accumulation of intelligence from various points, by which his character is more fully understood and illustrated.

Indeed I cannot conceive a more perfect mode of writing any man's life, than not only relating all the most important events of it in their order, but interweaving what he privately wrote, and said, and thought; by which mankind are enabled as it were to see him live, and to 'live o'er each scene' with him, as he actually advanced through the several stages of his life. Had his other friends been as diligent and ardent as I was, be might have been almost entirely preserved. As it is, I will venture to say that he will be seen in this work more completely than any man who has ever yet lived.

And he will be seen as he really was; for I profess to write, not his panegyric, which must be all praise, but his Life; which, great and good as he was, must not be supposed to be entirely perfect. To be as he was, is indeed subject of panegyric enough to any man in this state of being; but in every picture there should be shade as well as light, and when I delineate him without reserve, I do what he himself recommended, both by his precept and his example. . . .

What I consider as the peculiar value of the following work, is, the quantity that it contains of Johnson's conversation; which is universally acknowledged to have been eminently instructive and entertaining; and of which the specimens that I have given upon a former occasion, have been received with so much approbation, that I have good grounds for supposing that the world will not be indifferent to more ample communications of a similar nature. . . .

I am fully aware of the objections which may be made to the minuteness on some occasions of my detail of Johnson's conversation, and how happily it is adapted for the petty exercise of ridicule, by men of superficial understanding and ludicrous fancy; but I remain firm and confident in my opinion, that minute particulars are frequently characteristic, and always amusing, when they relate to a distinguished man.

The Nineteenth Century

Samuel Taylor Coleridge

*An inquisitiveness into the minutest circumstances and casual sayings of eminent contemporaries, is indeed quite natural; but so are all our follies, and the more natural they are, the more caution should we exert in guarding against them. To scribble trifles even on the perishable glass of an inn window, is the mark of an idler; but to engrave them on the marble monument, sacred to the memory of the departed great, is something worse than idleness. The spirit of genuine biography is in nothing more conspicuous, than in the firmness with which it withstands the cravings of worthless curiosity, as distinguished from the thirst after useful knowledge. For, in the first place, such anecdotes as derive their whole and sole interest from the great name of the person, concerning whom they are related, and neither illustrate his general character nor his particular actions, would scarcely have been noticed or remembered except by men of weak minds: it is not unlikely, therefore, that they were misapprehended at the time, and it is most probable that they have been related as incorrectly, as they were noticed injudiciously. Nor are the consequences of such garrulous biography merely negative. For as insignificant stories can derive no real respectability from the eminence of the person who happens to be the subject of them, but rather an additional deformity of disproportion, they are apt to have their insipidity seasoned by the same bad passions, that accompany the habit of gossiping in general; and the

* From 'A Prefatory Observation on Modern Biography', *The Friend*, No. 21, Thursday, 25 January 1810, pp. 338–9. Reprinted with minor changes as 'The Principles of True Biography' in the 1818 collected edition.

misapprehensions of weak men meeting with the misinterpretations of malignant men, have not seldom formed the ground work of the most grievous calumnies. In the second place, these trifles are subversive of the great end of biography, which is to fix the attention and to interest the feelings of men, on those qualities and actions which have made a particular life worthy of being recorded. It is, no doubt, the duty of an honest biographer, to portray the prominent imperfections as well as excellencies of his hero; but I am at a loss to conceive, how this can be deemed an excuse for heaping together a multitude of particulars, which can prove nothing of any man that might not have been safely taken for granted of all men. In the present age (emphatically the age of personality!) there are more than ordinary motives for withholding all encouragement from this mania of busying ourselves with the names of others, which is still more alarming as a symptom, than it is troublesome as a disease. The reader must be still less acquainted with contemporary literature than myself—a case not likely to occur—if he needs *me* to inform him, that there are men, who trading in the silliest anecdotes, in unprovoked abuse and senseless eulogy, think themselves nevertheless employed both worthily and honourably, if only all this be done '*in good set terms*,' and from the press, and of *public* characters: a class which has increased so rapidly of late, that it becomes difficult to discover what characters are to be considered as private. Alas! if these wretched misusers of language and the means of giving wings to thought, and of multiplying the presence of an individual mind, had ever known, how great a thing the possession of any one simple truth is, and how mean a thing a mere fact is, except as seen in the light of some comprehensive truth; if they had but once experienced the unborrowed complacency, the inward independence, the homebred strength, with which every clear conception of the reason is accompanied, they would shrink from their own pages as at the remembrance of a crime. For a crime it is (and the man, who hesitates in pronouncing it such, must be ignorant of what mankind owe to books, what he himself owes to them in spite of his ignorance) thus to introduce the spirit of vulgar scandal and personal inquietude into the closet and the library, environing with evil passions the very sanctuaries, to which we should flee for refuge from them! For to what do these publications appeal, whether they present themselves as biography or as anonymous criticism, but to the same feelings which the scandal-bearers and time-killers of ordinary life seek to gratify in themselves and their listeners? And both the authors and admirers of such publications, in what respect are they less truants and deserters from their own hearts, and from their appointed task of understanding and amending them, than the most garrulous female chronicler of the goings-on of yesterday in the families of her neighbours and townsfolk?

James Field Stanfield

* The *end* proposed to be attained by this Essay is—to take such a view of biography, as may assist in developing the principles of man's active and moral nature; and in applying that knowledge to his practical improvement.

The *means* proposed to accomplish this, are certain arrangements, inductions, and observations, which have been derived from an attentive study of biography; from a patient and extensive survey of living character, in various countries and stages of civilization; and from an early and constant exercise of considering *self-movements*, in all their springs, courses, and apparent destinations.

The *motive*, which impelled both to the Essay, and to the resolution of laying it before the public, was, and is—a sincere desire to promote, in students as well as writers, through the medium of biography, a more attentive examination of the principles of the human character; and a very ardent hope, that the effects of such investigation may be actively applied to the improveable points of education and conduct.

It may appear presumptuous to engage in a didactic treatise on biography, at a time when that species of writing is so generally cultivated; and when so many elaborate compositions of the kind are brought before the established literary tribunals—to have their principles, arrangement, and execution, investigated and decided on by the received laws of biographical criticism. But, though the lives of celebrated men have become, more than formerly, the subjects of literary labour, and

* Excerpts from *An Essay on the Study and Composition of Biography* (Sunderland, 1813), pp. v–vii, 1–2, 15–17, 54, 59–60, 62–63, 65–69, 134, 139–40, 145–6, 149–53, 162, 164–6, 175–6, 185, 325–7.

though such works, from their frequency, have attracted critical animadversion, yet, no regular compact dissertation on the general subject of biographical composition has ever yet appeared.

The author of the present Essay does not, in the extended view he wishes biography to be considered, feel himself competent to supply this vacancy: but if his effort can be an instrument of directing to this interesting subject the attention of those more qualified to undertake the task, he has gained one important point of his general purpose. . . .

Man's natural faculties, his education, the progressive intercourse and mutual impression between him and surrounding circumstances, with the habits, course, and conduct of life, resulting therefrom, offer the principal materials to the discerning biographer. These can never be furnished with certainty and exactness, but from the genuine stores of a man's own consciousness. There can be no perfect biography but that which is written by a man's self; who, not only has it in his power to trace with accuracy and connection the continued progression of his pursuits and actions, but is, also, competent to view with conscious certainty the motives which produced them, and the ends to which they were directed. But, as our supply of genuine self-biography is but scanty, and as we shall have occasion to remark more particularly on that part of the subject in the course of the Essay, we must, for the present, take a view of the materials which generally furnish the stock of personal history. We must take them as they present themselves; connected or detached, shining or ordinary, interesting or futile, consistent or unequal: and, in this view, we must consider also the disadvantages which have attended them, from casualty and circumstances. . . .

There are very many, even among supposed biographers, who vainly imagine, that the delineation of a man's life, from his birth to his demise, is an agreeable, easy task,—requiring small pains in the preparation, and little effort in the performance. Such persons would feel surprise, were they requested to draw the likeness of the most familiar face, without having first acquired the general principles of the art of painting, and without having, by long and assiduous exercise, brought those rules into practical execution. Such surprise would be, obviously, well founded; and yet these scrupulous personages would not at all hesitate to attempt, not the description of a single incident of a man's life, but, the full and accurate representation of his faculities, habits, opinions, and manners; his particular passions, and his general conduct.

They would undertake to exhibit his motives, objects, and pursuits; the transactions he was engaged in, with the circumstances that influenced, and the consequences that followed; in short, the whole series of a connection of purposes and events, which link together the varied, yet regular, continuity of human existence. And all this would be presumptuously ventured upon, without any previous study of the general nature of man; without a knowledge of the dominion of physical and moral causes, the power of the passions, or the phenomena of the strange but accountable shiftings of the human character.

Such a writer, unskilled in the regular succession of connecting particulars, as well as the distinctive prominencies of human agency, will, in his collection of materials, be confused and indiscriminate; either producing a disorderly accumulation of all that could be gathered, or an incoherent display of such as appeared to be most shining or extraordinary. A mere relater of anecdotes, not a writer of lives, his account will be perplexed, because he does not know how to arrange—will be inaccurate, because he does not know what to select.

Without a previous knowledge of the nature of man, his general pursuits, his essential propensities, and common habits of acting, it is impossible to give a connected and regular history of particular transactions. A set of disjointed passages, however lively in themselves and in the manner of their exhibition, does not constitute historical narration: they must be threaded together, to give continuity to the subject, and direction to the mind. How different soever the various incidents of life appear, they have their classes, their dependencies, and connections. The ordinary acts of producing these relations, or of generating one from another, have such a definite identity, that a true biographer may apply his terms of connection with such precision, as to derive very great assistance towards the devolving of causes, as well as towards the tracing of successive effects. Whereas, from the writer's ignorance of these hidden links which connect events with agency, and these general elements which impress similitude on the human character, the truth of biographical representation is distorted, and all attempts at characteristical investigation are defeated or confounded.

* * *

To delineate with force and truth, the writer must enter intimately into the character he would exhibit—he must, for the time, endeavour to see things in the same point of view, and conceive sentiments of the same nature and feeling. But, whilst he describes with perspicuity, it is not his office to defend what he represents, and change the historian into the apologist, much less to blacken the party or characters that are found in opposition to the opinions and practices of his hero. . . .

Modern composition, from a superabundance of materials, and from facility of access to them, frequently suffers more under this redundancy than is perceived in the coherent and individual representations of former times. A conspicuous name, and the delineation of an extraordinary character, in the present day, is often assumed to give the author an opportunity of indulging in remote discussion, and extraneous incident. The rage of accumulating anecdotes gives enjoyment to the collector; and the exhibition gratifies those who look for the reiteration of amusement, but who would feel fatigued by the attention requisite to follow a series of facts and events, collected by patient observation, strung together by the laws of agency and consequence, and by the progressive principles which influence the direction and force of human action.

If the character be a literary one, the temptations for the gathering of anecdotes are multiplied. Every tale, incident, or saying, that can be collected, is seized upon with avidity; sometimes having relation to, and often totally unconnected with the person, whose memoir is supposed to be before us. Should these extrinsic matters be insipid or tedious, they still abstract attention from the proposed object; and if they be lively and well told, they transfer the interest from the subject to themselves, and engage the reader in a desultory course of literary gossiping, whilst the essential narration, the promised transactions and character, are passed by and neglected. . . .

A detailing particularity in description brings tediousness and languor:—to be too concise is to be dry and uninteresting. But, whilst remarking on the propensity of loading the page with minute particulars, and on the fastidiousness which rejects essentials because minute, it is proper to observe, that those light circumstances which appear unnecessary or tedious appendages to a character of the present time, may be received as valuable matter for the investigation of the future student; and will acquire importance from the remoteness of the period and estimation of the character. The *Critical Review*, animadverting on Whitelock's Journal of the Swedish Embassy, remarks that 'the work, so far as it extends, may be considered as the most copious fund of minute incidents that we meet with in biographical writings. But they are unimportant;—and, in his life-time, would not be interesting. At this period they derive a degree of veneration, from the distance at which they are placed, and from the integrity of the author.' Those circumstances, which may be generally known amongst contemporaries, are not, on that account, to be pretermitted. Posterity will desire to be acquainted with the minutest appearances that have attached to a great character. The familiar habits, the convivial and domestic manners, the times and modes of study, business and enjoyments, the very dress and idle propensities, of such men, are valuable in preservation; and must not be confounded with those unmeaning and extraneous trifles, liable to the present exception. . . .

When the materials are clear, copious, and genuine, and the mind of the writer well informed and free from prejudice, biography will still fall short of its legitimate aim, if the method of composition be not perspicuous and conducive to the purpose.

Plutarch, the great master of the art, has, generally, followed the chronological order; narrating rather according to the succession of time, than the connection of things: and in this mode he has been followed by the generality of biographers. Suetonius, Melchior Adam, and a few more, have aimed to give a kind of connection and wholeness to actions, by collecting the circumstances under certain general heads. And others have divided their histories by separate accounts of the public and private transactions. Each of these methods, considered singly, may possess peculiar advantages; yet being followed strictly and exclusively, the limitation will produce deficiency and incoherence.

There can be no distinctness presented, and scarcely the appearance of continuity preserved, by the feeble links of the chronological series. Unity and interest are generally inseparable;—to fix their mutual impression, leading pursuits or transactions of magnitude might be kept in view to their accomplishment, with little interruption. By continuing a pursuit, passion, or production, as closely as possible, through its rise, progress, and completion,—confusion is avoided—curiosity and attention are gratified and engaged—and, as Gibbon says of his method of grouping his pictures by distinct nations, 'the seeming neglect of chronological order is compensated by the superior advantage of interest and perspicuity.' . . .

Following the order of time, day by day, like the journal of a diarist (the routine of common circumstances mixing with the gradual progression of purpose, and broken by the hourly intervention of accident) presents nothing but a chequered display of occasional incident and habitual occurrence; resembling life in the mere glance at appearances, but utterly unlike it in a close view of that seemingly-interrupted, yet *persevering pursuit of objects*, which constitutes the very essence of rational being, and is, indeed, the principle of all voluntary action. Much is certainly due to the minute and laborious annalist, as a collector of valuable materials, though without arrangement or direction; but for connection and design, for lucid order and accurate classification, we must have recourse to the genius and talents of a different operator.

By advancing so much in favour of connecting particular pursuits or passions, it is not, by any means, intended to lose sight of the advantages of the chronological order, or to shut our eyes to the inconveniencies of collecting dispersed matters into compact and distinct divisions, without having due regard to time and situation. Though history, as in the elaborate work of Dr. Henry, may have attempted such an arrangement on a comprehensive scale, it must not be omitted —and it is the principle scope of this essay to inculcate—that, the leading object of biography should be to hold in view to the student or reader one faithful, perspicuous, and continued LIFE. The aim is to recommend a regular and uninterrupted detail of individual action, and a perfect and full delineation of individual character. But, to accomplish this end, it is also submitted to the attention of the biographer, that action should be concatenated, and character developed; that where an interesting process occurs, it should be pursued through the links of purpose, progress, and attainment, shutting out, for a time, the synchronous incidents, which would divert the attention to confused objects, and break the clue of rational investigation; that it is his province not only to describe, but connect; not only to narrate, but philosophize.

In the view of thus uniting the succession of time with the direction and continuity of pursuits, we might venture to think, that the chronology of a true biographer should be—an accurate knowledge of the prevailing passions and propensities, which are generally attendant on the different stages and conditions of human life; their relations among themselves, together with their influence on occurrences and situation; and the regular series of action, commonly generated by such combination. This mental computation should be held as much in view as the marginal 'Anno Domini': and, although, in so comprehensive a study, variations may be expected to arise, yet, on the whole, it may be found a useful scale to apply to the progression of events, discovery of principles, and investigation of character. . . .

The form and the end of biography are founded on one principle, and that is utility: and utility can only proceed from faithfulness of representation. The requisites leading to fidelity are independence and industry; the one giving a freedom of mind, fitted for the reception and promulgation of truth, and the other powers of attention for its investigation. Without a noble independence of mind, removed equally from sordid fear as from favourable expectation, the search, and even the knowledge, would be fruitless. The biographer should be under no control; free in his researches, unrestrained in his function, sacred in his character, exalted in his views, about the reach of power, and out of the prospects of favour. . . .

An historian (as is well expressed in a letter from Dr. Robertson to Mr. Gibbon) *should feel himself a witness giving evidence upon oath*. The biographer is indispensably obligated by the same law. He is bound, fairly and firmly, to advance what he himself has gathered from actual observation, or what he has impartially collected from the unsuspected testimony and accounts of others. To the principles of impartial justice and innate love of truth, inseparable from his own character, he must join a penetrating and discriminative spirit of enquiry into the views and modes of thinking, which may influence the decisions and representations of those, whose authorities and opinions he has to work upon. He must not only correct the accounts, that are communicated or written in the spirit of evident partiality, but he must also be on his guard in considering and appreciating the narrations of those, who suppose themselves to be incapable of advancing any thing, but within the bounds of the strictest veracity. Though it may be mortifying to the pride of presumed accuracy, yet experience too frequently declares, that, even in circumstances where they have been ear and eye-witnesses, and full of confidence in their fidelity and judgement, men will often furnish descriptions and accounts very wide of the real state of facts, when their minds are biased by the imperceptible warpings of opinion and prejudice. . . .

The two great ends of biography are—to obtain a deeper insight into the principles of the human mind, and to offer examples to practical observation and improvement. For the one, accurate fidelity is necessary; and for the other, moral illustration. Were we a generation of philosophers or profound thinkers, perhaps the accuracy of minute narration would be only wanting; but when we consider, that as, from the entertaining and interesting nature of personal history, it finds its way to the closets and bosoms of the young and unthinking,—in such possible circumstances, to send vice abroad in the specious colours it so generally assumes, without exposing its deformity and loathsomeness, would be seduction and not warning—would be to deteriorate and not to improve and instruct. . . .

The administration of the censorial power has been regarded as an indispensable duty by most of those great men, whom we look up to, as leaders in this important walk of literature. Nor can this moral dispensation be, in any instance, abandoned, if we would preserve to biography, that station it seems so well entitled to among the nobler sciences; not merely as a school of speculation and curiosity, but as an institute, deciding upon the nature of actions and their causes, pointing the influence of example to practical operation, and from a thorough knowledge of the whole case, in all its ethical relations, marking the issue with the eternal stamp of reprobation or renown. . . .

The biographer thus claims the right of free judgement on the motives, means, and actions of men. This judicial power is not exercised in solitary instances, but is directed to a whole series of events and conduct; not confined to certain inferior classes, but reaching to the great, the eminent, and the powerful; pronouncing on the virtues and on the crimes of all, and fixing their moral character with posterity.

The office being of such importance, and the decisions involving such interesting consequences, the most patient attention and scrupulous impartiality must be exerted. The judgements are not to be delivered unqualified and dogmatic; but should arise from a candid and temperate display of particular actions and circumstances, with their value balanced in the fair scale of ethical justice. In those instances, care must be taken that praise do not rise into panegyric, or reprehension degenerate into satire;—and it must not be forgotten, that this practice of interposing the moral judgement should be used sparingly, and with discretion, and can be rarely admitted with safety, but when the magnitude of the case demands the tribute or decision of the biographer, or when the exposure throws more light on the prominent features and peculiar form of the character.

Many are apt to judge and decide on the actions and conduct of men by the prevailing regulations of their own times, by their own particular scale of right and wrong, or by the disproportionate test of local prejudice and arbitrary association. These partial decisions will, in many cases, be injurious, and in most cases inapplicable; especially when the characters are removed by time, by country, or by degree of civilization, from the standard of our own practice and opinions. Giving appellations to the conduct and notions of men, according to our own estimation, or the opinions of the present day, is not the fair light in which to set a biographic picture. We often find that names and terms are adopted according to the feelings of party or variation of circumstances; and the religious man, attached to his peculiar persuasion, is, by an adverse pen, branded with the appellation of bigot; and what, in one case, is called rebellion, is, by a different class of writers, softened into the less-degrading term of revolution. In express political writings, or on the pages of controversy, such representations are admitted; but are essentially foreign to the nature and purpose of biography, whose province it is to produce the likeness of man as he is, modified, certainly, by locality and circumstances, but drawn accurately with his own distinctive features, and according to the established rules of general nature—and not distorted by the notions and peculiar practice of the artist.

Dionysius Halicarnassus ranks decency as a primary virtue in an historian. This is the becoming principle that represents with clearness the characters of the personages exhibited, and preserves the dignity of the actions under consideration. Admitting the above, the question will arise—how far, consistent with a regard to the operation of this principle, in the course of his official duty, the biographer may proceed in his investigation and exposure of such vices as may come in review before him;—vices, deforming the possessors, and calling on him for just censure and marked abhorrence?

In one of the fifteen theorems, proposed by Paul Beni, in his work on the manner of writing history, the question is agitated—'whether the foul and gross particulars of transactions should be narrated?'—and the answer is in the affirmative; but with this essential qualification, that the accounts, so given, be cloathed in modest and general terms. With this decision every unpolluted mind must most sincerely accord. Vice, even in its ramifications and recesses, may, and ought to be exposed, in order to show its hideousness, and secure its punishment in the detestation of posterity; but it is not to be grossly uncovered, or dwelt upon with meretricious implication and minuteness. On these accounts, and in this modest spirit, censure must unreservedly fall on the particular and disgusting views, given by Suetonius, in his account of the abominable lives of some of the Roman emperors: nor will the qualifying antithesis, said to be St. Jerome's, that he had written the lives of those monsters with the same freedom with which they had led them, supply any vindication; it can, at best, but place his descriptions on a level with *their* brutality. . . .

In some instances, a minuteness of representation has been condemned: the selection therefore requires both penetration and discretion. The practice should be judiciously limited, by not admitting every irrelative, idle story, that can be gleaned, nor rejecting any passage, however minute, which may serve to throw a ray of light on individual peculiarity, or can direct to any distinct aspect of the general human character. . . .

Detached, insulated facts offer no matter for delineation or development. Every prominent incident in life follows and is dependent on those which have preceded. The business of the biographer is, to trace the links by which they were united: and by every such process of investigation we advance one step further in a distinctive appreciation of general character—one degree more in the important science of cause and consequence.

What are those links? They must be acts or thoughts. If acts, they must be certain minor incidents interposed and connected with those that are more conspicuous; and, as such, should be examined, as well according to their own particular nature, as in their conjunctive relation to the events immediately preceding and following. If thoughts, they must consist of certain peculiar views taken of occurring circumstances, estimation of their relative interest and importance, and the resulting volition which determines to action.

But in this investigation, both skill and close attention are necessary, lest juxta-position be taken for association, and exception adopted instead of principle. Facts which do not accord with the general congruity of succession, as guided by the known principles of the character and conduct in question, must be looked on with suspicion, and minutely scanned by the laws of connective probability.

Where it is difficult to reconcile appearances to the circumstances of the situation presented, not only the peculiar condition of the principal personage is to be studied with deep attention, but also the views, power, and relation of those characters, which possess, by their agency or connection, an influence in the general effect. . . .

Letters are to biography what state-papers are to history; and what Ralph, the historian, ascribes to the latter, may be fairly applied to the utility of the former—that they are the very chart and compass of biography. And, though familiar letters, like those on state affairs, 'may and must partake of the private views, passions, prejudices, and interests of the writers', yet, in the delineation of individual history, all this is of advantage, and the very personalities that may be discovered will assist in throwing distinct lights upon the character. . . .

Letters, written in the genuine confidence of self-disclosure, offer, certainly, the most important materials to biographical composition. They are even beyond what could be supplied by the opportunity of a constant observation of the whole series of designs, pursuits, and attainments: for observation can only furnish us with the view and tenure of a man's ostensible actions; but letters lay open the communication of his very thoughts and purposes.

It must be obvious to every one engaged in this kind of study, that in examining facts and opinions in epistolary compositions, much cool discretion will be necessary. The mind must be guarded against an indiscriminate respect or partiality towards the endowments of the author, or too implicit an admiration of the merit of his writings. The character, foibles, and general designs of the man, should be taken into account. The relation subsisting between him and his correspondent—whether any particular purpose or any certain opinion is to be accomplished or enhanced by the expression and purport of his letters—and whether they are designed to meet other eyes than those of the correspondent, or laboured and finished with a view to future publication;—all of these circumstances should be carefully weighed, and accurately appreciated. Under the correction of such considerations, epistolary writings may be consulted with safety and advantage. . . .

The scrupulous delicacy of modern criticism does not admit the introduction of dialogue into regular biography. Yet where it has been ventured upon, the advantages and beauties, gained by such a mode of exhibition, have almost outweighed the questionable right of their admission. Could conversation be retained with such a degree of accuracy, as to give a *presumptive* confidence in the fidelity of the reporter's statement, the information, as well as the spirit, imparted by this valuable addition, would appear to advance the composition of biography almost to a state of perfection. When it is recollected that many, if not most, of the essential scenes of life have been transacted in this form, their representation, if warranted by sufficient authority, would not only exhibit the external form, but would also lay open the internal springs and genuine operations, which disclose and generally determine the character: and it was on this account, and under this point of view, that attention to the best scenes of our higher dramatic writers was recommended, as a useful auxiliary among the preparatory studies. . . .

The rage for indiscriminate biographical reading has been animadverted upon, as indicating the frivolous taste of the present times. When the mind is excited to this species of reading by a fondness of anecdote and an expectation of variety, little more seems necessary for the purpose of the author or peruser, than what might fairly be demanded from the writer and reader of a fictitious history. Indeed, with regard to solid improvement, the judicious narrator of feigned transactions, when compared with some of our biographers, appears to have greatly the advantage. The novelist, for example, may not only command the succession of events, and the association of condition, into such an orderly train of dependence as will best elucidate the view he means to exhibit of human life and conduct; but he can also create such characters, and adjust such relations between them, as may serve to fit them to situations calculated to discover the effects of circumstances on dispositions, and the consequences that are produced upon even established modes of conduct, by the occurrence of extraordinary incident or violent intrusion. But the biographer must take his facts and transactions as they actually are. He is bound to follow them in the succession of time, connect them by the arbitrary ties of fortuitous occurrence, or the stubborn associations of condition and humour—and 'pursue utility in no track but that of historical truth'.

These seeming detriments are not inherent in the composition and study of biography, considered merely as such. The disadvantages hitherto attendant on biographic delineation, are found to spring from circumstances purely accidental or extraneous. The chief obstructions have been seen to consist in the difficulty of gaining access to a sufficient store of materials for selection, and a want of skill in the artist to give them body and arrangement. To combat these obstacles, a course of study has been recommended; such as would have the effect of suggesting helps in difficult cases, and, by persevering practice, inspire a peculiar spirit to direct the completion. . . .

John Gibson Lockhart

* Voltaire, indeed, has said, 'no man that ever lived deserved a quarto to himself'; and one illustrious writer of our own time has lately protested against the copious style of biography, with reference especially to poets, in language which, were it but for the beauty of it, our readers would thank us for transcribing. Commenting on some cruel details in Dr. Currie's Life of Burns, Mr. Wordsworth, in his letter to Mr. James Gray, thus expressed himself:—

'Your feelings, I trust, go along with mine; and, rising from this individual case to a general view of the subject, you will probably agree with me in opinion that biography, though differing in some essentials from works of fiction, is nevertheless, like them, an *art*,—an art, the laws of which are determined by the imperfections of our nature, and the constitution of society. Truth is not here, as in the sciences, and in natural philosophy, to be sought without scruple, and promulgated for its own sake, upon the mere chance of its being serviceable; but only for obviously justifying purposes, moral or intellectual.

'Silence is a privilege of the grave, a right of the departed: let him, therefore, who infringes that right, by speaking publicly of, for, or against those who cannot speak for themselves, take heed that he opens not his mouth without a sufficient sanction. *De mortuis nil nisi bonum*, is a rule in which these sentiments have been pushed to an extreme that proves how deeply humanity is interested in maintaining them. And

* From a review of Croker's edition of Boswell's *Life of Johnson*, in *Quarterly Review*, November 1831, pp. 20–24. Wordsworth's 'A Letter to a Friend of Robert Burns' appeared in 1816.

it was wise to announce the precept thus absolutely; both because there exist in that same nature, by which it has been dictated, so many temptations to disregard it,—and because there are powers and influences, within and without us, that will prevent its being literally fulfilled—to the suppression of profitable truth. Penalties of law, conventions of manners, and personal fear, protect the reputation of the living; and something of this protection is extended to the recently dead,—who survive, to a certain degree, in their kindred and friends. Few are so insensible as not to feel this, and not to be actuated by the feeling. But only to philosophy enlightened by the affections does it belong justly to estimate the claims of the deceased on the one hand, and of the present age and future generations, on the other; and to strike a balance between them.—Such philosophy runs a risk of becoming extinct among us, if the coarse intrusions into the recesses, the gross breaches upon the sanctities, of domestic life, to which we have lately been more and more accustomed, are to be regarded as indications of a vigorous state of public feeling—favourable to the maintenance of the liberties of our country. Intelligent lovers of freedom are from necessity bold and hardy lovers of truth; but, according to the measure in which their love is intelligent, is it attended with a finer discrimination, and a more sensitive delicacy. The wise and good (and all others being lovers of licence rather than of liberty are in fact slaves) respect, as one of the noblest characteristics of Englishmen, that jealousy of familiar approach, which, while it contributes to the maintenance of private dignity, is one of the most efficacious guardians of rational public freedom.

'The general obligation upon which I have insisted, is especially binding upon those who undertake the biography of *authors.* Assuredly, there *is no cause why the lives of that class of men should be pried into with the same diligent curiosity, and laid open with the same disregard of reserve, which may sometimes be expedient in composing the history of men who have borne an active part in the world. Such thorough knowledge of the good and bad qualities of these latter, as can only be obtained by a scrutiny of their private lives, conduces to explain not only their own public conduct, but that of those with whom they have acted. Nothing of this applies to authors, considered merely as authors. Our business is with their books,—to understand and to enjoy them.* And, of poets more especially, it is true—that, if their works be good, they contain within themselves all that is necessary to their being comprehended and relished. It should seem that the ancients thought in this manner; for of the eminent Greek and Roman poets, few and scanty memorials were, I believe, ever prepared; and fewer still are preserved. It is delightful to read what, in the happy exercise of his own genius, Horace chooses to communicate of himself and his friends; but I confess I am not so much a lover of knowledge, independent of its quality, as to make it likely that it would much rejoice me, were I to hear that records of the Sabine poet and his contemporaries, composed upon the Boswellian plan, had been unearthed among the ruins of Herculaneum. You will interpret what I am writing, *liberally*. With respect to the light which such a discovery might throw upon Roman manners, there would be reasons to desire it; but I should dread to disfigure the beautiful ideal of the memories of those illustrious persons with incongruous features, and to sully the imaginative purity of their classical works with gross and trivial recollections. The least weighty objection to heterogeneous details is that they are mainly superfluous, and therefore an incumbrance.'

We have marked by *italics* that part of the above passage in which we find it most difficult to believe that this wise, no less than eloquent man has expressed the settled and deliberate conviction of his mind. It is admitted that it may be expedient to submit to a minute scrutiny the private life of persons who have 'borne an active part in the world', and asserted that 'nothing of this applies to authors, merely as authors'. Now, that 'nothing of this applies' to some, or to many, or even to the case of most authors, may possibly be true (though we do not think so); but on what principle it should be said of authors who, though not bearing what is familiarly called 'an active part in the world', have, as exerting their talents on practical questions, bringing understandings of remarkable strength to bear, in permanent shapes, on subjects of moral and political interest, and consequently filling a part, above all others, both active and influential, in determining the opinions, sentiments, and actual conduct of those of their fellow mortals who are immediately concerned in the great movements of public affairs, as well as of all who have to sit on judgement, whether at the time or ages afterwards, on these prominent actors of the busy stage of life—on what principle Mr. Wordsworth should conceive that '*nothing* of this applies' to such authors as the moralist or the poet, who, by his single pen, exercises perhaps wider and more lasting sway over the tone of thought and feeling throughout whole nations, than a regiment of kings and ministers put together;—this indeed is what we cannot pretend to understand. It is scarcely possible to put the question seriously

—but where is the mere statesman of the last age who at this moment, even if Boswell had never written, would have filled so large a space in the contemplation of any considerable section of mankind, as Dr. Johnson himself—or the details of whose private life, had they been preserved with Boswellian fidelity, would have found one reader for fifty that are continually poring over the pages before us? If we measure either the importance or the interest of personal details, by the extent to which the individual recorded has influenced the intellect, the feelings, the character of his countrymen, and consequently in fact the fortunes of the nation itself, we shall assuredly place those connected with the man who, by exertions in whatever walk of literature—no matter at what a distance from the gaudy surface of external pomps and vanities these may have been conducted, no matter in how mean a hovel he may have wielded his quill—has achieved anything at all approaching to the authority of a Johnson, far and infinitely far above all that the prying diligence of either friend or foe could ever have accumulated concerning the private sayings and doings of the most eminent so called 'public man' of the same generation. It is in vain, on questions of this kind, to oppose the suggestions of a refined meditative delicacy, such as breathes throughout the whole of the 'Letter' we have quoted, to the broad instinctive impetus and determined taste of the species at large. Neither does it seem to us that Mr. Wordsworth is over happy in the cases he selects, or in the logic with which he applies them. It is by no means true, for example, but lamentably the reverse, that all the details which Horace gives us about the private proceedings of himself and his associates, are 'delightful'; too many of them are loathsome and disgusting; but if the greater part be, as all must acknowledge, 'delightful', upon what principle are we to decide that it would have been otherwise than delightful to have had a great deal more of the like quality? Mr. Wordsworth is enchanted with the *Iter ad Brundisium*; would he have regretted the circumstance had the poet, 'in the happy exercise of his own genius', left us half-a-dozen more such *itinera*? or would he have been seriously displeased had either 'rhetor comes Heliodorus' or 'Fonteius—ad unguem factus homo', in the exercise of such ability as heaven had pleased to bestow, indited an account of the actual progress, bearing to Horace's the same sort of relation that Boswell's Hebridean Journal does to the Doctor's own immortal 'Tour'.

Surely the lamentable circumstance is, not that the Boswellian style should have been applied to the history of one great man, but that there should be so few even of the greatest men whose lives could be so dealt with without serious injury to their fame. 'There never,' says Mr. Croker, 'has existed any human being, all the details of whose life, all the motives of whose actions, all the thoughts of whose mind, have been so unreservedly brought before the public; even his prayers, his most secret meditations, and his most scrupulous self-reproaches, have been laid before the world.' They have all been sifted, too, and commented on, it may now be added, with as deliberate an exercise of studious acuteness as ever frightened a conscious imagination. All that curiosity could glean, or enthusiasm garner, philosophic penetration has bolted to the bran. 'There are, perhaps,' (Mr Croker says elsewhere) 'not many men who have practised such self-examination as to know themselves as well as every reader knows Dr. Johnson.' And what is the result?—that, in spite of innumerable oddities, and of many laughable and some few condemnable weaknesses, when we desire to call up the notion of a human being thoroughly, as far as our fallen clay admits the predication of such qualities, good and wise; in the whole of his mind lofty, of his temper generous, in the midst of misery incapable of *shabbiness*, 'every inch a *man*',—the name of Samuel Johnson springs to every lip. Whatever our habits of self-examination may have been, we certainly know him better than we are ever likely to do most of our own friends, and feel that, in one instance at least, the adage about heroes and their valets-de-chambre does not hold. The character is before us bare, and throughout it stands erect, sincere, great; the thoughts habitually turned on great things, and yet the observation of the world equally keen and broad; the sympathy with human passions, interests, and occupations almost boundless; and the charity for frailty, and feebleness, and sin, most Christian.

* * *

* I never thought it lawful to keep a journal of what passes in private society, so that no one need expect from the sequel of this narrative any detailed record of Scott's familiar talk. What fragments of it have happened to adhere to a tolerably retentive memory, and may be put into black and white without wounding any feelings which my friend, were he alive, would have wished to spare, I shall introduce as

* From *Memoirs of Sir Walter Scott* (1838) [Macmillan edition, 1900, III, 185–6].

the occasion suggests or serves; but I disclaim on the threshhold anything more than this; and I also wish to enter a protest once for all against the general fidelity of several literary gentlemen who have kindly forwarded to me private lucubrations of theirs, designed to Boswellize Scott, and which they may probably publish hereafter. To report conversations fairly, it is a necessary prerequisite that we should be completely familiar with all the interlocutors, and understand thoroughly all their minutest relations, and points of common knowledge, and common feeling, with each other. He who does not, must be perpetually in danger of misinterpreting sportive allusion into serious statement; and the man who was only recalling, by some jocular phrase or half-phrase, to an old companion, some trivial reminiscence of their boyhood or youth, may be represented as expressing, upon some person or incident casually tabled, an opinion which he had never framed, or if he had, would never have given words to in any mixed assemblage—not even among what the world calls *friends* at his own board. In proportion as a man is witty and humorous, there will always be about him and his a widening maze and wilderness of cues and catchwords, which the uninitiated will, if they are bold enough to try interpretation, construe, ever and anon, egregiously amiss—not seldom into arrant falsity. For this reason, to say nothing of many others, I consider no man justified in journalizing what he sees and hears in a domestic circle where he is not thoroughly at home; and I think there are still higher and better reasons why he should not do so where he is. . . .

Thomas Carlyle

* Man's sociality of nature evinces itself, in spite of all that can be said, with abundant evidence by this one fact, were there no other: the unspeakable delight he takes in Biography. It is written, 'The proper study of mankind is man'; to which study, let us candidly admit, he, by true or by false methods, applies himself, nothing loath. 'Man is perennially interesting to man; nay, if we look strictly to it, there is nothing else interesting.' How inexpressibly comfortable to know our fellow-creature; to see into him, understand his goings-forth, decipher the whole heart of his mystery: nay, not only to see into him, but even to see out of him, to view the world altogether as he views it; so that we can theoretically construe him, and could almost practically personate him; and do now thoroughly discern both what manner of man he is, and what manner of thing he has got to work on and live on!

A scientific interest and a poetic one alike inspire us in this matter. A scientific: because every mortal has a Problem of Existence set before him, which, were it only, what for the most of it is, the Problem of keeping soul and body together, must be to a certain extent *original*, unlike every other; and yet, at the same time, so *like* every other; like our own, therefore; instructive, moreover, since we also are indentured to *live*. A poetic interest still more: for precisely this same struggle of human Freewill against material Necessity, which every man's Life,

* From a review of Croker's edition of Boswell's *Life of Johnson*, in *Fraser's Magazine*, April 1832, pp. 253–9; reprinted in *Critical and Miscellaneous Essays* (1887), II, pp. 247–60. Carlyle's characteristic capitalization has not been changed.

by the mere circumstance that the man continues alive, will more or less victoriously exhibit,—is that which above all else, or rather inclusive of all else, calls the Sympathy of mortal hearts into action; and whether as acted, or as represented and written of, not only is Poetry, but is the sole Poetry possible. Borne onwards by which two all-embracing interests, may the earnest Lover of Biography expand himself on all sides, and indefinitely enrich himself. Looking with the eyes of every new neighbour, he can discern a new world different for each: feeling with the heart of every neighbour, he lives with every neighbour's life, even as with his own. Of these millions of living men, each individual is a mirror to us; a mirror both scientific and poetic; or, if you will, both natural and magical;—from which one would so gladly draw aside the gauze veil; and, peering therein, discern the image of his own natural face, and the supernatural secrets that prophetically lie under the same!

Observe, accordingly, to what extent, in the actual course of things, this business of Biography is practised and relished. Define to thyself, judicious Reader, the real significance of these phenomena, named Gossip, Egoism, Personal Narrative (miraculous or not), Scandal, Raillery, Slander, and suchlike; the sum-total of which (with some fractional addition of a better ingredient, generally too small to be noticeable) constitutes that other grand phenomenon still called 'Conversation'. Do they not mean wholly: *Biography* and *Autobiography*? Not only in the common Speech of men; but in all Art too, which is or should be the concentrated and conserved essence of what men can speak and show, Biography is almost the one thing needful.

Even in the highest works of Art, our interest, as the critics complain, is too apt to be strongly or even mainly of a Biographic sort. In the Art we can nowise forget the Artist: while looking on the *Transfiguration*, while studying the *Iliad*, we ever strive to figure to ourselves what spirit dwelt in Raphael; what a head was that of Homer, wherein, woven of Elysian light and Tartarean gloom, that old world fashioned itself together, of which these written Greek characters are but a feeble though perennial copy. The Painter and the Singer are present to us; we partially and for the time become the very Painter and the very Singer, while we enjoy the Picture and the Song. Perhaps too, let the critic say what he will, this is the highest enjoyment, the clearest recognition, we can have of these. Art indeed is Art; yet Man also is Man. Had the *Transfiguration* been painted without human hand; had it grown merely on the canvas, say by atmospheric influences, as lichen-pictures do on rocks,—it were a grand Picture doubtless; yet nothing like so grand as *the* Picture, which, on opening our eyes, we everywhere in Heaven and in Earth see painted; and everywhere pass over with indifference,—because the Painter was not a Man. Think of this; much lies in it. The Vatican is great; yet poor to Chimborazo or the Peak of Teneriffe; its dome is but a foolish Big-endian or Little-endian chip of an egg-shell, compared with that star-fretted Dome where Arcturus and Orion glance forever; which latter, notwithstanding, who looks at, save perhaps some necessitous star-gazer bent to make Almanacs; some thick-quilted watchman, to see what weather it will prove? The Biographic interest is wanting: no Michael Angelo was He who built that 'Temple of Immensity'; therefore do we, pitiful Littlenesses as we are, turn rather to wonder and to worship in the little toybox of a Temple built by our like.

Still more decisively, still more exclusively does the Biographic interest manifest itself, as we descend into lower regions of spiritual communication; through the whole range of what is called Literature. Of History, for example, the most honoured, if not honourable species of composition, is not the whole purport Biographic? 'History', it has been said, 'is the essence of innumerable Biographies.' Such, at least, it should be: whether it is, might admit of question. But, in any case, what hope have we in turning over those old interminable Chronicles, with their garrulities and insipidities; or still worse, in patiently examining those modern Narrations, of the Philosophic kind, where 'Philosophy, teaching by Experience', has to sit like owl on housetop, *seeing* nothing, *understanding* nothing, uttering only, with such solemnity, her perpetual most wearisome *hoo-hoo*:—what hope have we, except the for most part fallacious one of gaining some acquaintance with our fellow-creatures, though dead and vanished, yet dear to us; how they got along in those old days, suffering and doing; to what extent, and under what circumstances, they resisted the Devil and triumphed over him, or struck their colours to him, and were trodden under foot by him; how, in short, the perennial Battle went, which men name Life, which we also in these new days, with indifferent fortune, have to fight, and must bequeath to our sons and grandsons to go on fighting,—till the Enemy one day be quite vanquished and abolished, or else the great Night sink and part the combatants; and thus, either by some Millennium or some new Noah's

Deluge, the Volume of Universal History wind itself up! Other hope, in studying such Books, we have none: and that it is a deceitful hope, who that has tried knows not? A feast of widest Biographic insight is spread for us; we enter full of hungry anticipations: alas, like so many other feasts, which Life invites us to, a mere Ossian's 'feast of *shells*',—the food and liquor being all emptied out and clean gone, and only the vacant dishes and deceitful emblems thereof left! Your modern Historical Restaurateurs are indeed little better than high-priests of Famine; that keep choicest china dinner-sets, only no dinner to serve therein. Yet such is our Biographic appetite, we run trying from shop to shop, with ever new hope; and, unless we could eat the wind, with ever new disappointment. . . .

Meanwhile, quitting these airy regions, let any one bethink him how impressive the smallest historical *fact* may become, as contrasted with the grandest *fictitious event*; what an incalculable force lies for us in this consideration: The Thing which I here hold imaged in my mind did actually occur; was, in very truth, an element in the system of the All, whereof I too form part; had therefore, and has, through all time, an authentic being; is not a dream, but a reality! We ourselves can remember reading, in *Lord Clarendon*, [*History of the Rebellion*, iii, 625] with feelings perhaps somehow accidently opened to it,—certainly with a depth of impression strange to us then and now,—that insignificant-looking passage, where Charles, after the battle of Worcester, glides down, with Squire Careless, from the Royal Oak, at nightfall, being hungry: how, 'making a shift to get over hedges and ditches, after walking at least eight or nine miles, which were the more grievous to the King by the weight of his boots (for he could not put *them* off when he cut off his hair, for want of shoes), before morning they came to *a poor cottage, the owner whereof, being a Roman Catholic, was known to Careless*'. How this poor drudge, being knocked-up from his snoring, 'carried them into a little barn full of hay, which was a better lodging than he had for himself'; and by and by, not without difficulty, brought his Majesty 'a piece of bread and a great pot of buttermilk', saying candidly that 'he himself lived by his daily labour, and that what he had brought him was the fare he and his wife had': on which nourishing diet his Majesty, 'staying upon the haymow', feeds thankfully for two days; and then departs, under new guidance, having first changed clothes, down to the very shirt and 'old pair of shoes', with his landlord; and so, as worthy Bunyan has it, 'goes on his way, and sees him no more'. Singular enough, if we will think of it! This, then, was a genuine flesh-and-blood Rustic of the year 1651: he did actually swallow bread and buttermilk (not having ale and bacon), and do field-labour: with these hobnailed 'shoes' has sprawled through mud-roads in winter, and, jocund or not, driven his team a-field in summer: he made bargains; had chafferings and higglings, now a sore heart, now a glad one; was born; was a son, was a father; toiled in many ways, being forced to it, till the strength was all worn out of him; and then—lay down 'to rest his galled back', and sleep there till the long-distant morning!—How comes it, that he alone of all the British rustics who tilled and lived along with him, on whom the blessed sun on that same 'fifth day of September' was shining, should have chanced to rise on us; that this poor pair of clouted Shoes, out of the million million hides that have been tanned, and cut, and worn, should still subsist, and hang visibly together! We see him but for a moment; for one moment, the blanket of the Night is rent asunder, so that we behold and see, and then closes over him—for ever.

So too, in some *Boswell's Life of Johnson*, how indelible and magically bright does many a little *Reality* dwell in our remembrance! There is no need that the personages on the scene be a King and Clown; that the scene be the Forest of the Royal Oak, 'on the borders of Staffordshire': need only that the scene lie on this old firm Earth of ours, where we also have so surprisingly arrived; that the personages be *men*, and *seen* with the eyes of a man. Foolish enough, how some slight, perhaps mean and even ugly incident, if *real* and well presented, will fix itself in a susceptive memory, and lie ennobled there; silvered over with the pale cast of thought, with the pathos which belongs only to the Dead. For the Past is all holy to us; the Dead are all holy, even they that were base, and wicked while alive. Their baseness and wickedness was not *They*, was but the heavy and unmanageable Environment that lay round them, with which they fought unprevailing: *they* (the ethereal god-given Force that dwelt in them, and was their *Self*) have now shuffled that heavy Environment, and are free and pure: their life-long Battle, go how it might, is all ended, with many wounds or with fewer; they have been recalled from it, and the once harsh-jarring battle-field has become a silent awe-inspiring Golgotha, and *Gottesacker* (Field of God)!—Boswell relates this in itself smallest and poorest of occurrences: 'As we walked along the Strand tonight, arm in arm, a woman of the town accosted us in the usual enticing manner. "No, no, my girl," said Johnson; "it won't do." He, however, did not treat her with harshness; and we talked of the wretched life of such women.' Strange power of *Reality*! Not even this poorest of occurrences, but now, after seventy years are come and gone, has a meaning for us. Do but consider that it is *true*; that it did in very deed occur! That unhappy Outcast, with all her sins and woes, her lawless desires, too complex mischances, her wailings and her riotings, has departed utterly; alas! her siren finery has got all besmutched, ground, generations since, into dust and smoke; of her degraded body, and whole miserable earthly existence, all is away: *she* is no longer here, but far from us, in the bosom of Eternity,—whence we too came, whither we too are bound! Johnson said, 'No, no, my girl; it won't do'; and then 'we talked';—and herewith the wretched one, seen but for the twinkling of an eye, passes on into the utter Darkness. No high Calista, that ever issued from Story-teller's brain, will impress us more deeply than this meanest of the mean; and for a good reason: that *she* issued from the Maker of Men.

It is well worth the Artist's while to examine for himself what it is that gives such pitiable incidents their memorableness; his aim likewise is, above all things, to be *memorable*. Half the effect, we already perceive, depends on the object; on its being *real*, on its being really *seen*. The other half will depend on the observer; and the question now is: How are real objects to be *so* seen; on what quality of observing, or of style in describing, does this so intense pictorial power depend? Often a slight circumstance contributes curiously to the result: some little, and perhaps to appearance accidential, feature is presented; a light-gleam, which instantaneously *excites* the mind, and urges it to complete the picture, and evolve the meaning thereof for itself. By critics, such light-gleams and their almost magical influence have frequently been noted: but the power to produce such, to select such features as will produce them, is generally treated as a knack, or trick of the trade, a secret for being 'graphic'; whereas these magical feats are, in truth, rather inspirations; and the gift of performing them, which acts unconsciously, without forethought, and as if by nature alone, is properly a *genius* for description.

One grand, invaluable secret there is, however, which includes all the rest, and, what is comfortable, lies clearly in every man's power: *To have an open loving heart, and what follows from the possession of such.* Truly, it has been said, emphatically in these days ought it to be repeated:

A loving Heart is the beginning of all Knowledge. This it is that opens the whole mind, quickens every faculty of the intellect to do its fit work, that of *knowing*; and therefrom, by sure consequence, of *vividly uttering-forth*. Other secret for being 'graphic' is there none, worth having: but this is an all-sufficient one. See, for example, what a small Boswell can do! Hereby, indeed, is the whole man made a living mirror, wherein the wonders of this ever-wonderful Universe are, in their true light (which is ever a magical, miraculous one) represented, and reflected back on us. . . .

*   *   *

* One thing we hear greatly blamed in Mr. Lockhart: that he has been too communicative, indiscreet, and has recorded much that ought to have lain suppressed. Persons are mentioned, and circumstances, not always of an ornamental sort. It would appear there is far less reticence than was looked for! Various persons, name and surname, have 'received pain': nay, the very hero of the biography is rendered unheroic; unornamental facts of him, and of those he had to do with, being set forth in plain English: hence 'personality', 'indiscretion', or worse, 'sanctities of private life', &c., &c. How delicate, decent is English biography, bless its mealy mouth! A Damocles' sword of *Respectability* hangs for ever over the poor English life-writer (as it does over poor English life in general), and reduces him to the verge of paralysis. Thus it has been said, 'there are no English lives worth reading except those of Players, who by the nature of the case have bidden Respectability good-day.' The English biographer has long felt that if in writing his Man's Biography, he wrote down anything that could by possibility offend any man, he had written wrong. The plain consequence was that, properly speaking, no biography whatever could be produced. The poor biographer, having the fear *not* of God before his eyes, was obliged to retire as it were into vacuum; and write in the most melancholy, straitened manner, with only vacuum for a result. Vain that he wrote, and that we kept reading volume on volume: there was no biography, but some vague ghost of a biography, white, stainless; without feature or substance; *vacuum*, as we say, and wind and shadow,—which indeed the material of it was.

No man lives without jostling and being jostled; in all ways he has

* From a review of Lockhart's *Life of Scott* in *The London and Westminster Review*, January 1838, pp. 299–301.

to *elbow* himself through the world, giving and receiving offence. His life is a battle, in so far as it is an entity at all. The very oyster, we suppose, comes in collision with oysters: undoubtedly enough it does come in collision with Necessity and Difficulty; and helps itself through, not as a perfect ideal oyster, but as an imperfect real one. Some kind of remorse must be known to the oyster; certain hatreds, certain pusillanimities. But as for man, his conflict is continual with the spirit of contradiction, that is without and within; with the evil spirit (or call it with the weak, most necessitous, pitiable spirit), that is in others and in himself. His walk, like all walking (say the mechanicians), is a series of *falls*. To paint man's life is to present these things. Let them be represented, fitly, with dignity and measure; but above all, let them be represented. No tragedy of *Hamlet*, with the part of Hamlet omitted by particular desire! No ghost of a Biography, let the Damocles' sword of Respectability (which after all is but a pasteboard one) threaten as it will! One hopes that the public taste is much mended in this matter; that vacuum-biographies, with a good many other vacuities related to them, are withdrawn or withdrawing into vacuum. Probably it was Mr. Lockhart's feeling of what the great public would approve that led him, open-eyed, into this offence against the small criticizing public: we joyfully accept the omen.

Perhaps then, of all the praises copiously bestowed on his work, there is none in reality so creditable to him as this same censure, which has also been pretty copious. It is a censure better than a good many praises. He is found guilty of having said this and that, calculated not to be entirely pleasant to this man and that; in other words, calculated to give him and the thing he worked in a living set of features, not leave him vague, in the white beatified ghost-condition. Let it be so. Several men, as we hear, cry out, 'See, there is something written not entirely pleasant to me!' Good friend, it is pity; but who can help it? They that will crowd about bonfires may, sometimes, very fairly, get their beards singed; it is the price they pay for such illumination: natural twilight is safe and free to all. For our part, we hope all manner of biographies that are written in England will henceforth be written so. If it is fit that they be written otherwise, then it is still fitter that they be not written at all: to produce not things but ghosts of things can never be the duty of man. The Biographer has this problem set before him: to delineate a likeness of the earthly pilgrimage of a man. He will compute well what profit is in it, and what disprofit; under which latter head this of offending any of his fellow-creatures will surely not be forgotten. Nay, this may so swell the disprofit side of his account, that many an enterprise of biography, otherwise promising, shall require to be renounced. But once taken up, the rule before all rules is to do *it*, not to do the ghost of it. In speaking of the man and men he has to deal with, he will of course keep all his charities about him, but also all his eyes open. Far be it from him to set down aught *untrue*; nay, not to abstain from, and leave in oblivion, much that is true. But having found a thing or things essential for his subject, and well computed the for and against, he will in very deed set down such thing or things, nothing doubting,—*having*, we may say, the fear of God before his eyes, and no other fear whatever. Censure the biographer's prudence; dissent from the computation he made, or agree with it; be all malice of his, be all falsehood, nay, be all offensive avoidable inaccuracy, condemned and consumed; but know that by this plan only, executed as was possible, could the biographer hope to make a biography; and blame him not that he did what it had been the worst fault not to do.

Allan Cunningham

*The penury of British biography was remarked by Johnson; he did much, indeed, to remove the reproach, and succeeding writers have added largely to the structure which he may be said to have commenced. We had, before his day, individual biographies, such as Sprat's *Life of Cowley*, and Cibber's *Apology*, remarkable for elegance of eulogium and liveliness of detail, but we had no connected series of Lives before those of the Poets, and even in these, some of the greatest poets England has produced, are omitted. It was the object of Johnson to exhibit the genius as well as the persons of the poets; to give us their mental picture along with their bodily, and I know of no writer who has equalled him. He knew it was by their intellect that they had purchased the distinction of biography; succeeding biographers, and among them Boswell, have thought differently; we have diaries rather than memoirs, and letters substituted for characters. The importance of the individual in the eyes of the world, has not at all been attended to; instead of forty pages, we have four hundred, and instead of a hundred, a thousand. Men about whom the world had no solicitude, have come into the market with their 'Life and Times', and we have been deluged with accounts of writings that were never read, and of books published but to be forgotten. Boswell's *Life of Johnson* led to these inflictions; but then, Johnson was long at the head of our literature—was for many years the 'Triton of the minnows',

*From 'Biographical and Critical History of the Literature of the Last Fifty Years', *The Athenaeum*, 14 December 1833, pp. 851–2; reprinted (Paris, Baudry's Foreign Library, 1834), pp. 213–15, 258–9.

and renowned besides, over the civilized world, for the wit and wisdom of his sayings. It is not that he said lively and witty things, but that he said wise ones also, that we peruse the minute account of his biographer with a pleasure which never tires. The great beauty of the Memoir of Johnson is, that the sage is recalled to life, placed at our side, and we are made to see as well as hear him—not scattering his pearls in solitude, but surrounded by the choice spirits of his day—Burke, Reynolds, Percy, Goldsmith. The chief fault of the performance is, that it wants the splendid summary, and final judgement of character, which forms the crowning glory to the *Lives of the Poets.* We are left to draw our own conclusions from the anecdotes and indications of Boswell, and the consequence is, that every one forms a mental character according to his abilities or prejudices, and nothing is fixed or defined. . . .

The most perfect piece of biography in the language is the *Life of Nelson,* by Robert Southey: it is as complete and well-proportioned as the finest statue; all is handsome, graceful, and expressive; there are no parts weak and languid, and none more colossal and massive than strict harmony allows. Those who wish to excel in biography would act wisely in studying this noble work: they will see with what wonderful, and all but invisible art, it is composed, and yet feel that all is so simple, so easy, and so natural, that art is out of the question. In the conception of the Memoir, the author has, like a skilful gardener who inoculates a barren bough with a bearing bud, brought collateral matter to give life to the duller or less interesting parts; nor has he, out of a false love for his hero, painted his character in the Sir Charles Grandison style of perfection; he has spoken of the failings of the man with deserved compassion, and of the nobleness of his nature with merited rapture. . . .

Anonymous

*In considering biography as an art distinct in a great measure from history, we naturally inquire, first, what are the aims of biography; and secondly, by [what] qualities they may be accomplished.

It is not an idle, flippant curiosity that excites in men a desire to learn the private as well as the public character and actions of their fellow-men. It is rather an universal sympathy, interesting all men, even the most callous and misanthropic, in whatever concerns their neighbours. Specially, does mankind experience this thirst after a knowledge of the private life of those favoured individuals to whose lot it has befallen to act a conspicuous part in the great drama of life. In accordance with that sympathy, the first aim of biography is to furnish an elaborate picture of the character of the men whose lives are under consideration. . . .

Biography professes to bring the reader into intimate personal association with each of its characters, to draw aside the veil that conceals from the world their domestic life, and to exhibit all their actions, great and small, without reservation, without exaggeration.

But while the biographer, by combining the details of public and private life, attempts a faithful delineation of individual character, he intends to afford the reader something more than a source of mere pleasure. Portraits of distinguished men are eloquent in their teachings

* From 'Biography', *Southern Literary Messenger* (Richmond, Virginia), October 1856, pp. 282–8. I have not, with certainty, been able to identify the author.

to posterity. The historical painting set before us has not simply the merit of being a representation of an entire character; to the connoisseur, or even to the comparatively ignorant, the features speak volumes. The attentive observer cannot fail to discover that pride and meanness may be united; that basement is often a companion of greatness; that the men whom the world most admires and applauds are sometimes most miserable, and often, least deserving of admiration and applause; that great men are after all human,—creatures with the same follies and crimes and sorrows that chequer the experiences of their less fortunate brethren. The most beneficial effect of all this is to diminish that blind admiration for men which is appropriately named hero-worship. No branch of letters is so well fitted as biography to teach the important lesson that the difference between the greatest and the humblest man is, at best, trifling. . . .

The two leading faculties of the mind—those to which all others are subservient—are reason and imagination. The office of reason in biography seems to consist chiefly in tracing to their sources individual actions, and in pursuing generalizations to discover the farthest limit of their influence. It is employed in elucidating facts and events; in connecting hitherto apparently isolated occurrences by the relation of cause and effect; and in deducing from all such data those maxims of wisdom and experience which it is the peculiar boast of all history to furnish. Whatever instruction is contained in brief and incidental remarks on political science, in the lives of statesmen; whatever maxims of war are given in the cursory treatment of military affairs, in the lives of warriors; whatever profound reflection and philosophic observation are embodied in biography at all, are due to the exercise of this faculty. Reason is further to discriminate between fact and fiction; to decide what credence is to be given to traditions, anecdotes, and other species of information poorly authenticated; to weigh opposing testimony and conflicting authorities on all contested questions;—to enable the biographer to select, from the mass of materials in his possession, such only as are true, and such as are adapted to his purpose. Many occurrences are regarded in one age as exerting a marked effect on the affairs of the world, which in a succeeding age are unnoticed and forgotten. Reasoning powers of unusual clearness and vigour are needed to prevent the biographer from overloading his pages with such useless facts, which, while they cause him to neglect others on which may have hinged the destiny of the individual, and through him, perhaps, the destiny of the state, weary the reader with their details and ultimately consign the book to oblivion.

But something more than reason is requisite to produce a good life of any man. Imagination, the great antagonist faculty to reason, is intimately concerned in every successful record of men's lives. A bare narration of the story of the gifted man, accompanied by such observations as the subject and incidents might naturally suggest to a philosophic mind, would, beyond a doubt, contain much valuable instruction; but how much more intensely interesting would such a narrative become in the hands of an imaginative artist? That aim of biography which is first of all others can be effected only by the aid of imagination. Happy delineation of character, individual and national; pictorial descriptions of men and scenery, of manners and customs, of events and their accessories, of battles, sieges, marches, of great assemblies, and of the calm delights of domestic life depend on the presence of imagination, watching over and impressing its character on the composition of the book. This faculty spreads a kind of enchantment over every thing it touches. Its office here is not to originate new and unheard of combinations, but to so combine existing and actual materials in proportions that have already existed, that, while absolutely true, they shall possess all the novelty of original conceptions.

If the foregoing be true, it follows that biography should occupy an intermediate space between the broad and rugged, but productive field of reason, on the one hand, and the brilliant-hued and enchanting garden of imagination on the other. Neither faculty should be exclusively employed. The one or the other should predominate according to the character of the life to be unravelled. The Sistine Chapel, at Rome, was reared by an architect from solid materials; Michael Angelo was employed to decorate the walls and ceiling with fresco-paintings, which should shadow forth the gigantic character of his mind; the result of this combination of the labours of two distinct and widely dissimilar artists was a chapel, whose beauty the lapse of four centuries has not impaired, whose grandeur still strikes the visitor with admiration and awe. So in biography, reason should lay the foundation and rear upon it the superstructure; while the decorations, the frescoes, the paintings, and the other ornaments, external and internal, should be the work of imagination.

Where these two faculties are properly combined, biography is most perfect, and is, to a healthy mind, the most delightful reading in the whole range of literature. Nor is this difficult to explain. One peculiar advantage which, independent of all others, biography possesses, and which will always render the dullest specimens of it more or less interesting, is its Reality. We know that the man, whose life we are reading, is not the creation of a novelist's brain; that the incidents affecting us variously are real incidents; that the actions and achievements, the successes and failures, the sufferings and misfortunes, the weaknesses, frailty, and humanity, or the pride, meanness and cruelty, which are recorded of the hero, have been actual existences and actual experiences—in a word, that the book is not a hypothetical view of human nature, elaborated in all its characters and incidents to establish the theory of some fiction-writing philosopher, but the authenticated life of a man who really existed and suffered and sinned and died, at some period, on this great world. The writer of fiction is successful in proportion as he reproduces nature, either when describing natural scenery and occurrences, or more especially when delineating human character, in doing both of which, he depends mainly on imagination. Now with the same powers of imagination, a genuine biography may be made as intensely interesting and far more instructive than the most powerful modern novel. It is all a mistake to imagine that fiction is, in and of itself, more entertaining than fact. There never could be a more absurd notion. The charm that chains the reader of fiction spell-bound to the brilliant page is wholly produced by art. The same art, employed in connecting and embellishing the actual experiences of an eventful life, will produce a similar charm, differing from the other, only by being more healthful, and being stripped of all meretricious and dangerous qualities.

The biographer should be as truly an artist as the sculptor, the painter, or the novelist, for his works are just as susceptible of criticism according to rules of art as are the works of the others. His art consists in the judicious selection and arrangement of materials, in the disposition of the light and shade, of the foreground and background. A little reflection will show that half a dozen different narratives of the same life may be constructed, each of which shall contain facts and facts only, while none of them shall furnish either a true account of the man's life or a true picture of his character. In the hands of Mr. J. Parton, that compound of Brownslow-billingsgate and Theodore Parker-raving commonly yclept Horace Greeley, becomes a great man, a Christian, a philanthropist; in the same hands John C. Calhoun would probably become another Aaron Burr, ambitious to subvert the government of his country. This arises from the fact, that as all, or even the greater part, of the occurrences of a life could not be recorded in any reasonable limits, the biographer necessarily confines himself to such as are, in his opinion, most worthy of mention. The art of the biographer should enable him to make a selection of materials which, in artistic combination, shall produce an effect most nearly similar to what the whole mass of incidents would produce, if it were possible for them to be minutely represented. It is principally the want of this art of selection that floods the world with specimens of worthless biography.

Fidelity and impartiality are qualities so imperatively demanded, that without them, or an appearance of them, a biography, faultless in other respects, would be condemned and ostracized. The very nature of the undertaking to write lives of other men supposes the possession of these qualities. Otherwise, there would be no reliability in anything recorded, we would receive the author's statements and remarks with suspicion, if not with positive unbelief, and this whole art would degenerate into ordinary fiction. . . .

When cultivated powers of reasoning, a brilliant pictorial imagination, an artistic skill in the selection and disposition of incidents, and scrupulous fidelity and impartiality are united in one person, that fortunate individual is fitted to excel in the noble art of biography. A mind like this is rarely, if ever, found, but we may be sure that a biographical production of it would prove a treasure, the value of which few other books equal, and none surpass. . . .

Thomas Love Peacock

* This appetite for gossip about notorieties being once created in the 'reading public', there will be always found persons to minister to it; and among the volunteers of this service, those who are best informed and who most valued the departed will probably not be the foremost. Then come biographies abounding with errors; and then, as matter of defence perhaps, comes on the part of friends a tardy and more authentic narrative. This is at best, as Mr. Hogg describes it, a 'difficult and delicate task'. But it is always a matter of choice and discretion. No man is bound to write the life of another. No man who does so is bound to tell the public all he knows. On the contrary, he is bound to keep to himself whatever may injure the interests or hurt the feelings of the living, especially when the latter have in no way injured or calumniated the dead, and are not necessarily brought before the tribunal of public opinion in the character of either plaintiffs or defendants. Neither if there be in the life of the subject of the biography any event which he himself would willingly have blotted from the tablet of his own memory, can it possibly be the duty of a survivor to drag it into daylight. If such an event be the cardinal point of a life; if to conceal it or to misrepresent it would be to render the whole narrative incomplete, incoherent, unsatisfactory alike to the honour of the dead and the feelings of the living; then, as there is no moral compulsion to speak of the matter at all, it is better to let the whole story slumber in silence.

* From 'Memoirs of Percy B. Shelley', *Fraser's Magazine*, June 1858, p. 643.

Grant Goodrich

*In my opinion you are the last man who ought to attempt to write a life of Abraham Lincoln—Your long and intimate association with him unfits you for the task. No one holding the intimate relations to another, which you did to him, ever has succeeded. There may be exceptions, but I cannot now remember one. They are mere eulogists —or having known him in other conditions than on those fields, or in those departments where his fame was won, he regards and exhibits him in those humble and different aspects and characteristics in which the public have no taste, and which brings him down from the high sphere of his triumphs, and the humdrum everyday affairs of life which are stale and insipid to the public. To enter into the private everyday life of ordinary or extraordinary men can only [*sic*] be made endurable to readers, or safe to the fame of the subjects, without the most discriminating taste and art; and no one is safe to undertake it without much practice and knowledge of the public taste. Again, contact with great men always dispels something of the awe with which they are contemplated at a distance. In intimate association we fix upon some characteristic or peculiarity, and fail to catch other lineaments. We can only regard them as the kind friend, amusing companion, and generous mind. In the distance we see the bold outline of the mountain; its summits wrapped in sunshine, or swathed in cloud. When we approach it, we catch a view of the deep, it may be

* From a letter to William H. Herndon, 9 December 1866. Original manuscript in the Library of Congress, Herndon-Weik Collection of Lincolniana, Group IV, Vol. 17.

dark gorges, the rugged cliffs, the lean rocks and distorted outlines. So in the characters of our dearest friends. See how Boswell, with all his literary abilities, failed in his Life of Johnson. No blow so severe was ever struck at Johnson. Think on these things.

If I am to judge of what your production will be by the publication of a portion of your Salem lecture, I am more solicitous still. I fear you did not realize what an injury and injustice you did to the memory of your dead friend, and mortification you caused his friends, but especially his widow and children. Ask yourself, if he were living, whether he would not have revolted at the uncovering to the public gaze that drama of his life? And shall his friends exhibit what we know he would have preserved in sacred privacy? If the facts are truly stated, I should as soon [have] thought of exposing his dead body, uncoffined, to the vulgar gaze of the public eye—It should never have been dug up from the grave, when time had buried it.

Margaret Oliphant

* The cynic principle, as applied to biography, is, however, to the credit of human nature, of far more rarity than that of the enthusiast. Perhaps this fact gives it, when it appears, the greater power. But there is a difficulty at the very outset in explaining what motive a writer can have in choosing as his subject a character of which his moral estimate is very low. Friends there are, no doubt, who love without approving; and it cannot be questioned that the prodigal in a family, the black sheep in a group of companions, is very often the individual whom the others regard with the greatest tenderness. But in most cases their faults are those of youth; they produce almost invariably tragic consequences, and they are often compatible with qualities so genial and lovable that the judgement refuses to condemn, and the heart clings to the victims of their own folly, those who themselves are the greatest sufferers by their imperfections. Save in such instances as these, however, it is difficult to understand why a biographer, himself a man of intellect and character, should voluntarily seek the society living, or devote himself to the elucidation of the life when ended, of a warped and gloomy soul, whose temper is odious to him, and whose defects he sees in the clearest light. The meaning of the enthusiast's work is simple, but not that of the detractor. We ask ourselves, What is its motive? Is it a cynic's gratification in proving that to be the 'wisest, meanest' of mankind is possible to more than one historical personage, and that no one can be more petty and miserable than he

* From 'The Ethics of Biography', *Contemporary Review*, July 1883, pp. 82–84, 88–91.

who is most great? Is it a pleasure in associating moral deformity with genius, and showing, in one who has strongly demanded veracity as a condition of life, a character ignoble and untrue? These are questions somewhat apart from the question we set out by asking, Whether a work executed in this spirit can fulfil the true objects of biography? But they are inevitable questions. Impartially, the cynical record is no more biography, in any true sense of the word, than is the enthusiast's; but it is almost impossible to be impartial in such a discussion, and we must add that, according to all our capabilities of judging, it is less so. For the enthusiast by turns justifies himself by discovering the latent nobleness of a man whose motives have been misconstrued, and at all times is likely to serve the ends of justice better by thinking the best, than he can ever do who thinks the worst. For it is more often in performance than in intention that men go astray. Save in the very worst cases there is a certain ideal, a shaping of better things in the mind, which love divines, but which hate, dulling the finest insight, is unconscious of. We all set out with a better intention than our performance comes up to, and our defender is at all times more nearly right than our detractor.

Neither of the two, however, attains the true objects of biography, which are twofold—for the individual and for the world. In both cases the biographer holds an office of high trust and responsibility. In all likelihood, if he is at all equal to his subject, permanent public opinion will be fixed, or at all events largely influenced, by the image he sets before it. It will be his to determine how far the man of whom he writes carried out his own creed, and was worthy of his greatness, or departed from the ideal which he set up for others, yet was indifferent to in his own person. A mere record of facts will not satisfy either the reader or the conditions under which such a writer ought to work. He is expected to enable us to surmount or to correct such momentary impressions as we may have taken up from chance encounter with his subject, and to give guidance and substance to such divinations of character or life as we may have gleaned from the public occurrences in which he was involved, or the works he has left behind. While we stand without, eager to gain a glimpse through an opened door or window of the object of our interest, he is within, in the very sanctuary, free to examine everything; and he is consequently bound to spare no pains in eliciting that truth which is something more and greater than fact, which it is possible even may be almost contradictory in its development, and which is of far greater permanent importance than any mere occurrence. In every portrait the due value of differing surfaces and textures must be taken into account, and we must be made to perceive which is mere drapery and apparel, and which the structure of the individual beneath. If this is true of the pictured history which represents but one movement and one pose, it is much more true of the whole course and progress of a life, which it is the office of the literary workman to set forth, not according to momentary and easily recognized tricks of manner, but according to the real scope and meaning which pervade and inspire it. That which is accidental, and due to the force of circumstances, is thus on a different *plan* from that which is fundamental. The most patient may be subject to a burst of passion, which, seen unconnected with the rest of his life, would give a general impression of it, in reality quite false, though momentarily true. Thus Moses, the meekest of men, might possibly be known to the carping Jew by the one act of scornful impatience which marred his public life, rather than by all the long-suffering with which he endured the continual vagaries of his stiff-necked people. Nor is it less easy to disentangle the character from the little web of petty susceptibilities which often, to the cursory observer, throw a mist over the most generous and noble spirit. The biographer must be in no respect cursory. It is his business to preserve us from being deceived by appearances, and still more to guard himself from superficial impressions. And if he is unfortunately compelled, by evidence which he cannot resist, to form an unexpectedly unfavourable judgement, it is the merest commonplace of honourable feeling to say that the most scrupulous care must be taken in testing that evidence, and that anything that is mere opinion must be discarded and left entirely out of the question.

Towards the world his duties are scarcely less important. To give an erroneous impression of any man, living or dead, to the mind of his country and generation, is the greatest of social sins. But the living may outlive every misrepresentation; and the most unpardonable offender in this respect is the man who persuades a whole community into injustice towards the dead. Without even going so far as this, a biographer has to discriminate between the legitimate and noble interest which mankind takes in every man sufficiently distinct in character or genius as to have identified himself from the crowd, and that prying curiosity which loves to investigate circumstances, and thrust itself into the sanctuaries of individual feeling. The question of how far the world should be allowed to penetrate into those sanctuaries, and to invade the privacy which every soul has a right to guard for itself, is one in which the delicacy of his perceptions and that good taste of the heart, which no artificial standard can supply, will be severely tested. . . .

Thus the position of the biographer carries with it a power which is almost unrestrained, the kind of power which it is doubly tyrannous to use like a giant. Not even the pulpit is so entirely master; for we all consider ourselves able to judge in respect to what the clergyman tells us; and we have his materials in our hands, by which to call him to account. If we must let him have his say at the moment, it is only for the moment, and we are always ready to hear all that is to be said on the other side; but the biographer has a far more assured place, and if he is not restrained by the strictest limits of truth and honour, there is nothing else that can control him in heaven or earth.

To those who have stepped out beyond the ranks of their fellows it must thus become a terrible reflection, that they may one day be delivered over helpless into the hands of some one, who, with no power in the world to call him to account, will give what view he pleases of their life and career and all their most private relationships. He may be a man without that power of penetrating beneath the surface into the character of another, which is sympathy, imagination, genius, all in one. He may be one of those who understand only what is spoken, to whom everything has a rigid interpretation, who take *au pied de la lettre* utterances intended for anything rather than that matter-of-fact statement. He may be incapable of appreciating the special conditions of another's education or habits of living, and from his different point of view may find only in the familiar facts entrusted to him material for dishonouring a memory. This may well give a sting to death among those who cannot fail to be aware that their lives will have an interest to mankind. . . .

The biographer alone can interrupt the operation of this rule of natural equity. He stands, in the first instance, in the place of posterity, for those who, with a touching confidence, thus await its decision. He has it in his power to guide the final deliverance, like that judge whose summing up so often decides the verdict. And hence there arises a weighty question in which we think much is involved. If a man, on the eve of so important an undertaking, finds that the idea he has formed of the person whose good name is in his hands is an unfavourable one, and that all he can do by telling the story of his life is to lessen or destroy that good name—not indeed by revealing any system of hypocrisy or concealed vice, which it might be to the benefit of public morals to expose, but by an exhibition of personal idiosyncrasies repulsive to the ordinary mind and contradictory of the veneration with which the world has hitherto regarded a man of genius—is it in such a case his duty to speak at all? Is the necessity of producing another book among many so imperative that the natural reluctance, which any honourable man must feel, to put forth accusations which can only be answered at second-hand, and which the person principally concerned is powerless to reply to, must be disregarded? There are cases of perverted intelligence in which the detractor does not perceive the moral bearing of the statements he has to make, and thus maligns his subject without being sensible of it, with a certain innocence of mind, perhaps even glorying in the shame he originates. But this can scarcely be the case, except in an obtuse understanding and uninstructed judgement. We can imagine that in such circumstances a high-minded man, alarmed by his own discoveries—which we must suppose to have been made after the death of his hero, since it is scarcely possible that any one should love and frequent, and identify himself with, a character of this description—would seek every means of getting rid of the ungracious task set before him; that he would, in the first place, anxiously consult every authority, and test and compare every piece of evidence, and try every method of dispelling the painful shadows which were gathering between him and the object of his trust; and that, finally, rather than be the instrument of ruining a virtuous reputation, and betraying the secret weakness of a man whom the world held in honour, he would retire from the field altogether, and leave with a sad heart the work which he could only execute in this way to some less severe moralist, who might be able to throw upon it a gentler light. This is the view which we believe most good men would take of a position so painful. In private life most of us would rather not hear new facts disadvantageous to our friends who are dead, and would consider the publication of them a breach of every delicate sentiment. To bring a great man, who has lived in the common daylight without reproach during his life, to the bar of this world's opinion after his death, is in itself a painful act. The defendant is, in all cases, silenced by English law;

but, at least, he has the privilege of communicating all the facts in his favour to his advocate, and furnishing explanations of his conduct for counsel's use. But the dead have no such safeguard; they have no longer any privacy; their very hearts, like their desks and private drawers and cabinets, can be ransacked for evidence to their disadvantage. Is it in any conceivable case a biographer's duty to do this? If the question, as one of literary and social morals, were submitted to any competent tribunal, or jury of his peers, the answer, we think, would be unanimous. Should something more powerful than any private sentiment demand the performance of so painful a duty; should there exist other and darker accusations that might be made were not these acknowledged and established, an argument which might perhaps have held in the case of Byron, for instance; should the scandal be so great that investigation was imperative—then with patience and care, waiting till the fumes of passion had died away, and every privilege of perspective had been attained, the work should be done. But if there were no such necessity, it is impossible that a man could be compelled to criminate his friend, or to soil an established reputation entrusted to his care. In this case his plain duty would be to refrain. . . .

George Saintsbury

*All biography is obviously and naturally divided into two kinds. There is the biography pure and simple, in which the whole of the materials is passed through the alembic of the biographer, and in which few if any of these materials appear except in an altered and digested condition. This, though apparently the oldest, is artistically the most perfect kind. Its shortest examples are always its best, and some of the best and shortest are among the best things in literature. The *Agricola* of Tacitus at one end of the list and Southey's *Nelson* almost at the other may save us the trouble of a long enumeration of the masterpieces; while nobody needs to be told that the list ranges from masterpieces like these down to those that *ego vel Cluvienus* may write. There has always been a considerable demand for this sort of thing; but it is not quite the kind of biography which has been specially popular for the last century, and which has produced the famous books to which I have already alluded. This is the kind of 'applied' or 'mixed' biography, including letters from and to the hero, anecdotes about him, and the like, connected and wrought into a whole by narrative and comment of the author, or, as he sometimes calls himself, the editor. To this belong more or less wholly the great biographies which I shall take for texts, Boswell's *Johnson*, Moore's *Byron*, Lockhart's *Scott*, Carlyle's *Sterling* (much smaller than the others, for reasons, but distinctly on the same lines with them), and, of books

* From 'Some Great Biographies', *Macmillan's Magazine*, June 1892, pp. 97–107; reprinted in *Collected Essays* (1923), I, 409–12, 432–3.

more recent, Sir George Trevelyan's *Macaulay*. And to this class also, for reasons very easy to understand, belong almost all the biographies recently produced of men recently living. The reasons I say are easy to find. There is the great popularity of the great examples: there is the demand arising from this popularity; but most of all there is the fatal facility of the proceeding in appearance, and in appearance only.

There can of course be no doubt that to the inexperienced it looks easy enough. In the first kind of biography the writer must to some extent master a considerable quantity of matter and subject it to some kind of intellectual or quasi-intellectual process of his own. At the very worst, the absolutely least, he must frame a sufficient number of sentences in his own head and (unless he dictates) write them with his own fingers—a number sufficient to fill the space between the covers of the book. And, unless he is a quite abnormally stupid or conceited man, he will be more or less conscious that he is doing this well or ill, sufficiently or insufficiently. He cannot to any great extent merely extract or quote. He must create, or at any rate build, or do something that may at least cheat himself into the idea that he is building or creating.

The second path is in comparison quite a primrose one. In most cases the biographer by hypothesis finds himself in possession of a certain, often a considerable, stock of material in the way of diaries, letters, and what not. Even if he has struck out the notion of the book for himself and is not ready furnished with his materials by executorship, appointment of friends, and the like, his own unskilled labour or that of a few jackals at public and other libraries will generally stock him amply with all the stuff he wants. Very often this stuff is, in part at least, really interesting. What more simple than to calendar it; to omit whatever is more than is wanted to fill the one, two or three volumes ordered or accepted by the publisher; to string the rest together with a 'John-a-Nokes was born on the —th of ——. Of his earliest years we find' and so on; to insert here and there a reference, a reminiscence, a reflection, or a connecting narrative; and, if the operator be very conscientious, to wind up with an appreciation or summary, 'We have thus followed a remarkable (or a painful, as the case may be) career to its close. Had this', and so forth? What, I repeat, more simple?

'It is not more stiff than that,' says the engaging idiom of the Gaul. At any rate there is certainly a large and apparently an increasing number of persons, many of them educated, presumably not unintelligent, certainly not unacquainted with books, things, and men, who consider that there is no greater 'stiffness' in it. Any competent critic, even any tolerably intelligent reader who dutifully studies or skims his new volumes from Mudie's, could name books of this kind within the last few years, nay, within the last few months, some of which had no justification whatever for their existence; others which a really skilful hand would have reduced to a small volume or even to an ordinary quarterly essay; others which, though capable of having been made into books of the right sort by the right treatment, had only been made into books of the wrong sort by the wrong treatment. Anybody on the other hand who remembers many thoroughly satisfactory books of the kind for some years past must either be a much more fortunate or a much less fastidious reader and critic than I can pretend to be. . . .

It is quite possible that the materials for biography are not so promising as they used to be. Some persons pretend that the cry about the decay of letter-writing is nonsense. The cautious arguer will confine himself to replying that at any rate there are great temptations not to write letters. Telegrams, postcards, correspondence-cards, letter-cards—all of these things the truly good and wise detest and execrate; it is not quite so certain that they abstain from them. I believe that the habit of keeping a diary has really gone out to a great extent. Too often moreover nowadays the unauthorized person steps in with his privateering before the authorized person is ready for sea; and then the authorized person too often indulges in undignified chasings and cannonadings of his predecessor. Above all there seems to have been lost, in this and other things, the all-important sense of proportion in books, and we get 'Lives' that would have been excellent in one volume watered out into two, 'Lives' that would have been pleasant places in two, becoming pathless deserts in four. These things have had a bad effect on the class of persons who are likely to find biographers. One hears of their destroying materials with a 'Please God, nobody shall deal with *me* as —— dealt with ——'. Or else, as was the case with Cardinal Newman, they enjoin a method of dealing with their materials, which, though it permits any one of tolerable intelligence to construct a biography for himself with comparatively little difficulty, does not give him the biography actually made. For it cannot be too often repeated that a real biography ought to be something more than the presentation of mere materials, however excellently calendared, something more than Memoirs, Letters, Diary and so forth. The whole ought to be passed through the mind of a competent and intelligent artist, and to be presented to us, not indeed in such a way that we are bound to take his word for the details, but in such a way that we see a finished picture, a real composition, not merely a bundle of details and *data*.

Charles Whibley

* For many years in England the follies of great men have been held the property of the fool. No sooner is genius laid upon its bier than the vultures are ready to swoop, and to drag from the dead bones two (or more) volumes of what were once most worthily described as 'remains'. Neither cancelled cheques nor washing-bills are discarded, and if research may uncover a forgotten scandal the bird of prey is happy indeed. With an energy amazing only for its misdirection the 'collector' wanders abroad that he may purchase the secrets of poets he never knew, and may snatch a brief notoriety from the common ridicule, wherein he involves an unapproachable talent. Thus, by a curious ingenuity, Shelley has become a hero of intrigues. The amateur of letters overlooks the poet, the intrepid champion of lost causes, the fearless fighter of other men's battles. Nor does he interest himself in the gay, irresponsible, pleasure-seeking adventurer, quick to succour others and to imagine fantastic plots against himself. No, he merely puts him in the dock upon a charge of marital infidelity, and constituting himself at once judge and jury, condemns him (in a lecture) to perpetual obloquy. Thus, too, the gimlet glance of a thousand Paul Prys pierces the letters which John Keats destined only for the eye of Fanny Brawne. Thus, too, through the indiscretion of pretended friends, Rossetti has been pictured now as a shivering apostle of sentiment, now as an astute, even an unscrupulous, driver of hard bargains. . . .

* From 'The Limits of Biography', *The Nineteenth Century*, March 1897, pp. 428–36.

Reticence being at an end, you may note everywhere the same fury of detection. The reviews fatten upon the dead with a ghoulish ferocity; it is almost impossible to discover a journal free from the prevailing frankness; no man's letters are thought too insignificant for print; and the Bibliothèque Nationale will soon be too small to contain the vast array of books and pamphlets which disclose hitherto inviolate secrets. . . .

Is it, then, out of respect that secrets are divulged? Hardly: respect does not show itself in the wanton advertisement of unimportant frailty, in the reckless publication of letters which the writer would have given his hand to suppress. If the thousands who assume a fervent interest in the love affairs of Shelley or Musset were sincere in their respect, they would avoid eavesdropping and devote themselves to the study of the poet's works. Nor is the lust of truth a sufficient excuse for these chafferers in private scandal. The result of their research is, and must ever be, falsification. Their zeal and energy are of no account, since the more they collect the more helpless becomes their confusion. They set their idol in a hideous light, and perforce destroy the proportion of his career. Having crowded a brief year with inglorious strife, they leave a decade blank, and so provide a perfect opportunity to mislead the envious. Musset's life is focussed (so to say) in his sojourn at Venice. He goes down to posterity as the lover of George Sand, and the facts that he parted from his Lélia, and that he wrote plays and novels and poems, do not touch the common imagination. 'I tell you he was in love with George Sand', says the student of literature, and there's an end of it. Above all the authority of letters is suspect. Printed long after the occasion which prompted their composition, read with the cold eye which takes no account of the preceding tumult and excitement, they lose the meaning which once was theirs and become the easiest instrument of falsehood and distortion. It is idle, therefore, to attribute the modern madness for biography to knowledge, or loyalty, or truth. It is not by the heedless accumulations of biography's raw material that truth is established or art is prospered. It is only the general curiosity which prompts the opening of drawers and the glance over the shoulder that demands satisfaction, and satisfaction it finds in half-digested memoirs and unselected correspondence.

Biography, none the less, is the most delicate of the arts, and its very delicacy renders interesting some definition of its limits. But the definition is difficult, because it must be framed with an equal regard to art and to behaviour. If the subject exacts a frank and free discussion of his foibles, his biographer is guarded against reproach, and succeeds or fails merely by his workmanship. Carlyle, for instance, desired an open exposition of his life, and it is hypocrisy to condemn Froude on any other than an aesthetic ground. So, also, memoirs are exempt from the censorship of manners. Every writer is justified in taking his own life as the material of his art, and Pepys no less than Saint-Simon may be credited with a perfect masterpiece.

Byron, on the other hand, shows the reverse of the medal. His strength and weakness alike demand description. He represented not only the poetry but the character of his age, and so openly was his life given to the public that his smallest action was criticized by thousands who knew him not. He was, in fact, a social problem made concrete, even in his lifetime, and thus he anticipated the vogue of Shelley. For him a frank biography is not an indiscretion; it is the necessary response to past libels. That he felt this necessity is evident from the studied Memoir composed by himself and most treacherously destroyed by Moore, whose sin upon the side of caution is less easily pardoned than the clumsiest revelation. Moreover Byron lived a life of energy and action outside his poetry, and his adventures are admirably characteristic of his romantic epoch. So that not only is his career memorable for its fancy and excitement, but every effort should be made to atone for the heedless crime of Moore. This truth has been realized by Mr. Henley, Byron's latest editor, who has undertaken in his commentary no less a task than the portraiture of Byron's 'dissolute yet bigoted' contemporaries.

The irresponsible biographer, then, must pass before this double tribunal, nor can he be acquitted until he satisfy it that his performance is excellent on both counts. He must prove first that he is guiltless of indiscretion, that he has betrayed no secret which his hero (or his victim) would have chosen to keep. He must exercise to the dead the same courtesy and reticence which he owes to the living, and from this prime duty no ingenuity shall absolve him. It is irrelevant to plead love of truth in excuse for betrayal, since truth (were it possible) is not of supreme value, and since truth which is half told (and it is seldom wholly told outside heaven) is indistinguishable from malice or falsehood. And then he must prove that he has fulfilled the aesthetic aim of biography, which is portraiture with a retrospect.

He must prove that he is capable of suppressing his documents, and catching from a thousand letters a vivid, separate impression. For literature transmutes experience, and takes no account of unimportant facts, and, alas! it is the workman's habit to sweep his raw material into a heap and call it biography.

The man of genius is above and beyond criticism; he is exempt from punishment, and enjoys the free and undisputed privilege of law-breaking. Boswell's *Life of Johnson* is magnificent, because for once in the world's history genius seized its opportunity with single-hearted devotion. The result is obtained by the most laborious method. The general impression is contrived by an infinitude of details, which in less skilful hands would inevitably have destroyed the portrait. But Boswell escaped triumphantly from the failure which had awaited a man of lesser talent, and his book remains a masterpiece not only of biography but of literature. So also Lockhart defies censure; yet his example is not for the herd, since to few men is given the tact or the occasion which carried his *Life of Scott* to perfection. These two transcend the rules of art, but for the rest the biographer's first necessity is invention rather than knowledge. If he would make a finished portrait of a great man, he must treat him as he would treat the hero of a romance; he must imagine the style and habit wherein he lived. He must fill in a thousand blanks from an intuitive sympathy; should he use documents in his study he must suppress them in his work, or pass them by with a hint; thus only will he arrive at a consistent picture, and if he start from an intelligent point of view he is at least likely to approach the truth.

A quick understanding may divine what a thousand unpublished letters would only obscure. When Mr. Pater drew his imaginary portrait of Watteau he excluded from the perfected work all the sketches and experiments which had aided its composition. There was no parade of knowledge or research, and such research as discovered the quality of the artist was held severely in reserve. This, then, is the ideal of biography: an imagined portrait stripped of all that is unessential, into which no detail is introduced without a deliberate choice and a definite intention. . . .

Early Twentieth Century

Edmund Gosse

* The great cause of difference of opinion on this subject of the limits and direction of biographical portraiture is the radical hostility of the groups of people for whose behoof the portrait is made. No successful biography of a recent person was ever written, it is fair to suppose, in which the contests of interests did not come to the front. There is always, besides the majority, whose curiosity is to be entertained, and whose legitimate interest is to be stimulated, a minority, few in number, but very influential and very respectable, whose object is to curtail intimate revelations, and defy all curiosity so far as it is possible to do so. We may argue for ever on one side or the other, on behalf of publicity or in favour of privacy, and yet come to little or no result, because each single case is morally independent of all possible precedents, and needs to be examined from its own new standpoint. Meanwhile those who are not related by blood or friendship or interest to the deceased shout for truth, the whole truth, and nothing but the truth; but each shouter, if he becomes personally involved in a 'life', instantly comes over to the other camp, and pleads for extreme caution and reticence.

We shall arrive, therefore, at no moral decision of the least practical value, unless we are persuaded, quite frankly, to accept a compromise. It is not possible to write a biography of any man, and still less of any woman, which will at once be valuable and amusing and yet palatable to every one who knew or was indebted to the subject. Cervantes wittily says, in one of his 'Exemplary Novels', that you cannot catch

* From 'The Ethics of Biography', *The Cosmopolitan*, July 1903, pp. 317–23.

trout, and yet keep your breeches dry. The adventurer in biography has to make up his mind to the commission of certain sins of indiscretion. He need not attempt to tell his story, if his only solicitude is to give nobody cause of offence. I will go further, and say that his anxiety should be, not how to avoid all indiscretion, but how to be as indiscreet as possible within the boundaries of good taste and kind feeling. He should start determined to reveal as much as possible, to drag his coy and retreating subject as far as can be done into the open light of day. We have all become so ultra-refined nowadays that we pursue the opposite course; we conceal this, and we tell lies about the other, and we make such a pother about reticence and professional secrecy, that when a trait of nature does struggle to the light, as it is bound to do now and then, we scream with horror at the solecism of it.

The more a human figure deserves biographical study, the more delicate and individual are its features, the more it seems, as a rule, to shrink from discovery. It crouches away in the darkness, as Claudius cowered under the heavy curtains of his palace while the murderers of Caligula were searching for him to make him Emperor of Rome. The biographer has to drag the reserve away, to open letters, to unclasp diaries, to catch the fleeting spirit of the man down the winding galleries of his concealments. He does it, not to shame him, not to satisfy his own curiosity, but because the world requires another leader. Here the figure lies, clinging to a pillar, its robe thrown over its face; tear the veils away, and Ave, Imperator! This, I admit, is a flamboyant apology for indiscreet biography. It may be coldly suggested that there is not, in every case, a certainty that the figure, when discovered and unearthed will present the features of an emperor. But I say that, even if he is but of the stature for a tribune or a mere poor senator, such as he is, so far as he goes, what he consists of, will not be appreciated unless we do some violence to his feelings, or what his relations are pleased to imagine that they would have been.

If the reader will but bear with me so far as to endure the thesis that the first theoretical object of the biographer should be indiscretion, not discretion, I will concede almost everything practical to delicacy. But this must be granted to me: that the aim of all portraiture ought to be the emphasizing of what makes the man different from, not like, other men. It is the specific, the individual, view that we want to catch. Some people have an inborn objection to the particular. Their one desire is to be, and to appear to be, exactly like everybody else.

The Widow, whom I have in another place ventured to describe as an instance of the survival of the unfittest in biographical literature, almost always desires that her deceased hero should be represented as exactly like all other respectable men, only a little grander, a little more glorified. She hates, as only a bad biographer can hate, the telling of the truth with respect to those faults and foibles which made the light and shade of his character. . . .

There is a terrible fear that this or that touch, of a homely, vivid kind, will lessen the dignity of the subject, will make us treat him less respectfully, and so he is presented to us as though he spent his whole life standing, pressed in a tight frock coat, with a glass of water at his hand and one elbow on a desk, in the act of preparing to say: 'Ladies and Gentlemen!' I have been glancing through a number of comparatively recent lives of illustrious Americans, and I am struck by the lack of anything like anecdotal impropriety which surrounds them all. Each man is presented to us as if the readers of his 'life' were a class and he was the professor, with something definite to teach, and no opportunity for displaying the smallest individuality of behaviour.

When I was a young man, and frequented the Pre-Raphaelites, I used to notice that Rossetti had a very curious way of tilting a glass or cup out of which he was drinking, and gulping down the last drops in a great hurry. I have never heard or seen this trick noticed by anyone else, and it is so trivial that I have never thought of recording it myself. But there it is, in my memory; the feverish, swarthy face turned upward in profile, and the large lips eagerly supping down the stream of liquid. I don't know why, but in that trifle I see Rossetti again after all these years; there is something, to me, characteristic, personal, unique, in the habitual gesture. Are we not glad to know, on the authority of those who had seen him, that Bacon had a nut-coloured eye, like the eye of a snake, and that he would not allow any of his servants to wear boots of Spanish calf because he hated the smell of it? Is it not satisfactory to be told that the celebrated Dr. Isaac Barrow was so dreamy that he would mount the stairs of the pulpit, and address a fashionable audience, with his collar unbuttoned and his hair uncombed? I cannot tell why it is that the modern biographer is so afraid of letting us into these little picturesque secrets. . . .

A belief in the uniformity of human character is one main cause of dull and false biography. You label a man 'good' or 'great', and you are bound to present him as great or good all through and upon every side. But not only was this theory refuted centuries ago by the Puritan general, Lambert, when he said—so excellently—that 'the best of men are but men at their best', it ignores that subtle law of human ethics which decrees that a sensitive person shall be 'all things to all men'. The complexity of human nature in its attitude to other specimens of the race is the stone upon which the majority of novelists stumble. They clap a ticket on their heroine, and make her act under identical impulses upon all occasions. But, if a woman is not a wax-work dunce, she is under the superficial control of many minds, and, though she is essentially one and the same, she is 'nice' to this person, and 'horrid' to that one. But the novelist rarely realizes this, and the biographer perhaps more rarely still, so that what was the result of some caprice or of some prejudice is laboriously explained away until all sense of spontaneity is gone.

We must not, however, exaggerate the importance of the anecdote in biography. A much more serious question is involved in the revelation or concealment of facts and conditions which have made a lasting mark on the character and the career of a man. We shall perhaps understand more clearly the ethical crux, if we put a definite, although imaginary, instance before us. Let us suppose that the biographer of a very eminent man is placed in possession of all the documents required to illustrate his life, and has had access to persons who knew the facts, and recounted them to him fairly and dispassionately. While docketing and confirming a large number of data which are highly to the credit of Mr. A., and place him in a light which is wholly attractive, the biographer also becomes aware of certain matters which are not so agreeable. We may tabulate these less-admirable data as follows:—

1. Mr. A. married very early, and his first wife was 'an objectionable person', who upset his life a great deal, and disturbed him so much that for several years he worked under a serious disadvantage.

2. In consequence of family troubles, he became from time to time the victim of intemperance, and injured his prospects by this.

3. His temper was extremely bad, and he did himself harm by giving way to it. In particular, an unjustifiable hatred of one of his aunts led to a very serious pecuniary disappointment, which hampered him.

4. He had good features, but a distressing birthmark on the left cheek destroyed his appearance on that side of his face. He was very sensitive to this, and his portrait was therefore always taken, in profile, from the right.

5. Mr. A. was very witty, but he could not restrain himself from saying things that gave pain to others, or, being repeated, produced great offence. He was habitually selfish in his dealings with people younger than himself.

Taken alone, these characteristics give the impression of an ugly and unattractive personality. But I must ask the reader to think of them as combined with elements of force and brilliancy and high native ability sufficient to make Mr. A. a proper, or indeed an irresistible, theme for biography.

Suppose that as we are sitting down to write the life of this man, who may have been an illustrious lawyer, an intrepid traveller, a splendid artist,—how should these five heads be treated? All five were of real importance in the evolution of the man's character and public usefulness, although not of equal importance. All add colour to his history, each is what he would either have denied or desired to conceal. (I have been careful to suggest nothing extraordinary or sensational; these are faults and misfortunes which are of every-day occurrence.) In the case of a modern biography, raised by relatives, it is almost certain that not one of the five would be so much as referred to, although, as the personal appearance of a man is not of much importance to anybody but the man himself—not even to his wife—some vague allusion to number four might be admitted. But it would be indelicate to speak of number one; a breach of professional etiquette to hint at number two; number three would not seem interesting to a modern biographer (although so deeply human); and number five would be the subject of direct, and what is considered pious, falsehood. The way in which nineteen out of twenty modern biographers would treat number five would be to say that Mr. A., 'though such a conversational sparkler, held his tongue ever in restraint lest it might unconsciously wound a friend; and that he was always eagerly looking out for merit in those younger than himself—"the generation knocking at the door!" as he would often playfully exclaim'.

But, if we examine these heads more closely, we shall see that they have a very various moral significance. Number four, which I have pointed out as that which would most easily pass the censorship of relatives, seems to me to be the one about which morality is most indifferent. If the poor man preferred the world to see one side of his face and not the other, he was after all not responsible for his left cheek, and may surely be allowed a posthumous preference for his right one.

On the other hand, for number five he was directly responsible, and I am of the opinion that it is not a matter of choice with the biographer, but a matter of duty, to expose, without rancour, without emphasis, but unmistakably, this fault, which was a direct outcome of a certain sensitiveness, a certain want of balance, inextricably connected with his peculiar genius, whatever it was. If a man possessed splendid talents, and gets the full credit of them, it is immoral to conceal defects which were the corollary of his genius and the result of its excessive qualities. It is wrong, as well as absurd, to paint a man of disagreeably intense egotistic force as though he were a sister of mercy on wheels.

About number three I do not feel so confident as about number five. It would, perhaps, not be proper to tell the incident of the aunt, although an aunt may be so very trying and although so very excellent a person as she whom the poet Gray called the 'Dragon of Wantley'. I think that the characteristic of the peppery temper ought to be indicated, and the fact that Mr. A. did himself harm by giving way to it not wholly concealed. After all, temper is not a deadly sin. The kitchen proverb tells us that 'all good cooks have bad tempers', and perhaps Mr. A. would not have done whatever it was he did do so well if he had been less irascible. On the whole, I think we ought to be told frankly about his temper. But numbers one and two stand in an entirely distinct category. There the responsibility of the biographer is complicated, as it is not in numbers three, four, and five, with the possible effects of what he writes upon other persons who neither claim nor desire the high light of publicity. Numbers one and two, therefore, require our special consideration.

As I said before, the moral aspect of biography is involved in difficulty by the fact that each individual instance needs a law unto itself. In dealing with number one, for example, it is impossible to decide whether it should be concealed or confessed until we know a variety of cognate circumstances, such as whether Mrs. A. died long before her husband, or is still alive, whether she had children or not, if she had, whether they are still alive, and what her final relations were with her husband. Each shade of difference in these conditions lays a fresh obligation on the biographer as towards her or towards his public. He has to weigh in the balance the sensitiveness or legitimate self-respect of survivors against what is due to art and truth in the treatment of his subject. If he is a writer of any skill, he will probably find means of indicating all the essential points contained in number one without producing a scandal and without needlessly wounding anyone's feelings. He should certainly endeavour to make this indication; if the circumstances had a strong influence on the character and career of his subject, it seems to me that it is his bounden duty to do so, but with all reasonable care in avoiding needless vexation to survivors.

In number two, I have suggested the existence in the subject of biography of a definite moral weakness of a humiliating order. I have taken intemperance as being one of the least abnormal of such weaknesses, but the experienced reader will easily think of others. The careers of men of high genius have not been exempted from these moral maladies, and we have learned to think with nothing but indulgent regret of the sadder passages in the lives of Coleridge and Lamb, of Burns and Edgar Poe, even of Villon and Verlaine. In some of these cases the frailty, whatever it was, could not be concealed; in others the piety of biographers fought for the legend of their subject's immunity, stubbornly, inch for inch, with the result—as eminently in the instance of Charles Lamb,—of bringing at last a blaze of attention to it. In all such matters, the shock of discovery is the worse; we get accustomed to everything, and the judgement finds its level in reflection. It seems to me that here, also, the question of pain to survivors should be paramount. If a man of distinction and talent leaves sons and daughters behind him, they are deeply wounded if the world is informed, in crude terms, that their father was a drunkard. But we should never use crude terms about anything, and the legitimate scruples of private persons must, in a matter of this kind, be respected. Yet, even here, I think that respect should never extend so far as to the telling of a deliberate lie. We must not say that Mr. A. was a strong upholder of teetotalism; still less must we say (and this is the favourite formula of the official biographer in such cases) that Mr. A. was particularly anxious for the spread of temperance among the lower classes and the young. With a certain legitimate regret, as of one who is not permitted to paint a wen on a rugged face, the biographer must make up his mind entirely to omit any reference to the subject of intemperance; but he is justified in firmly refusing to tell the smallest falsehood on the subject. . . .

George Santayana

*Our ignorance of the life of Lucretius is not, I think, much to be regretted. His work preserves that part of him which he himself would have wished to preserve. Perfect conviction ignores itself, proclaiming the public truth. To reach this no doubt requires a peculiar genius which is called intelligence; for intelligence is quickness in seeing things as they are. But where intelligence is attained, the rest of a man, like the scaffolding to a finished building, becomes irrelevant. We do not wish it to intercept our view of the solid structure, which alone was intended by the artist—if he was building for others, and was not a coxcomb. It is his intellectual vision that the naturalist in particular wishes to hand down to posterity, not the shabby incidents that preceded that vision in his own person. These incidents, even if they were by chance interesting, could not be repeated in us; but the vision into which the thinker poured his faculties, and to which he devoted his vigils, is communicable to us also, and may become a part of ourselves.

* From *Three Philosophical Poets* (Harvard University Press, 1910), p. 20; reprinted with the title, 'Against Prying Biographers', in *Little Essays Drawn from the Writings of George Santayana*, ed. Logan Pearsall Smith (1921), p. 159. Included by permission of Constable and Co.

Lytton Strachey

*It is not by the direct method of a scrupulous narration that the explorer of the past can hope to depict that singular epoch. If he is wise, he will adopt a subtler strategy. He will attack his subject in unexpected places; he will fall upon the flank, or the rear; he will shoot a sudden, revealing searchlight into obscure recesses, hitherto undivined. He will row out over that great ocean of material, and lower down into it, here and there, a little bucket, which will bring up to the light of day some characteristic specimen, from those far depths, to be examined with a careful curiosity. Guided by these considerations, I have written the ensuing studies. I have attempted, through the medium of biography, to present some Victorian visions to the modern eye. They are, in one sense, haphazard visions—that is to say, my choice of subjects has been determined by no desire to construct a system or to prove a theory, but by simple motives of convenience and of art. It has been my purpose to illustrate rather than to explain. It would have been futile to hope to tell even a *précis* of the truth about the Victorian age, for the shortest *précis* must fill innumerable volumes. But, in the lives of an ecclesiastic, an educational authority, a woman of action, and a man of adventure, I have sought to examine and elucidate certain fragments of the truth which took my fancy and lay to my hand.

I hope, however, that the following pages may prove to be of interest from the strictly biographical no less than from the historical

*'Preface', *Eminent Victorians* (1918). Reprinted by permission of Chatto and Windus and Harcourt, Brace and Co., publishers.

point of view. Human beings are too important to be treated as mere symptoms of the past. They have a value which is independent of any temporal processes—which is eternal, and must be felt for its own sake. The art of biography seems to have fallen on evil times in England. We have had, it is true, a few masterpieces, but we have never had, like the French, a great biographical tradition; we have had no Fontenelles and Condorcets, with their incomparable *éloges*, compressing into a few shining pages the manifold existences of men. With us, the most delicate and humane of all the branches of the art of writing has been relegated to the journeymen of letters; we do not reflect that it is perhaps as difficult to write a good life as to live one. Those two fat volumes, with which it is our custom to commemorate the dead—who does not know them, with their ill-digested masses of material, their slipshod style, their tone of tedious panegyric, their lamentable lack of selection, of detachment, of design? They are as familiar as the *cortège* of the undertaker, and wear the same air of slow, funereal barbarism. One is tempted to suppose, of some of them, that they were composed by that functionary, as the final item of his job. The studies in this book are indebted, in more ways than one, to such works—works which certainly deserve the name of Standard Biographies. For they have provided me not only with much indispensable information, but with something even more precious—an example. How many lessons are to be learnt from them! But it is hardly necessary to particularize. To preserve, for instance, a becoming brevity—a brevity which excludes everything that is redundant and nothing that is significant—that, surely, is the first duty of the biographer. The second, no less surely, is to maintain his own freedom of spirit. It is not his business to be complimentary; it is his business to lay bare the facts of the case, as he understands them. That is what I have aimed at in this book—to lay bare the facts of some cases, as I understood them, dispassionately, impartially, and without ulterior intentions. To quote the words of a Master—'Je n'impose rien; je ne propose rien: j'expose.'

Robert Littell

* *Biographer*—We are both in the same business.

Novelist—How do you make that out?

Biographer—We are both writing about people.

Novelist—But your people have actually existed, while mine are made up inside my head.

Biographer—That difference is not as real as it seems on the surface. The people you believe you have invented get their start from people you have known in real life, or have read about. And the statesmen or adventurers whose lives I choose to retell are in great part my own creations.

Novelist—Which amounts to an admission that you are a very poor sort of biographer indeed.

Biographer—Not at all. But perhaps you had better explain your notion of a biographer.

Novelist—Certainly. I should remind you that I used to take a whack at biography myself. I would try to draw a picture of a particular person which should correspond with the facts I had collected about him. Taking a bird's eye view of these facts, I attempted to make of them an artistic whole. I could never work out a single pattern which satisfied me both as a pattern and as a rearrangement of certain facts adding up to the known truth. If I left out what would not fit, the picture was incomplete. If I put it in, the picture was blurred. I saw no way out of the dilemma, so I turned to fiction, where nobody but myself knew all the facts, and where I was free to change, invent, and eliminate them so as to correspond with only one truth—the truth inside my own head, which I was at perfect liberty to change, and which

* 'Truth is Stranger', *The New Republic*, 16 December 1925, pp. 112–13. Reprinted by permission of the author and the publisher.

did change as I went along, whether I wanted it to or not. My desertion to the ranks of fiction was of course partly due to laziness, but I must give myself credit for a certain amount of honesty. This brings me to that definition of a biographer you asked for. He must be honest; he must be loyal to the facts, even when they tell him nothing. My duty as a novelist is the opposite—I must above all be loyal to the image of my character, and choose only those facts which support it. You know as well as I do that every biographer is faced with quantities of material which he cannot explain. He cannot ignore this material, though it will spoil his pattern, blur his picture, and force blank spaces upon an otherwise intelligible narrative. He must record the truth, the whole truth, and nothing but the truth, even when, as often happens, the truth is quite meaningless.

Biographer—You were right to turn to fiction, because as a biographer either your honesty or your imagination would have given way. Your counsel is one of perfection, and that alone is reason enough to reject it. You ask the biographer to stick to the facts he has accumulated, to incorporate all of them, and to let them speak for themselves, even when what they say is incomprehensible. If it were possible to arrive at something like all the truth about the subject of a biography, I might agree with you. But the biographer, after years of research, after digging up all the lost letters, after interviewing all the surviving friends and associates, has at best only a very small fraction of the facts. If we rely on the memory of contemporaries, we must recognize that memories are selective, and keep for us, not all the facts, but only those which for some psychological reason, were chosen to survive. If we rely on recorded acts, we must weigh against them all acts unrecorded, acts stillborn in the will, acts resolved upon, acts refrained from. In the long movie that was a life, all that remains to us are a few disconnected stills. And, as you suggest, even if we knew all, we would still not be able to make sense of it. Our job is to make sense: that is the new biography. We recreate our own conception of likeness out of the facts by using our imagination. Of course the imagination distorts anything it touches, but only through imagination can the thing touched live at all. Do you suppose that Lytton Strachey's Queen Victoria is faithful to everything the old lady said and did? I doubt it very much, but I don't care. I vastly prefer Strachey's act of creation, which will make Victoria live for ever, to a more self-effacing, honest and archæological effort. An attempt to set down everything of importance would wander over the canvas until its sprawling diversities could no longer be framed. And biography should be a frame.

Novelist—You ought to be writing fiction instead.

Biographer—I might, but for a public-spirited streak in me which demands that certain characters in history I have become fond of should not for ever lie buried under the facts loyally collected by the old-style biographer. If the essential character is to stick its head out above the facts, facts must be shaped, manipulated, thrown away. The whole question for me is whether the character is to survive or not. To that end I bend everything, including the truth. I will burn up a lot of little dead truths to make one big live truth: a distinct and memorable character.

Novelist—We are dangerously near a discussion of the nature of truth itself.

Biographer—I agree that nothing could be more futile. But allow me to make a few footnotes. As to a given character whose life we want to re-create, there is not, nor has there ever been one truth, except in some impossible heaven of omniscience. A few bare facts aside—and these are likely to be the least important things in a re-creation—nothing is absolutely certain. The character certainly lied to himself about himself, and had all sorts of different impressions of himself and his own acts at different times. The sum total of all those intimate impressions—the least discoverable item to a biographer—is one leg of the centipede of truth. Think of the other legs: the impressions of all the people who knew him, listened to him, witnessed his deeds. No two of them are alike, yet each of them amounts to a sort of truth, and the sum of them is still another kind of truth. What truth then can the biographer be faithful to other than his own? It is born as he explores the character, and grows according to what it feeds on. Some food it rejects, other food it builds up into the final character. And this finished product is judged and interpreted by readers in many different ways. The character is created again, but, as in his own lifetime, he relives different lives in the minds of different people. And the whole truth—since truth is subjective—is a sum of impressions of the sum of other impressions which changes so long as the book has readers, or the character vitality.

Novelist—It was a good thing that I deserted biography for fiction. Whatever diverse impressions my readers may have, at least I have a clear idea of what I was trying to do.

Biographer—I wouldn't be so sure about that.

Virginia Woolf

*Through the influence of Boswell, presumably, biography all through the nineteenth century concerned itself as much with the lives of the sedentary as with the lives of the active. It sought painstakingly and devotedly to express not only the outer life of work and activity but the inner life of emotion and thought. The uneventful lives of poets and painters were written out as lengthily as the lives of soldiers and statesmen. But the Victorian biography was a parti-coloured, hybrid, monstrous birth. For though truth of fact was observed as scrupulously as Boswell observed it, the personality which Boswell's genius set free was hampered and distorted. The convention which Boswell had destroyed settled again, only in a different form, upon biographers who lacked his art. Where the Mrs. Hutchinsons and the Izaak Waltons had wished to prove that their heroes were prodigies of courage and learning the Victorian biographer was dominated by the idea of goodness. Noble, upright, chaste, severe; it is thus that the Victorian worthies are presented to us. The figure is almost always above life size in top-hat and frock-coat, and the manner of presentation becomes increasingly clumsy and laborious. For lives which no longer express themselves in action take shape in innumerable words. The conscientious biographer may not tell a fine tale with a flourish, but must toil through endless labyrinths and embarrass himself with countless documents. In the end

*From 'The New Biography', *New York Herald Tribune*, 30 October 1927; reprinted in *Granite and Rainbow* (1958), pp. 150–2, 154–5. © 1958, by Leonard Woolf. Included by permission of Mr. Leonard Woolf and Harcourt, Brace and Co.

he produces an amorphous mass, a life of Tennyson, or of Gladstone, in which we go seeking disconsolately for voice or laughter, for curse or anger, for any trace that this fossil was once a living man. Often, indeed, we bring back some invaluable trophy, for Victorian biographies are laden with truth; but always we rummage among them with a sense of the prodigious waste, of the artistic wrongheadedness of such a method.

With the twentieth century, however, a change came over biography, as it came over fiction and poetry. The first and most visible sign of it was in the difference in size. In the first twenty years of the new century biographies must have lost half their weight. Mr. Strachey compressed four stout Victorians into one slim volume; M. Maurois boiled the usual two volumes of a Shelley life into one little book the size of a novel. But the diminution of size was only the outward token of an inward change. The point of view had completely altered. If we open one of the new school of biographies its bareness, its emptiness makes us at once aware that the author's relation to his subject is different. He is no longer the serious and sympathetic companion, toiling even slavishly in the footsteps of his hero. Whether friend or enemy, admiring or critical, he is an equal. In any case, he preserves his freedom and his right to independent judgement. Moreover, he does not think himself constrained to follow every step of the way. Raised upon a little eminence which his independence has made for him, he sees his subject spread about him. He chooses; he synthesizes; in short, he has ceased to be the chronicler; he has become an artist. . . .

And here we again approach the difficulty which, for all his ingenuity, the biographer still has to face. Truth of fact and truth of fiction are incompatible; yet he is now more than ever urged to combine them. For it would seem that the life which is increasingly real to us is the fictitious life; it dwells in the personality rather than in the act. Each of us is more Hamlet, Prince of Denmark, than he is John Smith of the Corn Exchange. Thus, the biographer's imagination is always being stimulated to use the novelist's art of arrangement, suggestion, dramatic effect to expound the private life. Yet if he carries the use of fiction too far, so that he disregards the truth, or can only introduce it with incongruity, he loses both worlds; he has neither the freedom of fiction nor the substance of fact. Boswell's astonishing power over us is based largely upon his obstinate veracity, so that we have implicit belief in what he tells us. When Johnson says 'No, sir; stark insensibility', the voice has a ring in it because we have been told, soberly and prosaically, a few pages earlier, that Johnson 'was entered a Commoner of Pembroke, on the 31st of October, 1728, being then in his nineteenth year'. We are in the world of brick and pavement; of birth, marriage, and death; of Acts of Parliament; of Pitt and Burke and Sir Joshua Reynolds. Whether this is a more real world than the world of Bohemia and Hamlet and Macbeth we doubt; but the mixture of the two is abhorrent.

* * *

* The art of biography, we say—but at once go on to ask, Is biography an art? The question is foolish perhaps, and ungenerous, certainly, considering the keen pleasure that biographers have given us. But the question asks itself so often that there must be something behind it. There it is, whenever a new biography is opened, casting its shadow on the page; and there would seem to be something deadly in that shadow, for after all, of the multitude of lives that are written, how few survive!

But the reason for this high death rate, the biographer might argue, is that biography, compared with the arts of poetry and fiction, is a young art. Interest in our selves and in other people's selves is a late development of the human mind. Not until the eighteenth century in England did that curiosity express itself in writing the lives of private people. Only in the nineteenth century was biography fully grown and hugely prolific. If it is true that there have been only three great biographers—Johnson, Boswell, and Lockhart—the reason, he argues, is that the time was short; and his plea, that the art of biography has had but little time to establish itself and develop itself, is certainly borne out by the textbooks. Tempting as it is to explore the reason—why, that is, the self that writes a book of prose came into being so many centuries after the self that writes a poem, why Chaucer preceded Henry James—it is better to leave that insoluble question unasked, and so pass to his next reason for the lack of masterpieces. It is that the art of biography is the most restricted of all the arts. He has his proof ready to hand. Here it is in the preface in which Smith,

* From 'The Art of Biography', *Atlantic Monthly*, April 1939, pp. 506–10; reprinted in *The Death of the Moth* (1942), 187–97. Copyright, 1942, by Harcourt, Brace and Co. Included by permission of Mr. Leonard Woolf and Harcourt, Brace and Co.

who has written the life of Jones, takes this opportunity of thanking old friends who have lent letters, and 'last but not least' Mrs. Jones, the widow, for that help 'without which', as he puts it, 'this biography could not have been written'. Now the novelist, he points out, simply says in his foreword, 'Every character in this book is fictitious.' The novelist is free; the biographer is tied.

There, perhaps, we come within hailing distance of that very difficult, again perhaps insoluble, question: What do we mean by calling a book a work of art? At any rate, here is a distinction between biography and fiction—a proof that they differ in the very stuff of which they are made. One is made with the help of friends, of facts; the other is created without any restrictions save those that the artist, for reasons that seem good to him, chooses to obey. That is a distinction; and there is good reason to think that in the past biographers have found it not only a distinction but a very cruel distinction. . . .

II

The figure of Lytton Strachey is so important a figure in the history of biography that it compels a pause. For his three famous books, *Eminent Victorians*, *Queen Victoria*, and *Elizabeth and Essex*, are of a stature to show both what biography can do and what biography cannot do. Thus they suggest many possible answers to the question whether biography is an art, and if not why it fails.

Lytton Strachey came to birth as an author at a lucky moment. In 1918, when he made his first attempt, biography, with its new liberties, was a form that offered great attractions. To a writer like himself, who had wished to write poetry or plays but was doubtful of his creative power, biography seemed to offer a promising alternative. For at last it was possible to tell the truth about the dead; and the Victorian age was rich in remarkable figures many of whom had been grossly deformed by the effigies that had been plastered over them. To recreate them, to show them as they really were, was a task that called for gifts analogous to the poet's or the novelist's yet did not ask that inventive power in which he found himself lacking.

It was well worth trying. And the anger and the interest that his short studies of Eminent Victorians aroused showed that he was able to make Manning, Florence Nightingale, Gordon, and the rest live as they had not lived since they were actually in the flesh. Once more they were the centre of a buzz of discussion. Did Gordon really drink, or was that an invention? Had Florence Nightingale received the Order of Merit in her bedroom or in her sitting room? He stirred the public, even though a European war was raging, to an astonishing interest in such minute matters. Anger and laughter mixed; and editions multiplied.

But these were short studies with something of the over-emphasis and the foreshortening of caricatures. In the lives of the two great Queens, Elizabeth and Victoria, he attempted a far more ambitious task. Biography had never had a fairer chance of showing what it could do. For it was now being put to the test by a writer who was capable of making use of all the liberties that biography had won: he was fearless; he had proved his brilliance; and he had learned his job. The result throws great light upon the nature of biography. For who can doubt after reading the two books again, one after the other, that the *Victoria* is a triumphant success, and that the *Elizabeth* by comparison is a failure? But it seems too, as we compare them, that it was not Lytton Strachey who failed; it was the art of biography. In the *Victoria* he treated biography as a craft; he submitted to its limitations. In the *Elizabeth* he treated biography as an art; he flouted its limitations.

But we must go on to ask how we have come to this conclusion and what reasons support it. In the first place it is clear that the two Queens present very different problems to their biographer. About Queen Victoria everything was known. Everything she did, almost everything she thought, was a matter of common knowledge. No one has ever been more closely verified and exactly authenticated than Queen Victoria. The biographer could not invent her, because at every moment some document was at hand to check his invention. And, in writing of Victoria, Lytton Strachey submitted to the conditions. He used to the full the biographer's power of selection and relation, but he kept strictly within the world of fact. Every statement was verified; every fact was authenticated. And the result is a life which, very possibly, will do for the old Queen what Boswell did for the old dictionary maker. In time to come Lytton Strachey's Queen Victoria will be Queen Victoria, just as Boswell's Johnson is now Dr. Johnson. The other versions will fade and disappear. It was a prodigious feat, and no doubt, having accomplished it, the author was anxious to press further. There was Queen Victoria, solid, real, palpable. But undoubtedly she was limited. Could not biography produce something of the intensity of poetry, something of the excitement of drama, and yet keep also the peculiar virtue that belongs to fact—its suggestive reality, its own proper creativeness?

Queen Elizabeth seemed to lend herself perfectly to the experiment. Very little was known about her. The society in which she lived was so remote that the habits, the motives, and even the actions of the people of that age were full of strangeness and obscurity. 'By what art are we to worm our way into those strange spirits? those even stranger bodies? The more clearly we perceive it, the more remote that singular universe becomes,' Lytton Strachey remarked on one of the first pages. Yet there was evidently a 'tragic history' lying dormant, half revealed, half concealed, in the story of the Queen and Essex. Everything seemed to lend itself to the making of a book that combined the advantages of both worlds, that gave the artist freedom to invent, but helped his invention with the support of facts—a book that was not only a biography but also a work of art.

Nevertheless, the combination proved unworkable; fact and fiction refused to mix. Elizabeth never became real in the sense that Queen Victoria had been real, yet she never became fictitious in the sense that Cleopatra or Falstaff is fictitious. The reason would seem to be that very little was known—he was urged to invent; yet something was known—his invention was checked. The Queen thus moves in an ambiguous world, between fact and fiction, neither embodied nor disembodied. There is a sense of vacancy and effort, of a tragedy that has no crisis, of characters that meet but do not clash.

If this diagnosis is true we are forced to say that the trouble lies with biography itself. It imposes conditions, and those conditions are that it must be based upon fact. And by fact in biography we mean facts that can be verified by other people besides the artist. If he invents facts as an artist invents them—facts that no one else can verify—and tries to combine them with facts of the other sort, they destroy each other.

Lytton Strachey himself seems in the *Queen Victoria* to have realized the necessity of this condition, and to have yielded to it instinctively. 'The first forty-two years of the Queen's life', he wrote, 'are illuminated by a great and varied quantity of authentic information. With Albert's death a veil descends'. And when with Albert's death the veil descended and authentic information failed, he knew that the biographer must follow suit. 'We must be content with a brief and summary relation', he wrote; and the last years are briefly disposed of. But the whole of Elizabeth's life was lived behind a far thicker veil than the last years of Victoria. And yet, ignoring his own admission, he went on to write, not a brief and summary relation, but a whole book about those strange spirits and even stranger bodies of whom authentic information was lacking. On his own showing, the attempt was doomed to failure.

III

It seems, then, that when the biographer complained that he was tied by friends, letters, and documents he was laying his finger upon a necessary element in biography; and that it is also a necessary limitation. For the invented character lives in a free world where the facts are verified by one person only—the artist himself. Their authenticity lies in the truth of his own vision. The world created by that vision is rarer, intenser, and more wholly of a piece than the world that is largely made of authentic information supplied by other people. And because of this difference the two kinds of fact will not mix; if they touch they destroy each other. No one, the conclusion seems to be, can make the best of both worlds; you must choose, and you must abide by your choice.

But though the failure of *Elizabeth and Essex* leads to this conclusion, that failure, because it was the result of a daring experiment carried out with magnificent skill, leads the way to further discoveries. Had he lived, Lytton Strachey would no doubt himself have explored the vein that he had opened. As it is, he has shown us the way in which others may advance. The biographer is bound by facts—that is so; but, if it is so, he has the right to all the facts that are available. If Jones threw boots at the maid's head, had a mistress at Islington, or was found drunk in a ditch after a night's debauch, he must be free to say so—so far at least as the law of libel and human sentiment allow.

But these facts are not like the facts of science—once they are discovered, always the same. They are subject to changes of opinion; opinions change as the times change. What was thought a sin is now known, by the light of facts won for us by the psychologists, to be perhaps a misfortune; perhaps a curiosity; perhaps neither one nor the other, but a trifling foible of no great importance one way or the other. The accent on sex has changed within living memory. This leads to the destruction of a great deal of dead matter still obscuring the true features of the human face. Many of the old chapter headings —life at college, marriage, career—are shown to be very arbitrary and artificial distinctions. The real current of the hero's existence took, very likely, a different course.

Thus the biographer must go ahead of the rest of us, like the miner's canary, testing the atmosphere, detecting falsity, unreality, and the presence of obsolete conventions. His sense of truth must be alive and on tiptoe. Then again, since we live in an age when a thousand cameras are pointed, by newspapers, letters, and diaries, at every character from every angle, he must be prepared to admit contradictory versions of the same face. Biography will enlarge its scope by hanging up looking glasses at odd corners. And yet from all this diversity it will bring out, not a riot of confusion, but a richer unity. And again, since so much is known that used to be unknown, the question now inevitably asks itself, whether the lives of great men only should be recorded. Is not anyone who has lived a life, and left a record of that life, worthy of biography—the failures as well as the successes, the humble as well as the illustrious? And what is greatness? And what smallness? He must revise our standards of merit and set up new heroes for our admiration.

IV

Biography thus is only at the beginning of its career; it has a long and active life before it, we may be sure—a life full of difficulty, danger, and hard work. Nevertheless, we can also be sure that it is a different life from the life of poetry and fiction—a life lived at a lower degree of tension. And for that reason its creations are not destined for the immortality which the artist now and then achieves for his creations.

There would seem to be certain proof of that already. Even Dr. Johnson as created by Boswell will not live as long as Falstaff as created by Shakespeare. Micawber and Miss Bates we may be certain will survive Lockhart's Sir Walter Scott and Lytton Strachey's Queen Victoria. For they are made of more enduring matter. The artist's imagination at its most intense fires out what is perishable in fact; he builds with what is durable; but the biographer must accept the perishable, build with it, imbed it in the very fabric of his work. Much will perish; little will live. And thus we come to the conclusion, that he is a craftsman, not an artist; and his work is not a work of art but something betwixt and between.

Yet on that lower level the work of the biographer is invaluable;

we cannot thank him sufficiently for what he does for us. For we are incapable of living wholly in the intense world of the imagination. The imagination is a faculty that soon tires and needs rest and refreshment. But for a tired imagination the proper food is not inferior poetry or minor fiction—indeed they blunt and debauch it—but sober fact, that 'authentic information' from which, as Lytton Strachey has shown us, good biography is made. When and where did the real man live; how did he look; did he wear laced boots or elastic-sided; who were his aunts, and his friends; how did he blow his nose; whom did he love, and how; and when he came to die did he die in his bed like a Christian, or . . .

By telling us the true facts, by sifting the little from the big, and shaping the whole so that we perceive the outline, the biographer does more to stimulate the imagination than any poet or novelist save the very greatest. For few poets and novelists are capable of that high degree of tension which gives us reality. But almost any biographer, if he respects facts, can give us much more than another fact to add to our collection. He can give us the creative fact; the fertile fact; the fact that suggests and engenders. Of this, too, there is certain proof. For how often, when a biography is read and tossed aside, some scene remains bright, some figure lives on in the depths of the mind, and causes us, when we read a poem or a novel, to feel a start of recognition, as if we remembered something that we had known before.

Emil Ludwig

*After a period which attempted to define man in terms of descent and breeding, we enter upon an era totally alien to the Darwinian mentality; once again we turn our attention to the personality *per se*, the personality almost devoid of temporal co-ordinates, considering the volume, intensity, and resistance of its vital forces, the restless fluid of its emotional configurations, and the balance between its impulse towards action and its repression through precept. Whereas our fathers asked, 'How did the individual harmonize with his world?' our first question is, 'Does he harmonize with himself?' Questions of success and responsibility have been shifted from the environment back to the individual, so that the analysis which was formerly expended upon the milieu now seeks to penetrate within. Further, the renewed interest in memoirs is biological: and perhaps the portraitist of today, who is first of all a psychologist, is much nearer to the biologist than to the historian.

And he has correspondingly greater freedom in his method of treatment. He can exploit the dramatic form, or the short essay, the detailed, exhaustive life history, or the editorial. He should be at home in all these methods of approach, and should select them in accordance with the subject and purpose of his work—just as his speechless colleague, the portrait-painter, makes use of oil, crayon or charcoal, etching needle or water colour.

* From 'Introduction: On Historical Portraiture', *Genius and Character* (1927), pp. 13–17. Reprinted by permission of Harcourt, Brace and Co. and Jonathan Cape. Copyright, 1927 by Harcourt, Brace and Co., renewed, 1954, by Kenneth Burke.

His problem remains a constant: it is the discovery of a human soul. Of course, the portraitist takes his basic material from the purely scientific biographer and is always indebted to him. With a kind of naïve cynicism, he appropriates the scientist's laboriously collated facts for purposes of his own: an artist who ransacks the flower-beds and leaves a pillaged garden behind for the grumbling gardener, while he himself goes off with a superb bouquet gleaming in his arms.

For if the philologist begins with an investigation and gradually assembles the picture of a man, the portraitist begins with the concept of a character and searches the archives for what is at bottom the corroboration of an intuition. But woe to him if he is tempted to improvise, to shift his dates ever so little, thereby encroaching upon the novelist! . . .

The nature of a man is summarized in his picture—and the great portrait-painters with pen or brush have all been great physiognomists. Pictures, those silent betrayals, provide the biographer with material as valuable as letters, memoirs, speeches, conversations—when the scientific investigator has found them authentic—or as handwriting. For this reason, a biography without a picture of its subject is impossible.

The same applies to the accounts of a man's daily habits. These were formerly inserted like curiosities, little bonbons for the reader's palate. Anecdotes were recorded sceptically, shamefacedly, and as though with a lowering of professional dignity. For us, today, the most trivial habit will often suggest the interpretation for some major trait of character, and the accredited anecdote becomes an epigram.

Scientific biographies, even now, occasionally close with a chapter designed to show us the hero 'as a man'—an appendix, like the diagram of a battle or the facsimile of a page from a note-book. But how is the portraitist to represent his subject except as a man? What is his task but to trace this man's every thought and act, every motive and impulse, back to the indivisible elements of his personality?

For this purpose, he must have more than the knowledge of a period: he must be versed in the study of man, must be a psychologist and an analyst. He must be skilled, through both intuition and training, in interpreting a character by the symptoms of its behaviour. Surely there are great biographers latent in great diplomats; and biographers could be profitably employed in diplomatic service.

Yet a knowledge of genius is demanded also—and herein lies the most formidable difficulty of all. To understand and interpret a poet, one must have the creative gift; to discuss the man of the world, a taste for worldly living is necessary; the biography of a statesman demands political insight; an understanding of women is called into play when an erotic character is analysed—in a word, subtlety of feeling is the condition of truthful representation. 'I take pleasure in the thought', wrote Vauvenargues, 'that the man who understands such great deeds would not have been incapable of performing them—and fate seems unfair in confining him to the mere recording of them'.

If we conceive of our task in so wide a sense and are determined to make our accounts of a human life serve also as an instance of the nature of genius, if we see in our hero merely a kind of pretext for tracing the outer limits of mankind, then we are immune to all dangers of partisanship: beyond chauvinism and other prejudices, we face our heroes with impartiality, avoiding—like the two creators of human beings, Shakespeare and Balzac—the strictures of any so-called philosophy of life. . . .

Frederick A. Pottle

★ What is the problem of a man who wishes to write a biography of an author whom he did not know in the flesh? (I am not speaking of critical essays, in which the method of divination is legitimate, but of professed lives.) His problem, is it not, is to form in the imagination a strong and trustworthy impression of the personality of his subject. It is the conviction which the biographer gives his reader of having a vital comprehension of the mind he is dealing with that determines whether his book is really a biography or not. Biographers have various ways of getting this impression of personality. One way is to read as you come to it everything you can find pertaining to your subject, to keep your mind open and simply collect facts. When you have read, as it seems to you, everything of importance, and have filled drawer after drawer with notes, you can make a dispassionate survey of your materials and form your imaginative reconstruction. You can, but I am sure no one ever did. If a man really could keep his mind open until he had assembled all the facts, he would find himself precisely in the plight of Mr. Casaubon with his materials for the mythology of all races. The imagination never makes a dead leap from a heap of facts. If it works at all, its processes are those of the growing snowball; facts come alive, cling together, and build up into a vital imaginative organism only as there is something for them to cling to. Of course many men being perhaps younger and more vigorous than Mr. Casaubon, have found themselves in his plight and

★ From *The Literary Career of James Boswell* (1929), pp. xviii–xx. Reprinted by permission of the author.

yet have published biographies—by the simple procedure of sorting their files of notes into chronological sequence and hurling them at the printer. Such biographies are amorphous; they are really not biographies but chronicles.

What happens in real biography is that the biographer, pretty early in his work, allows his imagination to form from only a partial reading of the evidence a trial impression of the personality he is attempting to reconstruct. He then collects his facts with this tentative reconstruction always in mind. If the facts fit, he uses them to fill in the picture; if they won't fit, he must modify his conception until they do. But he always builds up on this imaginative core; he does not simply collect facts and wait for something to quicken the chaos.

The danger is that he will get at the outset a mistaken impression which he will later be unable or unwilling to modify. He is especially liable, in the early stages of his reading, to see his subject in the light of one ruling passion and to present something much simpler than life. This is the fault of the majority of the truly brilliant books now offered to us as biographies. The authors of these works apparently gain their first impression by a swift reading of previous biographies, and especially of letters and diaries. From this material they catch up whatever is vivid and amusing, especially what readily adapts itself to an ironic purpose. Using these, perhaps unrepresentative, details they draw the outline of their sketch, and then in their subsequent reading deliberately select only such colours as will finish the picture. Whatever is discordant is simply ignored. The result is eminently readable, for it is highly artistic, but it deserves to be classed as fiction rather than as biography.

Is there no way to avoid the dullness of the amorphous biography on the one hand, and the specious brilliance of the impressionistic biography on the other? Can a biographer follow no course that will enable him to have from the first a conception of character which is not only objective and adequate, but also plastic? Scientific bibliography, while it cannot remove all the difficulties, seems to me to offer a real solution. If we make a serious study in strictly chronological order of everything our author wrote, so far as it is accessible, learning under what circumstances those works were conceived, what were their literary sources and the influences upon them (if certainly known), under what arrangements they were published, what revision they suffered, what reception they met at the hands of their contemporaries at home and abroad—if we do this, we shall find ourselves able to harmonize most of the discrepancies because we shall see them as the logical expression of a developing personality. The biographer who approaches an author in this way will have a definite conception of his subject's character as soon as he has read his first publication and pushed the lines of inquiry out to the lengths I have indicated. This conception will develop naturally as he goes on reading, just as the man's mind matured in life. When he has finished such an investigation he will be surprised to find how little there is left to consider, for the application of bibliography to a literary career, as I conceive it, leaves few of the pertinent facts unexamined. The biographer naturally will not introduce any technical bibliographical matter into his biography. The technicalities have been a means to an end. But I cannot agree with the most popular of our modern biographers, who seem to think that in writing the life of a man of letters one succeeds only as he makes the reader forget that the man he is reading about was an author. . . .

Ernest Boyd

* Describing the spate of so-called 'modern' biographies, 'novelized' lives, and so forth, one might say: 'The trick of biography seems to have fallen on prosperous times in Europe and America. A most scholarly and subtle branch of writing has been relegated to the sex circulationists of letters; we do not reflect that it is perhaps as easy to write a flashy biography as a cheap novel. Those octavo volumes with which it is our custom to vulgarize the dead—who does not know them, with their half-digested paucity of material, their "smart" style, their tone of tedious superiority, their lamentable lack of taste, of real knowledge, of honest purpose? They are as familiar as the case histories of the psycho-analysts, and wear the same air of spurious, psychological profundity.'

In other words, the overemphasis of the sex element in contemporary biography doubtless explains in large part the current vogue of that branch of writing. . . .

It is also a significant fact, for it raises the general question of the importance of sex in biography. Is it possible that we now exaggerate its importance? One may welcome the freedom of modern biography from hagiography while questioning its overemphasis upon sexual psychology. When Frank Harris was trying to make of his life of Bernard Shaw a volume comparable to his own ineffable and insufferable *My Life and Loves*, his victim escaped him by confronting him

* From 'Sex in Biography', *Harper's Magazine*, November 1932, pp. 753–6. Reprinted by permission of Mrs. Madeleine Boyd and the publisher.

squarely with unromantic facts, thereby confuting prurient conjecture. 'First, O Biographer,' he writes, 'get it clear in your mind that you can learn nothing about your sitter (or Biograph*ee*) from a mere record of his gallantries. You have no such record in the case of Shakespear, and a pretty full one for a few years in the case of Pepys; but you know much more about Shakespear than about Pepys. The explanation is that the relation between the parties in gallantries is not a personal relation. It can be irresistibly desired and rapturously executed between persons who could not endure one another for a day in any other relation'. And he adds: 'I found sex hopeless as a basis for permanent relations. . . . In permanence and seriousness my consummated love-affairs count for nothing beside the ones that were either unconsummated or ended by discarding that relation'.

Here we have the unusual spectacle of the subject of a biography definitely answering the question I have raised. Mr. Shaw is clearly of opinion that the part of sex in biography—not merely in *his* biography—is negligible. He even declares: 'If I were to tell you every such adventure that I have enjoyed, you would be none the wiser as to my personal, nor even as to my sexual, history'. From which it would seem to follow that even the sexual history of a biographer's subject is not to be explained merely by reference to the latter's sexual experiences. In other words, an intelligent view of biography may so far diverge from the current preoccupation with sex as to eliminate it altogether, as something wholly irrelevant.

Obviously the relevance of sex in biography must be largely determined by the character and temperament of what Mr. Shaw calls the 'biographee', rather than by the more or less morbid prepossessions of the biographer. If Mr. Shaw, for example, had been the kind of man whom Frank Harris so fatuously alleged himself to be in *My Life and Loves*, what purpose would be served by recording the facts? By his own admission such facts would be irrelevant, since 'gallantry is not a personal relation' and 'sex is hopeless as a basis for permanent relations'. Presumably it is precisely the permanent elements in the life of a human being which are of vital importance to the biographer. Consequently, the latter has to decide whether or not the sexual life of his subject is essential to an understanding of his career. Can that be decided arbitrarily, on the theory popularized by the Freudians, that we are such stuff as sexual psychoneuroses are made on, our little life is rounded with a complex? . . .

Thus we return to the question of the place of sex in biography. Where sex is an essential factor the first thing to be decided is whether the case is pathological or not. If pathological, the biographer becomes the scientist, as defined by Mr. Nicolson and M. Maurois, and biography as a work of art, as a means of expression, ceases to concern us. Where sex is not pathological, its importance is slight almost to the point of non-existence. The happiest sex life is one that has no history, and biography is neither more nor less concerned with sex than with digestion. Carlyle's indigestion, Gibbon's hydrocele, Napoleon's cancer, the erysipelas of Frederick the Great, add not one cubit to our knowledge, understanding, and appreciation of these men. Many obscure persons have suffered similarly and many people of like stature have been free of such suffering. The tedious novels of George Sand are not a whit more interesting because of her encounters with Jules Sandeau, Musset, Pagello, Chopin, and the rest of that 'necropolis', as an unkind lover called the 'cemetery' of her heart. Nor is the tedium of George Eliot's novels relieved by the thought of her exemplary life with George Henry Lewes, and her courageous unconventionality has not prevented us from preferring the works of the Brontë sisters and of Jane Austen, whose lives seemed models of decorum. . . .

. . . Sex in biography, as in life itself, is simultaneously essential and unimportant, save when nothing else of importance is afoot. The autobiographies of Mill, Newman, Gibbon, Herbert Spencer, Renan, dealing with the world of the mind and of ideas, are worth all the memoirs of all the Casanovas, great and small, real and imaginary, whose usually trivial exploits and conquests make one wish that more people had Mr. Shaw's keen realization of the fundamental valuelessness of such experiences as a commentary on life.

Bernard DeVoto

* Literary people should not be permitted to write biography. The literary mind may be adequately described as the mind least adapted to the utilization of fact. It is, to begin with, much too simple. The novelist, the dramatist, the poet, or the critic selects vivid phases of experience and co-ordinates them in such a manner that they give us an illusion of the whole. The significance, the ultimate value, of the process resides in its omissions. But biography cannot simplify and must not omit. The experience with which it deals is not simple. A novelist may invent a motive or a situation of magnificent simplicity; but that is fiction, and the motives and situations of fact are not simple but complex. The novelist deals with social organization only so far as he sees fit; but the subject of a biography was part of a web so intricate that only an objectification beyond the reach of fiction can comprehend it. The mathematics of a complex variable are forbidden to the literary mind.

That mind is also habitually, even professionally, inaccurate. Accuracy is not a criterion of fiction, drama, or poetry; to ask for it would be as absurd as to appraise music by its weight or painting by its smell. Hence the literary person is horribly inept at the practice of biography, whose first condition is absolute, unvarying, unremitted accuracy. He is subject to credulity—a reliance on intuition, on appearance, on rumour and conjecture and sheer imaginative creation. He

* From 'The Sceptical Biographer', *Harper's Magazine*, January 1933, pp. 184–92. Reprinted by permission of Mrs. Bernard DeVoto and the publisher.

is sometimes unable to read accurately and is nearly always unable to report what he has read. Some years ago a literary critic, writing the life of a novelist, demonstrated that he could not even read his subject's books. He ascribed words and actions of characters in them to other characters; he erred in summarizing the plots of books; he asserted that events happened in them which did not happen, which were even specifically denied; in general, he appeared unable to report either the geography or the events in them as they really exist. This form of illiteracy is buttressed by another defect in accuracy, unwillingness to turn a page. One grows weary of seeing passages quoted from letters, journals, and notebooks in support of ideas or sentiments which the next manuscript page, usually the same entry, categorically denies.

The literary mind, furthermore, is naïve. That is its charm. From this unspoiled freshness, this eager willingness to believe, this awe and wonder, the world's poems and romances are woven. But it disqualifies its possessor for biography, which requires an all-inclusive scepticism and a cynicism that are best cultivated in human intercourse. The artist is usually a simple, home-loving person, given to nerves or paternity or the cultivation of some bourgeois hobby. He has little experience of the great world and none at all of the world of action. He knows nothing about the conditions of practical life, the way in which members of trades and professions and businesses must conduct themselves. He is ignorant even of rudimentary organization, business, military, political, diplomatic, economic, or religious. He could not conduct a horse trade, a sales drive, a senatorial campaign, an order of battle, or a revival, and usually has never observed one. Yet when he essays a biography of Napoleon, St. Francis, Roscoe Conkling, or Jay Gould he must not only master these mechanisms but must also understand their laws. In a novel or a play the problem is simple: he may brood about Napoleon till his own special talents invent something that will give us an illusion. But it is not illusion that biography demands—it is fact. The literary mind can imagine a world for St. Francis but it cannot deal with the actual, the factual, world of St. Francis. It succumbs to fantasy, which is its proper medium. It is effective when it is evolving a world out of its own inner necessities, when it is creating its own material and data. But that is why the literary mind has worked so much stupidity in biography. We do not want illusion there, however convincing—we want reality. We do not want invented facts, created motives, phantasmally generated problems solved by intuition. We do not want anything whatever that imagination, intuition, or creation can give us. We want facts; and the literary mind is incapable of finding them, understanding them, and presenting them.

That is why the literary biographer has been victimized by preposterous methods. Unfitted to understand the nature of fact and bountifully endowed with credulity, he has relied on preposterous instruments for the ascertainment of fact. Most notably, in the last decade, on psycho-analysis.

Psycho-analysis has no value whatever as a method of arriving at facts in biography. No psycho-analytical biography yet written can be taken seriously—as fact. The assertion holds for the work of the master himself, whose study of Leonardo is absolute bilge uncontaminated by the slightest perceptible filtrate of reality, and for other biographies by professional analysts. But if the professional's rare excursions into biography are worthless, why has the method so gratified the literary?

The answer is that an acquaintance with the terminology of psycho-analysis gives the literary a means of transcending their limitations. It shifts the field of biography from the empirical world where the subject mingled with his fellows, lived, worked, struggled, and, it may be, loved. In that world there are all sorts of dark places, mysterious bare spots about which nothing can be found, lacunæ, ellipses, conflicts of testimony and narrative, contradictions in evidence, insoluble problems, and sheer chaos. The lay biographer, denied the resources of Freud, must deal with these as best he may—by the swink of a never-ending labour which terrifies his slumber with the dread that he may have missed something, and which enables him in the end to say only '*a* is more probable than *b*'. Labour and nightmare are spared the amateur psycho-analyst. He needs only the subject's letters and diaries, his books and speeches if he wrote any, the more intimate letters of his friends, and an earlier biography. Not all of these items are indispensable: much brilliant work has been done on the basis of the last alone. The external world is to be disregarded; the amateur Freud will devote himself to a far richer field, his subject's mind. He has, for the exploration of that field, an infallible instrument. It is the celestial virtue of psycho-analysis that it can make no mistakes. The amateur will never stub his toe on the discouragement of the biographer—he will never find that no evidence exists on a question he is trying to answer, or that the evidence which exists is insufficient. All of his subject's mind is of one piece and all his life is a unity, and so anything that is desired can be recovered from anything else. And if he finds a conflict of evidence, that too is simple. The principle of ambivalence tells him that all evidence means the same thing.*

The amateur begins with a set of necessities to which his subject must be fitted. The science he has acquired from a month's reading—more often from a couple of popular outlines—gives him a number of patterns and a series of keys. He knows before he begins that Diogenes, Brutus, or Cleopatra must have had this complex, or, if not, then that one. He knows in advance that inhibition must have been responsible for something, under-sublimation for something else, over-sublimation for still more. He knows that one kind of behaviour indicates a form of sublimated anal erotic interest, another kind, oral eroticism. The indices of sadism are given on page 114 of Tridon, those of masochism in the third chapter of Hinkle. The Œdipus complex (Freud's modernization of original sin) may be expected to show itself in one of certain catalogued ways. It will produce such other universals as the castration complex. These in turn will work out, sometimes through other complexes, in behaviour whose meaning and symbolism have been carefully charted. There remain such beautiful and versatile instruments as the death-wish to explain any chance fragment that might seem incommensurable with the rest. Or if something is still left over, the biographer has the blithe freedom of dropping Freud and picking up one of Freud's murderously incompatible opponents. Perhaps the uninterpreted residue of Caesar's unconscious had better be treated in the light of Jung's types, which are beautifully systematic and have recently been doubled for American use. Few biographers, however orthodox in their use of Freud, have been able to refuse the help of Adler's *Minderwertigkeit*—fewer still have used it to mean what Adler means. It is a reasonable expectation that few will hesitate to

* A lay psycho-analyst finds that the political philosophy of Thomas Jefferson was a product of Jefferson's infantile revolt against his father. He then says: 'It is significant that Jefferson's antipathy to his father was so infantile and deep-seated that it was scarcely ever raised to consciousness. He frequently speaks of his father in his writings in a reverential and awe-inspired attitude. This, of course, made the disguised and substituted forms of outlet for this repressed revulsion all the more vigorous and extreme.'

marry the death-wish to the birth-trauma when an adequate exposition of the former works into the outlines.

The rabbit, perceive, has been hidden in the hat. There remains only to pull it out with a smile of reassuring omniscience. It is obvious how unnecessary are the researches and verifications of the biographer. Conversations which no one ever recorded can be reproduced and explained. Interviews which no one ever witnessed can be described. Documents long since vanished from the earth can be re-created and interpreted. The method cannot make mistakes: it is, in literary hands, infallible. You have what the dead man wrote, what it is said he said, and what some people have said about him. Your method dissolves all doubts, settles all contradictions, and projects the known or guessed into absolute certainty about the unknowable. You wonder, perhaps, what Diogenes said at the grave of Keats or where Apollonius was and what he did on a certain fourth of July? If you are a historian you examine all possible sources of information and if you find no information, you report 'I don't know'. But if you are an amateur analyst, to hell with uncertainty. You have discovered that Diogenes possessed a mother fixation as the result of jealousy before his second birthday (evidence of what was in the mind of a child twenty centuries ago does not exist, but no matter), that he had a mania for overripe plums as the result of an incestuous admiration of his sister, and that his Id and Ego were abnormally at peace with each other. What, therefore, must Diogenes have said on the specific occasion? Where, therefore, must Apollonius have been? Obviously, where he must have been is where he was.

That *must* is the mechanism of psycho-analytical biography. It is the invention of the biographer, his deduction from an *a priori* principle. It has no relation to the subject of *The Life and Times*. It does not tell what did happen. It tells us instead what must have happened. Biography proper is not concerned with the *must* but only with the *did*. Between them is a sheer gulf which no theory can possibly bridge. Psycho-analysis cannot come into effective relationship, into any relationship, with a dead man.

Professionally, it does not try. The physician to diseased minds is engaged in a process whose aim is therapeutic—empirical. He practices an art whose entire condition is the mutual association of living minds. His technic requires a constant interplay of a myriad variables, a constant shift and adaptation, a constant accommodation and reexamination and reinterpretation—all of which are impossible to biography. Psycho-analysis is dynamic or it is nothing. The professional must deal with phenomena which his trade-jargon calls Displacement, Conversion, Resistance, Transference, and with similar psychic energies which perish when the patient dies. These phenomena never engage the attention of a biographer: no dead man exhibits them. The amateur does not hesitate to dispense with them. He has his pattern, his clues, his guidebooks, and they are enough. As the result of his skill, they create his patient for him.

The result may be, as our literary editor insisted, an interpretation in the highest degree entertaining. It may be a brilliant exposition of its author's sentiments or his talent for denunciation or his exhortatory power. When produced by an intelligent man it may approximate the art of the detective story, whose clues are also invented and whose deductions are also made to fit. But it exists always on the left side of a fixed line. On the right side of that line are the materials of biography. The findings of psycho-analysis, any findings whatever, belong forever on the left side, with guesses, improvisations, fairy stories, and mere lies. The obligation of a biographer is to find facts. When he employs psycho-analysis he cannot arrive at facts but only at 'interpretations', which is to say theory, which is to say nonsense. . . .

Biography is the wrong field for the mystical, and for the wishful, the tender minded, the hopeful, and the passionate. It enforces an unremitting scepticism—towards its material, towards the subject, most of all towards the biographer. He cannot permit himself one guess or one moment of credulity, no matter how brilliantly it may illuminate the darkness he deals with or how it may solace his ignorance. He must doubt everything. He must subject his conclusions and all the steps that lead to them to a corrosive examination, analysis, and verification—a process which he must hope will reveal flaws, for if it does he has added one more item of certainty to his small store. He has, apart from such negatives, very little certainty. His job is not dramatic: it is only to discover evidence and to analyse it. And all the evidence he can find is the least satisfactory kind, documentary evidence, which is among the most treacherous phenomena in a malevolent world. With luck, he will be certain of the dates of his subject's birth and marriage and death, the names of his wife and children, a limited number of things he did and offices he held and trades he practiced and places he visited and manuscript pages he wrote, people he praised or attacked, and some remarks made about him. Beyond that, not even luck can make certainty possible. The rest is merely printed matter, and a harassed man who sweats his life out in libraries, courthouses, record offices, vaults, newspaper morgues, and family attics. A harassed man who knows that he cannot find everything and is willing to believe that, for ever concealed from him, exists something which, if found, would prove that what he thinks are facts are only appearances.

From this quicksand and mirage he will derive facts. Only a few of them are unmixed fact, free of misunderstanding, misinformation, and plain ignorance. The rest he will grade in a hierarchy, and arrange them as their nature, value, and validity make necessary—not as some wish or religion of his own would like them arranged. In the end he can say, '*A* did this, and I think he did that, and for the rest I am ignorant and refuse to guess'. This is the act of judgement, and it contains three different stages, each one of them serviceable to his reader—who will use them, according to their degree, in his acquisition of knowledge. When he has said this much, the biographer has done his job. He will say, '*A* did this', but he will not try to say why. For that is speculative, the gate that lets the motive in, and with the motive enter all the guessing, hoping, and chicanery that have debauched his profession.

His result lacks brilliance. It is without the certainty of the ignorant and the psychological—the certainty that is the unmistakable hallmark of the theorist's cocksureness. It is without the ingenious nonsense of the interpreter. It is without the invective of the debunker, without the contrived, humanitarian unity of the hopeful, without the passion of the generous. It is without teaching, without preaching, without hope for a better world: altruistic desire does not come into it. It will not make life seem easier to optimists and has no bearing on reform or revolution. It is only an intelligent man's efforts to deal with facts. It is a faulty, imperfect picture, a blurred image, an uncompleted map. But such as it is, it is trustworthy: it looks towards reality. It establishes part of a pattern, makes out some lines of the obscured page, recovers something from the past. Like other controlled and tested knowledge, it is usable. It is an accounting, the settling of a stewardship. Momentarily, mists have partly blown away and the North Star, though blurred, has been visible. It is an effort in the direction of truth. Such an effort has a value that no ignorance, however brilliant, and no wishfulness, however kind, can offer in competition with it.

Lord David Cecil

* Biography is not an important form of literary art. But it has a special interest to the student of modern literature. For it is the only new form. We talk of modern poetry and modern novels, but these are only new variations on old forms: the poetry and fiction of the past are just as much forms of art as those of today. Not so biography. Art is primarily the expression of the artist's creative powers; he writes to express his personal vision; he chooses as his subject that which he thinks will best exhibit his particular talent. Now this is not true of the biographer of the past. His aim was not artistic, it was useful, he wanted to give people information. If he was a man of literary talent, like Boswell, for instance, his book was a work of art. But even if it had not been, it would not have failed. For its primary purpose had been, not to give an artistic impression, but to tell the truth. . . .

But for the typical modern biographer literature comes first. Mr. Lytton Strachey writes about Queen Victoria, not in order to give us information about her, but because he thinks her life an excellent subject for a work of art. The design of his book shows that its aim is to produce an artistic impression. . . .

One wonders why it should have been left to our age to write biography in this way. Partly because it is not favourable to the practice of other literary forms: our age is, first of all, scientific. The most important work today is done by scientists; the scientific spirit

* From Introduction to *An Anthology of Modern Biography* (1936), pp. ix–xvi. Reprinted by permission of the author and Thomas Nelson and Sons.

permeates every study. And this is a bad spirit for the creative artist. It is cool and critical, it checks the enthusiastic emotion, the exuberant fancy which is the life-blood of poetry, for example. But people are born with a desire to write, as much now as in the past. So that they try to find other forms of expression, and naturally they light on biography. For it is not out of sympathy with the scientific spirit. Though it can be used to convey a personal vision, it is also inevitably concerned to tell the truth. For the study of truth, a scientific spirit is essential. To give a convincing picture of a human being the writer must be as studious of detail, as skilled in investigation, as to give a true diagnosis of a disease. And he must survey his subject with scientific detachment. The biographers of the past tended to write with a strong bias for or against their subject; or if they were unbiased, their views were yet distorted by strong moral opinions that made them approach him as a judge. But the biographer is there to explain rather than to judge. To get a clear view of a man we do not need to be told if his actions were good—indeed, such comments tend to blur our vision—but how and why he came to do them. Once more the scientist's is the correct attitude. He does not bother to tell us that disease is a bad thing, but what its causes are, and how they show themselves. Moreover, we are better equipped to do this now than in old days. Here we come to the final reason why this is a favourable age for the biographer. The last forty years have seen an enormous advance in the study of psychology; the nature of human personality and the forces that actuate it, the influence of heredity and environment, are understood as never before. So that writers are able, as never before, to give a full account of human character.

Still, it is not just the spirit of the age that makes us biographers. Man is led by man; and we have been led by Mr. Strachey. . . . He it was who first saw the full possibilities of this new medium; he it was who evolved the technical equipment for its expression. We may extend his building, but we must always construct on his foundations. He was the man who established the form.

It is a complex form. From one aspect it is like the novel, dramatic. Its subject is the drama of a human life. Miss Toksvig's *Hans Andersen* shows us the drama of an innocent, romantic idealist in conflict with the humdrum forces that rule the world; Mr. Waugh's *Campion* that of a saint battling for his faith against heretic and persecutor. Again, like the novel, the modern biography is pictorial. Its author attempts to bring his drama before our mental eye, to make us see the faces of the characters, the scenery in which they lived. But—and this is where the biographer's task is more complex than that of the novelist—he is telling us a true story; and he must stick to the truth. His incidents and characters are given to him ready-made: he must present them as accurately as he is able, take care that they appear in the order and significance they had in fact. His creative impulse, therefore, has to express itself in a different way from that of the novelist. The novelist's shows itself mainly in invention, in his power to create scenes and characters; the biographer's shows itself in interpretation, in his capacity to discover the significance of a given story, to discern amid the heterogeneous mass of letters, diaries, memoirs, which are his raw material, that continuous theme which will compose them into a work of art. Like the maker of pictures in mosaic, his art is one of arrangement; he cannot alter the shape of his material, his task is to invent a design into which his hard little stones of fact can be fitted as they are. Further, his imagination appears in his ability to vitalize his material, to clothe the dry bones of truth in the breathing flesh and blood which make them living to the reader.

Biography, then, must stick to truth; but this does not entail a lack of variety. You could have two lives of the same person unlike each other, and both good. For facts assume a different complexion in different lights. The same story may be comic, pathetic, or simply curious, according as it is seen by the eye of the satirist, the sentimentalist, or the scientific investigator. . . .

Thus, in addition to choosing the point of view from which best to express his personal vision, the biographer must choose that which exhibits his subject in the truest proportion.

Indeed, he walks along a knife-edge. For he is under an equal obligation to art and to life, his book must be equally satisfying as picture and as likeness. It cannot be said that modern biographers have always kept this balance. Some have sacrificed art to life. They give us a great many facts, and present them pleasantly, but they have not composed them into an artistic unity. Their books are not pictures, but scrap books. More often they err on the other side, and sacrifice life to art. Their portrait is vivid, but it is not accurate. They omit essential facts; or they twist them from their true significance, in order to make them more effective; or they fill up gaps in their information with unfounded conjectures of their own. Even those accomplished authors, from whom it is my privilege to quote in the ensuing pages, have fallen sometimes into one or other of these errors. It is natural enough, the balance is so delicate. But it can be kept. Taken as a story or as a bit of history, *Queen Victoria* is equally admirable. If our age has done nothing else, it has bequeathed to posterity a model biography.

Jacques Barzun

* Every biography is something like a detective story: a few clues are handled, a few witnesses examined, and from them a complicated series of events is reconstructed. The pleasure of the chase is in it. Unfortunately the analogy conceals a trap. Because we are dealing with clues and witnesses, it is easy to think that we are pursuing a criminal. We then no longer discover our subject's motives; we catch him in the act. If we are tempted to excuse a fault, we resist as if asked to compound a felony. The consequence is that just as our grandfathers ran the risk of worshipping every famous man as a hero, so we, after half a century of debunking, run the risk of taking fame itself as a sure sign of moral and mental turpitude. All our swans, because they are swans, must be geese.

The fashion once established, each new biographic fantasia woven around some famous name (Byron is still the best) must lure the reader by promising him the antics of genius, and then satisfy his craving by seeing to it that genius shall perform as required. The clerk, the misunderstood man of business, the disappointed intellectual, all rise from the reading of such books pleasantly refreshed and thanking their stars that they, at any rate, are no Byron, no Swift, no Edgar Allan Poe.

It is not my purpose here to go into the why of this aberration, but rather to make concrete the many-sided problem it raises for the biographer, by taking a subject who illustrates its difficulties, the French

* From 'Truth in Biography: Berlioz', *The University Review: a Journal of the University of Kansas City*, Summer 1939, pp. 275–80. Reprinted with minor revisions by permission of the author and the publisher.

composer Hector Berlioz. When I mentioned to one of the shrewdest of our literary critics that I was working on a life of Berlioz, he said: 'A wonderful subject—only don't write about his music'. When I spoke of the same enterprise to a well-known composer, he said: 'A wonderful subject—if you only stick to his music and forget about his life.' The technicians will read musical (or poetical or pictorial) criticism; the general reader wants thrills and what it deceptively calls a portrait. Both groups, moreover, expect a new biography to confirm their previous ideas, gathered from hearsay or casual reading and treasured like gossip.

In the Berlioz 'literature' are all the materials for a truthful biography, but the pieces of it are so scattered, tucked away, or stuck upside down in an enveloping mass of fantasy, that no casual or even well-informed reader can be blamed for accepting as real the pseudo-Berlioz of biography and romance. What has happened is that the clues and witnesses have been misread and misinterpreted in the light of false principles, for the self-indulgence of readers and musicologists.

II

Up to a point this self-indulgence is legitimate. It is fun to read about a man who, as we are told, 'is the very stuff and substance of the Romantic Movement', who 'revolutionized music and created the modern orchestra', and who fought for his ideas in the company of men like Schumann, Liszt, Chopin, Paganini, Mendelssohn, Wagner, von Bulow, Delacroix, Victor Hugo, George Sand, Gautier, Balzac, and Flaubert—to mention only the best-known of the period. If we add to this a rich literary output as music critic and writer of entertaining artistic fictions; herculean labours as one of the first great orchestra conductors, the militant championing of the music of Beethoven, Weber, and Gluck; and a deep artistic influence reaching to the four corners of Europe as an opponent of philistinism and academicism, Berlioz deserves attention proportionate to the commotion he created while alive. Add again a temperament combining fire with conscious purpose, a great capacity for love and hate, with wit to salt his words and a rare sense of humour about himself, and you have a figure who will justify the reading and writing of many another book. Note in passing that in all this I have not mentioned the musical monuments which, beautiful or ugly as they may be thought, he found time and strength to erect in the midst of his headlong career.

Now we may ask in virtue of what biographical principle these facts of a productive life are made to yield a Berlioz who was emotionally unstable, egotistical, undisciplined; musically untrained and incompetent; who thought himself the greatest composer of all time; who lived a disordered, purposeless, and wayward life, hating everybody and incurring universal ridicule—a genius, to be sure, but one pathetically deceived about himself, the world, and his true place in it.

The question is not one of opinion but of fact. The world being what it is, can a man who successfully organizes and conducts a musical festival like that of the Paris Exposition of 1844, be a disorganized and incompetent man? Logic being what it is, can a man who repeatedly says that 'Beethoven has everything', who plays him again and again to a reluctant public, and prints detailed analyses of the nine symphonies, and who also admires dozens of other composers, living and dead—can such a man be held the most self-centred and conceited musician the world has even seen? The art of music being what it is, can a man who enjoyed the love and respect of all the performers who worked under him, who was consulted by instrument makers and sat on musical juries; who was spoken of by Wagner as an 'immense musical intelligence'; who has aroused the enthusiasm of the majority of great composers from Schumann a hundred years ago down to Hugo Wolf, Busoni, and Van Dieren in our own day—can this man have been a musical ignoramus?

The first principle of biography, whether it deal with a musician or a military man, is obviously, 'by their fruits shall ye know them'. It is the principle Lincoln used to confound Grant's enemies: if drinking whisky wins victories, let all the generals be given a pint of Scotch. But Grant was not a drunkard who happened to win battles. He was a military genius who happened to drink. Similarly, all our victims of biography are not idlers and profligates who were great artists on the side. They were artists whose characters were marred by adventitious elements precisely like certain other people that we all know. Daily and hourly to commit the fallacy of accident, is the first great cause of defective biographical tradition, and it is an evil that amounts to far more than a mere personal 'injustice' to Berlioz, Coleridge, or anybody else. It warps history, degrades art, and makes complacent humbugs of us all when we ought to be modest seekers after truth and grateful beholders of the genius of mankind.

Often, no doubt, it is because we seek a certain kind of truth that we become biographical vandals. In our eagerness to find the 'cause' of individual achievements we pounce upon the nearest clue that suggests physical or psychological factors at work. Nearly all the so-called psycho-analytic criticism of the present day is of that sort. It uses the words 'neurotic', 'hysterical', 'psychopathic' in the naïve belief that they are explanations. Unfortunately, these words not only do not explain but they are generally used ignorantly. To call Berlioz hysterical (as does his latest biographer) is easy on the basis of certain passages of the *Memoirs*, but this diagnosis at the fourth remove ought not to be made by a writer for whom hysteria is only a more impressive word for excitement. It so happens that Berlioz's nervous excitement was not hysterical, and that genuine hysterical patients are often known by their unnatural calm.

Does it follow that we must simply record what we can of a man's life, shaking our head over its mystery, and letting the facts speak for themselves? Would this be more 'scientific' than the pseudo-science of biographical psycho-analysis? Not a bit of it. The facts obviously do not speak for themselves. They remain dumb and meaningless until they are organized and interpreted. We must remember Sherlock Holmes and our detective analogy. Watson sees everything that Holmes sees, but only Holmes understands. This means using not only creative ability but standards of judgement. So much is commonly agreed. Dispute begins when the standards are enunciated and applied.

In theory, the standard for judging a man's work ought to be derived from his own expressed or implied intentions. We must not blame the explorer for his bad grammar, nor be scornful, as some affect to be, because Berlioz did not engage in politics. Even within a man's professed limits, biographers can err—witness those delusive 'summaries' in which it is said that Walt Whitman had not Wordsworth's natural piety, Keats' word magic, Shelley's idealism, or Emerson's conciseness. Why not add W. S. Gilbert's rhyming tricks and Tennyson's income? In a critical 'life' we want to know what a man had and was, not the endless might-have-beens that the finite creature entirely missed.

Moreover, the effect of such illicit comparisons is aesthetically and psychologically bad: they seem to leave Whitman holding but a leaf of grass between his fingers while all the other poets stand by, richly endowed. They vitiate the sense of due comparison, which says that only those things should be compared which are roughly identical except in respect of the quality under review. To the discriminating critic, for instance, it is not enough that Thackeray and Tolstoy are both novelists. They are at opposite poles and must be described as separate entities. But Thackeray and Meredith, as novelists similarly concerned with social life—and that chiefly in English drawingrooms—can be fruitful subjects of comparison.

These negative principles are not to be applied with inflexible rigour. They serve merely to prevent the too-common biographical scrambling of oddities and insights, the confusion of origins with results. In a man who was a worker, we must start with the work and pass judgement upon that. Much work or great work means a great worker, whether he accomplished it at a desk like Scott, or in bed like Mark Twain. The desk and the bed must not be metamorphosed into criteria of literary or moral judgement.

III

But the task still remains of judging a man apart from his work and of describing his conduct fairly, in its trivial as in its significant aspects. It is here that the biographer is most tempted and consequently most fallible. It is so easy to bring together a striking instance, a curious detail, a ludicrous act, and call the resulting still-life a portrait. Besides, the melodramatic instinct loves to see in the lift of an eyebrow at a crucial moment the key to human character. All this is pure quackery. We are bound to judge conduct by the social standards we accept; hence we must be aware of what they are and state them openly. At the same time we must recognize that events are many-faceted and that we are in honour bound to judge a man by the prevailing tendency of his acts, not by a single incident that we happen to think amusing or derogatory.

Even when we have done our utmost to see and speak justly, we should still remember that to put a fluid and dynamic thing like life between the covers of a book—or as publishers' slang funereally has it, 'between boards'—alters every time-and-space relationship. A paragraph represents a decade, or a love affair of six months' duration; it settles a question of loyalty or ingratitude on the basis of three documents and a good hunch. The reader rarely suspects that any links are missing, or worse yet, that the chain of reasoning starts from one accepted social standard and ends with another as, for example, in the assumption often made in discussing the relations of Berlioz and

Liszt, that the friends of music must necessarily like the music of their friends.

It was first pointed out by Tom S. Wotton, the great English authority on Berlioz, that most current opinions of the composer were based on a blurred impression of what he relates in his *Memoirs* as happening in his twenties. Helped by the thin logic that the child is father to the man, it follows that what Berlioz *seemed* in his twenties is true of his forties, fifties, and sixties. The lesson for us is that when we have carefully conned over our standards of art and morals, when we have taken care not to telescope the years or vulgarize the intentions of complex human beings, we are still at the mercy of two biasing elements—words and provincialism. There is a provincialism of period, as well as of place, and it is much more difficult to overcome. Who does not see that in our day we are never so naturally and righteously provincial as when discussing Romanticism? In our eyes the early nineteenth century has not yet become quaint and classic; it is still in the middle distance and profoundly irritating. It irritates us chiefly by its vocabulary, which we mistake for an attitude towards life; and by its purposes, which we mistake for affectations.

In these circumstances, any character who belongs to the period, like Berlioz, must be translated as it were out of his own words into ours. For it is true that he reveals, particularly in his youthful and autobiographical writings, the use and abuse of the period-vocabulary. It is a defect, no doubt, but since it is an historical constant, which applies as much to Addison as it will to T. S. Eliot, we must not let it paralyse our judgement. If we get closer to the main objects of Berlioz's life—music, art, intellectual honesty—we notice with pleasure that far from being the excessive and violent squanderer of adjectives that he is thought to be, he is on the contrary master of an utterance remarkably adequate to the occasion. Read, for example, his *Nine Symphonies of Beethoven* or his piece on the mediums who were trying to get a post-humous sonata from that composer by table-tipping; or best of all, consult the short passage in the Memoirs where Berlioz judges and characterizes his own music: sober, pointed, exact, are the only words to describe a style which there truly reflects an individual and not a period attitude.

When we have learned a man's words (noting by the way that whole modern nations use 'awful', *furchtbar* or *épouvantable* to describe an uncomfortable draft of air upon the neck) we must likewise persuade ourselves that the more sensitive an artist is, the greater will slight differences seem to him, and, usually, the wider will his range of perceptions be. To us, a sense of proportion may well be the ability to see things in an average, normal, institutional way; but we go to the man of genius presumably because his sense of proportion enables him to feel and convey differently from us such differences as he alone perceives. At times, indeed, he may liken the ocean to a drop of water; but that is again for the purpose of making us forget our utilitarian scale and making us adopt another, whose utility serves a neglected part of our nature.

Rising from these particulars to our final conclusion, we must assert what no one questions in theory and everybody violates in practice, namely that the complexity of life, taken both quantitatively and qualitatively, is greater than our documentary, chronological, and critical schemes allow for. The clues and witnesses are, to begin with, very numerous, taken as brute facts by themselves. But they are, even so, a vast oversimplification of the past. There are available for Berlioz's mature life an average of one document a week. But huge as this harvest of clues may seem, it is not enough. The Ariadne's thread is missing. It is found in no letter, no archive, no encyclopedia. It must be spun from one's inner consciousness, at great risk of error and on guard against cocksure superiority. Hence the need for *a priori* sympathy, in the exact meaning of that term: *feeling with.*

'Feeling against' is sure falsification, for life is lived by everyone on the assumption that it has meaning, that he who lives it is a rational being, honest, worthy, and human. The genius has the added awareness of special gifts, and if he mentions them we must not take for boasting that which, if he concealed it, would convict him of hypocrisy. To put oneself in another's place is difficult; all the more so when the other man is one who visibly does not think and act like the grocer's boy around the corner. This is of course the pragmatic justification for not applying to genius the standards of morals, intelligence, and 'normality' that would fit the grocer's boy. A multiple standard implies no weak snobbery, whereas the single standard surely betrays rigidity of mind and the urge to cavil masquerading as the critical spirit.

André Maurois

* The ethics of the biographer partake of those of the historian and of those of the portrait painter.

What is the duty of the portrait painter? (*a*) To paint a true portrait, because he entered into an engagement to produce a reasonable likeness of a definite individual. (*b*) To paint a beautiful portrait, because a work of art will give pleasure even to those who never knew the model, and also will add inside truth to the outside likeness.

What is the duty of the historian? (*a*) To record true facts because, if his facts are not true, he deceives us, causes us to bear unfair judgements, and may influence in a regrettable way our future action. (*b*) To arrange these facts in an intelligible order and to give his work an artistic form.

In the case of the portrait painter, the duty to produce an artistic work is paramount. A picture that would have likeness without beauty would be no better than a photograph, and probably not as good, whereas we do not care at all whether Leonardo da Vinci's Mona Lisa was or was not a striking likeness.

In the case of the historian, the order of precedence is reversed, and *he* may achieve useful work if he fulfils the first condition (truth) without fulfilling the second (beauty). There are books which are nothing

* From 'The Ethics of Biography', *English Institute Annual, 1942* (1943), pp. 5–28. This address to the English Institute in New York City was delivered before the appearance of M. Maurois' most important later biographies. Reprinted by permission of the author and the Columbia University Press.

but loosely connected collections of documents and facts, a
extremely helpful to workers interested in the subject. How
books do not make their author an historian, in the literary sense of the word, any more than the publication of a dictionary of rhymes would make its author a poet. On the other hand, a writer might conceivably compose about past events a book that would have artistic value without being true to facts. In such a case should we call the author an historian? If he is in good faith, we might call him a badly informed historian. If he deliberately alters or invents the facts, we might call him a pamphleteer, or a panegyrist, or a propagandist, or a novelist, but certainly not an historian.

The same is true of the biographer who practises a peculiar form of history, the object of which is the recording of facts referring to a definite individual, chosen for his importance in religion, leadership, literature, or any other form of notoriety. Biography, as Edmund Gosse said, is 'the faithful portrait of a soul in its adventures through life', which is a paraphrase of Carlyle's definition: 'A likeness of the earthly pilgrimage of man'. A faithful portrait. An honest biographer should sit in front of his documents as an honest painter sits in front of his model, thinking only: 'What do I see, and which is the best way to convey my vision to others?' His first duty is to produce a true portrait. Why is it his duty? Because he announces a portrait of Lincoln, or Churchill, or Napoleon, and not merely an imaginary character. This makes him responsible to us for the image we shall form of Lincoln, or Churchill, or Napoleon. He has no right to force upon us, under false pretences, his personal prejudices against, or in favour of his hero.

His second duty is to produce, to the best of his ability, a readable and, if possible, a beautiful book. Readable, because a book nobody ever reads remains useless; beautiful, because beauty, poetical beauty, will lead to a much deeper understanding of a soul than would a cold collection of facts. We have therefore to answer two questions. How should a biographer collect his facts? And how should he organize and present the facts once collected?

How should he collect his facts and find which are the facts to be collected? The obvious answer is: All the facts that are connected with the life of the hero; but this is more obvious than helpful. For, in a way, all the facts contemporary with the hero may have had a bearing on his life. If you write about Napoleon, there is hardly a

European country of which the history, at the beginning of the nineteenth century, was not part of Napoleon's life. If you write about any Frenchman who was in his twenties or thirties between 1914 and 1918, there is a chance that all the big events of World War I affected his thoughts in some way. Should you then turn a biography of Napoleon into a history of the French Revolution, or a life of François Mauriac into a history of the World War? Evidently not.

It seems to me that the problem should be faced in the same way as the portrait painter faces the problem of composing his picture. He has a right to choose between showing the painted figure isolated on a plain background, painting it in its familiar surroundings, or giving it an elaborate historical background. Whistler's portrait of his mother, or Manet's portrait of Cézanne, are examples of the first type; most of Holbein's portraits belong to the second type; the portrait of Bonaparte at Arcole by Gros, is an example of the third.

Also the painter has a right to leave a wider or smaller margin around the central figure. In a lady's portrait by Vuillard, you can see that the lady was nothing more to him than a coloured spot in the representation of her home, or of her garden. But there is a limit to the portrait painter's freedom of choice. If the margin is too large, or the background too important, there is a risk of killing the real subject. Then the picture would no more be a portrait; it might become a landscape, or an 'intérieur', or a battle scene.

In the same way, a biographer has a right to leave around his central figure a margin, more or less wide, of contemporary facts. Only, if he leaves the margin too wide, he runs the risk of no longer writing a biography, while not writing a good history either. Where should he draw the line, and how should he choose between facts? It seems to me that he should consider as relevant all the facts that had a direct influence on the formation of the hero, on the adventures of his soul, or on his personal actions.

Take, for example, the question of ancestry. In some instances, you could fill a whole volume with the story of your hero's forefathers. Such is the case of Byron. Yet what matters is not what happened to Admiral Byron, or to the Wicked Lord, or to Captain Jack Byron, but what *our* Byron inherited from them, and also what he could know of them, and the extent to which his own actions were influenced by such memories and precedents. It seems quite obvious that the knowledge of his tragic ancestry gave Byron a feeling of irresponsibility and fateful predestination, which helps to explain him. Therefore we are justified in speaking of that aspect of his family and in devoting a chapter to that extraordinary group of people.

Or, to take another example, read the life of Roger Fry by Virginia Woolf. She has a few pages about the Quakers, their creed, their habits, and she is right. Roger Fry belonged to a Quaker family, and it is quite impossible to understand him if one does not know the outlook on life given him by his education. For the same reason, it seems necessary to begin a life of Disraeli with a few pages about the Jews in England, and a life of Shelley with a description of Eton at the end of the eighteenth century. On the other hand, it would be irrelevant and absurd, in a life of Chateaubriand, to describe French court life at the time of the birth of Chateaubriand, because there was no strong influence of the one upon the other. The Court of Louis XVI ought to be described only at the time when young Chateaubriand saw it for the first time. It is legitimate, in a life of George Washington, to describe Indian life and Indian tactics, but only inasmuch as Washington knew them, and at the time he came in touch with them.

Let us now come to the facts that are actually part of the life of our hero: anecdotes about him, letters he wrote, diaries he kept. We must, of course, study as many of them as we can find. No source of information should be neglected. Then, having carefully collected all the available material, we should sift it out in order to retain only what is indisputably true. We all have heard, in our own times, apocryphal anecdotes about well-known men. We have heard stories about ourselves that we know to be untrue. Such experiences ought to render us, as biographers, prudent and even diffident. The evidence of a personal enemy, or that of an intimate friend, should be weighed with careful precision before we accept it. Contradictory documents and statements should be compared and submitted to a serious inquiry.

All such preliminary work being done, we find ourselves, if our subject has been a man (or woman) who played a great part, confronted with a mass of documentation which is ten times, or a hundred times, as much as any book can contain. . . . It becomes imperative to choose, and therefore to suppress.

Now what right have we to suppress evidence, and can we be

called truthful historians if we do so? I shall here take the liberty to quote the rules I have, on this subject, attempted to follow in my own work:

1. A biographer has a right to suppress all duplicate evidence. If there are ten testimonials to show that your hero was addicted to drink, choose the most significant one and leave it at that, unless one of the others suggests an entirely new aspect of the case.

2. A biographer has a right to distil the essence of a correspondence, or of a diary. There is always, in all such writings, a recurrence of a certain number of themes. It is in them, predominantly, that we are interested. In many instances twenty lines, if well chosen, should convey to the reader a very accurate idea of twenty long letters. Therefore, give a letter in full if it is a masterpiece of writing or analysis, or if it is a revealing document; in all other cases, quote well-chosen extracts.

3. Small and trivial facts are not necessarily unimportant. They may throw a sudden light on a hidden aspect of the personality. Any fact that adds to the physical knowledge of the hero, his diet, his familiar gestures, his way of speech, is important. Plutarch knew this as well as Harold Nicolson or Virginia Woolf.

4. A biographer has of course no right to suppress a fact because it goes against his preconceived idea of his hero. If you start with the theory that Wordsworth was a saint, and discover he had his frailties, do not hesitate to say so. If, for political reasons, you start with a favourable view of Samuel Adams and discover, in the course of your studies, that you do not admire him any longer, tell the truth. A faked image of your hero has no interest whatsoever. It is nobody's portrait. Not even is it a portrait at all, but rather a sort of abstract design of an inhuman figure.

5. In a few cases, a biographer may have to suppress a fact for ethical reasons: for instance if the hero of the biography is a contemporary of the writer, and if premature publication of a certain fact could injure a third party; or if it is against public interest to lessen the prestige of a man who still has an important part to play in public life.

As a matter of fact this last rule, though valid, shows how dangerous it is to write the life of a man while he is alive. I did it myself in the case of Marshal Lyautey and, though he proved very generous and open-minded about it, I cannot say my book represents the whole truth about him, as it will be written in fifty years time. What I have said is true, but there is much I left unsaid.

What happens if an author, having completed and published a biography, discovers (or is informed of) the existence of new material which modifies, or completely transforms his views about his hero? It seems to me that he should, as soon as other work and publishing facilities permit it, rewrite his book. He has no right to leave behind him a portrait he knows to be inaccurate. I, for one, should rewrite my life of Shelley. In the light of the discoveries made, first by Mr. Leslie Hotson and later by Professor Newman White, some of the facts I stated in 1923 are now proved untrue, the whole character of Shelley being altered by the 'lost letters', found at last in 1931. It is certainly my duty to say so, as I do today, and even to alter certain parts of my book as soon as circumstances will make it possible.

In the case of Byron, I had a very serious moral problem to solve. It was the question of incest. Incest had been denied by most of the biographers, and also by Lord Ernle, who had edited Byron's letters and journals and was then, in England, *the* great expert on the poet. When I met John Murray, the descendant of Byron's publisher, he told me (in perfect good faith, I am sure) he did not believe in Byron's love for his half-sister Augusta Leigh. But when the family papers were given to me, and when Lady Lovelace (widow of Byron's own grandson) allowed me to read the unpublished diary of Lady Byron, no place was left for doubt. The proof, the irrefutable proof of the guilty love was there. What was I to do? I had a consultation with Lord Ernle, who agreed with me that my duty was to contradict him and all others, and to tell the story of the incest as it appeared in the Lovelace papers. No moral objections could be made: Byron, his sister, their children and grandchildren were dead. The truth could not harm the memory of Byron who, during his lifetime, had always posed as a cynic; on the contrary, if it was told with human truth and sympathy, it could inspire pity for Byron, and also could help his readers to understand much better some of his poems, based on this forbidden love.

In the case of a national hero, like Washington in this country, or Nelson in England, one might say: anything written against them is harmful, because it deprives the youth of the country of a perfect image of courage and devotion which used to be an inspiration. But this is true only of systematic 'debunking', and I do not think a great man could be belittled, in the eyes of intelligent admirers, by the acknowledgement of a certain number of human weaknesses. On the contrary, it seems to me that his courage and devotion are all the more to be admired if he had other inclinations to fight in his own soul. That Admiral Nelson died gallantly for his country was certainly fine, but that he gave his life while he was passionately in love with Lady Hamilton, knowing that his death would leave both her and their daughter unsupported, was even more praiseworthy.

6. When the biographer gets hold of a whole set of new facts, he is of course tempted to publish them and it may be interesting to do so. Yet, outside exceptional cases and when the document itself makes good reading, I do not think this documentary evidence should slow down the movement of the book, nor alter the general balance of its design. A better arrangement is to give, in the body of the book, only the gist of the story, and to publish the full document in an appendix. That is, of course, if one attempts to write a biography having an artistic value. In fact two types of biography are conceivable: the work of art in which, of course, facts must be respected, but which admits of legitimate suppressions made for the sake of proportion or composition; and the scholarly biography, in which form is deliberately sacrificed to complete information, and where, therefore, suppression of facts for aesthetical reasons would not be justified.

So much for suppression of facts. And now what about the invention of facts? Here I can think of only one rule, and it is a very simple one: Under no account has the biographer a right to invent a single fact. He is writing history, not fiction, and witnessing under oath. He cannot even say that the weather, on such and such a day, was good or bad, if he has no evidence for it. He should not put into his hero's mouth, nor attribute to any character, sentences they have not spoken. In *Ariel*, I took the liberty, not to attribute to Shelley things he had never said, but to turn into dialogue conversations that we possessed, in indirect form, in his own letters. I have never done it since, nor do I approve of that method. It undermines the confidence of the reader, and also there is always a risk, even with the best of good will, of mutilating or deforming a thought. If you have a letter, quote it, or part of it; if a conversation has been preserved by a reliable witness, make use of it. But never indulge in imagination. Once you cross the line between biography and fiction, you will never be able to retrace your steps.

Yet, if the biographer has no right to invent his facts, he has a perfect right, and even a duty, to interpret the facts. Why? Cannot the facts speak for themselves? Very often they can, and if they do, the duty of the biographer is to state them, without commentary, and not to intervene. We are interested in his hero; not in himself or in his reactions. However, there are cases, and many cases, when the facts do not speak for themselves and when the reader is at a loss to understand them. In such cases, the biographer has a right to step in and to attempt an interpretation. Why? Because he had more time than the reader to give to a study of the texts and also because, having explored with care the whole background of the hero, he has a chance better to understand his motives, and those of his friends or enemies. . . .

In many instances, it is a question whether the man we study was a really great man or a rather base character. The biographer has to choose. He cannot write a complete life of a man without deciding whether he likes him or not, whether he trusts him or not. Of course he may decide that, like most human beings, his hero was a mixture of greatness and weaknesses, but that also is an interpretation. Take the case of Chateaubriand, sending his resignation to Napoleon after the murder of the Duke of Enghien. Was it a noble, well-meditated gesture? Or was it a fit of temper, soon regretted? Or was Chateaubriand only too pleased to quit a job he disliked? Or did he realize the prestige such an action could give him one day? Every one of these explanations gives a different view of Chateaubriand's character. And if we decide to blend them together, in the Strachey way, this again is an interpretation.

Could not the reader say: 'I do not care for your interpretations. I am just as able as you are to put two and two together'? Yes, of course, but it may happen that the biographer, just as the novelist, is a better connoisseur of human nature than the average reader. He may find either in his own experience, or in the lives of other people he observed or wrote about, ideas, situations, reactions, very similar to those of the hero. He may be able, thanks to such previous experiences, to form a sort of interior view of the mind he has to analyse and describe.

Also the biographer may be an expert in the same field as his hero. If a man of action, who happens to be at the same time a scholar, writes the life of a general or of a prime minister, he knows more than we do of the normal reactions of a commander on the battlefield, or of a statesman at the time of a crisis. If a writer writes the life of a man of letters, he understands the pangs of literary composition, the desire to free one's life, to disentangle it of all ties in order to work peacefully, and the healthy egotism of the creator which resembles so much that of the expectant mother. This does not mean that the man of action and the writer, when they write a scholarly life, will invent sentiments and attitudes. We have already refused them the right to do this, and also pointed out the danger of over specialization in biography, but if the man of action and the writer happen to be at the same time born biographers, then it means that amongst the innumerable details that can be found in a correspondence, in memoirs, in verbal testimonies, they will prove able to select the important and really significant ones. Anyone will admit that a man who has himself had various love affairs and has known many women (as far as they can be known) understands Liszt or Wagner much better than would a Puritan, or a home-secluded scholar. When Disraeli wrote about Bolingbroke, or about Lord George Bentinck, he knew what he was talking about. If General Marshall were to write a life of Foch, or Arthur Rubinstein a life of Chopin it would be absorbingly interesting.

But this raises another question: To what extent is it legitimate to make use of one's own experiences to write other people's lives? Under no account should we undertake to write a confession and call it a biography. It would probably be both a poor confession and a poor biography. Chateaubriand attempted, perhaps unconsciously, to do it in his *Life of Rancé* and all good judges agree that, while the book is admirably written, it is *not* a life of Rancé. On the other hand, it would be absurd to neglect, while writing a life, the lessons of Life. The scholar who reads these documents, this diary, is a man; he once suffered, wondered, despaired; he recognizes such feelings when he meets with their unmistakable signs. Why should he forget what experience taught him, at the time when he needs it most?

If the hero has been a writer, the interpretation of his writings, as sources for his biography, is a very thorny problem. What right have we to make use of his novels, when we attempt to understand his outlook on life, and his character? It is self-evident that a writer of fiction or poetry always puts something of himself in his works. Can we isolate that 'something' and unearth, amidst the sayings and adventures of the characters he created, what really was the expression of his own nature? Let us confess that this is, at its best, a dangerous and unsafe method. Having written fiction myself, I know how inextricably mixed are, in a novel, memories of my own life, stories I have been told, reminiscences, inventions. How could an outsider find his way in this labyrinth when we writers ourselves, after a year, would be at a loss to say whether we actually heard this sentence or invented it? All one can say is that, when a writer comes back to the same themes and repeats the same character under different names, there is very good ground to infer that he is obsessed by such themes and characters, and that they may be a clue to his most secret nature.

Freudian biographers have analysed the writings of Edgar Poe, the poems of Baudelaire, as they would the dreams of their patients. One cannot deny that some of their interpretations are striking; others seem to us far fetched and unlikely. At best they can be nothing but conjectures and therefore they are not very useful to the historian. A psycho-analysis may sometimes confirm a biographer in a view he already arrived at by other means. A complete and true life will always require much more direct evidence. 'As a matter of fact', says Mark Longaker, 'every good biographer is a good psycho-analyst, but every good psycho-analyst is not necessarily a good potential biographer'.

Interpretation is not the only possible deformation of facts. It must not be forgotten that the marshalling and grouping of facts is in itself an interpretation. If I say that Mr. Gladstone was absolutely opposed to Sunday travel, and then show him travelling on Sunday, no comment is necessary to inform the reader of my feelings as to Mr. Gladstone's sincerity. Facts, in the hands of a Lytton Strachey, become the most deadly weapons. You remember how he dealt with Bishop Manning's diary, or with Queen Victoria's letters: quotations, nothing but quotations, but chosen in such a perfidious way that there was not much left, after reading them, of the Bishop's good faith, or of the Queen's good judgement.

The biographer should never allow his prejudices nor his humour to govern the arrangement of facts. Strachey's *Queen Victoria* is a brilliant portrait; Strachey's facts are all true, and yet the portrait is unfair. Queen Victoria was a much greater 'king' than the book would lead us to believe. And how does Strachey's hostile bias assert itself? Mostly by juxtaposition of incongruous and discordant facts. An amusing process, but one that belongs to the technique of the pamphleteer rather than to that of the historian.

Can we formulate any rules as to the arrangement of facts?

1. That events should be presented to the reader in chronological order appears natural enough; yet a great many biographers do not seem to understand that the strict observation of this rule will greatly help to maintain the interest of the reader. They think it wise, while they deal with one aspect of the life of their hero, to study it extensively, and at all periods. Or they keep all the most significant personal characteristics and anecdotes for the chapter before last, with the result that the reader finds there, strangely mixed, stories which belong to different ages of the hero. Can they not see that, what is really interesting is the development of a personality, the successive deposits of ideas left by Time on the central kernel constituted by heredity, environment, and childhood. That, and that alone, is the great human adventure we all look for in a biography.

2. Some trouble should be taken by the biographer to discover, in the life he is studying, some sort of pattern, such as to give to the multiplicity of facts an intelligible support. If I am allowed to take a personal example, it helped me, when I wrote the life of Chateaubriand, to discover that Chateaubriand, after having long attempted to make of his life a work of art and having found the attempt hopeless, gave up such active ambition and replaced it by the desire to turn the story of his life into a work of art. Hence the *Mémoires d'outre-tombe*. This is not, of course, the only explanation of Chateaubriand, who was an extremely complex being, but I believe it to be a true explanation, and one that does help in the arrangement of facts, without distorting them in the least.

3. For the same reason it is important that the biographer should attempt to discover the main themes of the life he is writing. Just as, in music, the return of the same themes helps us to understand a symphony or a concerto, while their interplay gives us pleasure, there is always in a well-composed book some sort of mysterious rhythm. Life itself produces such recurrent themes. We meet, from time to time, the men and women we used to know in our childhood, the masters of our adolescence, our first loves, and the effect upon them of the passing years helps us to realize the flight of Time and our advancing age. Also the same traits of our character produce, periodically, the same effects. Heredity brings the father back to life in the person of the son. Such are the natural rhythms of nature and of history. If the biographer is at the same time an artist, he can make use of them to give his work a poetical beauty.

4. There is also a great deal of poetry in anything that evokes nature around men. No biographer of Disraeli should omit a description of Bradenham Park, and later of Hughenden Park. No biographer of Byron should miss the beauty of Newstead Abbey. Such strong impressions were part of the daily thoughts of the heroes. Queen Victoria would no more be Queen Victoria without a description of Windsor Castle, of Balmoral, of Buckingham Palace. Very often the hero or the heroine themselves have left sketches of their favourite *décors*. In that case the biographer should quote their own words, only using his discretion to suppress or condense. In the life of a painter, an effort should be made to convey the idea both of the countries he lived in and of the image he has given of them. Cézanne's Provence is not everybody's Provence, and in order to show his originality, both should be in the book.

5. What about poetry in the life of a poet? The problem of the proper balance to be kept between the actions and the works of a writer is one of the most difficult that confront a biographer. Of course the work of a writer is part of his life, of his flesh and blood. No book about him has any meaning if it does not give an idea of his books. In fact his strongest impulses express themselves through the written words much more readily than through his actions. On the other hand a biography must not turn into a literary study, into an essay. The books must be analysed, but in relation to the type of man who composed them. In the case of a poet, it will probably be necessary to quote at length from his poetry; poetry cannot be condensed or 'digested'. One of the worst faults of my own life of Shelley was a lack of quotations. But here the question of language was an obstacle. Writing in French, I could only quote in French, and to what extent is the translation of a poem a true image of the original? Yet I felt my mistake so keenly that, a few years later, in the case of Byron, I introduced in my text a great many quotations. They are the best part of the book.

Some have thought that a biographer should choose between poetry and history. This would imply that you cannot, at one and the same time, write a poetical and a true book. With such a view I entirely disagree. There is no reason why a reliable history should not be at the same time poetical. After all there is a great deal of poetry in real life, and all the biographer has to do is to extract from the life he is writing all the poetry it contains. No choice is necessary; no choice would be possible.

One last question: there was a time when lives were written with a moral purpose, to exemplify the rewards of virtue and the failures of wickedness. Is it part of the ethics of the biographer that he should teach a moral lesson? Modern biographers think, not without reason, that the true story of a man's life always contains a moral lesson, but that the reader should be left to discover it for himself.

What do most lives prove? That to be a man is at the same time very difficult and very easy—very difficult because nothing, in human affairs, is ever simple, because our wisest schemes will always be partly wrong, because there is no end in life's struggle, because 'the life of man is but a span', because 'life is too short to be little', because most of the choices are made for us by the Fates. Great lives show that, in spite of all, it is possible for a man to act with dignity and to achieve internal peace. That is true of saints, of philosophers, of poets, of artists; it is even true of men of action. Napoleon at Saint-Helena, Byron at Missolonghi, Washington at Valley Forge are human lessons in resignation, courage, and patience. It is the part of the biographer, not to make these lessons pedantic and stale by writing a sermon about them, but to tell such noble stories with reverence and simplicity. If the writer respects his hero, the reader will respect the writer.

Dumas Malone

* But nobody can tell the whole truth about any important person within the limits of a book. Some exclusion is unavoidable. It is not entirely correct to say that the historical approach to biography is objective, while the fictional is subjective, for there is a degree of subjectivity in every writer and this inevitably affects his selection of materials and his judgement of them. But there are perceptible differences between men in their fairmindedness, just as there are in their capacity for taking pains; and there are perceptible differences between writers who think first and most about fidelity to their subject and those who think first and most about interesting their audience.

Let us consider the question of sex. No one can deny that this is an immortal subject and perennially interesting to all save pre-adolescents. Without questioning the indispensability of sex in human life, one often suspects that certain novelists give a greater emphasis, or a different sort of emphasis, to it in their books than it has in the ordinary life of the average person. They do not take it for granted as something normal, but accentuate it for sociological or artistic or commercial purposes. Whether they do this or not, they may; as novelists it is their privilege.

A biographer might conceivably do the same thing, thus heightening interest while giving an entirely false impression about the subject

*From 'Biography and History' in *The Interpretation of History*, ed. Joseph R. Strayer (1943), pp. 133–5. Reprinted by permission of the author and the Princeton University Press.

of his book. The person whose life and character are described might be greatly surprised to read what is said about him. He might say that particular incidents upon which great stress had been laid were entirely true but that, taking his life as a whole, they were unimportant. In much the same way personal foibles may be so accentuated, to add interest to the tale, that people who knew the subject in the flesh would regard the alleged portrait as a caricature. A man may have a long nose without being a Cyrano de Bergerac. It is entirely possible for every given fact or characteristic that is mentioned in a book to be true and for the impression to be, none the less, wholly false. The features are all there but they are so out of proportion that the portrait is unrecognizable.

It isn't quite as simple as that, of course, when the biographer never knew the person he is attempting to describe and has to recover him by means of research and historical imagination. He can never be quite sure that he has found him. But what the historically-minded biographer tries to do is to live with his subject in spirit long enough and intimately enough to form definite impressions of the proportions of his character and personality. Then, when he runs across some incident, savoury or unsavoury, he can judge whether or not it is in character—whether it is a proper illustration of the nature of the man or is largely without significance. His use of such an incident would depend, not primarily on its appeal to the interest of the reader, but on his mature judgement as to its appropriateness.

In the course of my own studies I have come across some lurid stories about the personal life of Thomas Jefferson. These would make a chapter which would be read with avidity. One of my tasks is to try to determine whether or not these stories are true. Most of them emanated from a single poisoned source, the vitriolic pen of an unscrupulous journalist who had turned upon his benefactor; and most of them are not true. But let us say that some of them are true—Jefferson himself admitted that one was. None the less, it is my strong impression that he was fastidiously clean in his personal life. He was extraordinarily devoted to his wife while she was living and reverent of her memory after her early death, and he lavished upon his motherless daughters a tenderness which is hard to describe without sentimentality. What, then, shall I do with an unsavoury incident which, in my opinion, is out of character? The only thing I am sure of is that I should not accentuate it. Much depends on the length of the biography I am writing, but at all events I must try to depict the man in the proportions which I have perceived. These proportions may not be correct, for my judgement is fallible; they may not seem precisely the same to any two students; but it is my obligation to see them as clearly and as honestly as I can.

James Thomas Flexner

* Biography is a complicated art that combines things seemingly irreconcilable. Concerned with the depiction of personality, the biographer must be an imaginative writer; concerned with the resurrection of actual men and events, he must be a meticulous scholar. On one hand, he leans towards the technique of the novelist; on the other, towards the technique of the documentary historian. Somewhere between these two poles lies his own technique. Finding the golden mean which is most suited to his art is the fundamental problem which faces every writer of lives.

The easy way out is to go to one extreme or the other. Many a biographer, deeply conscious of his duty as a scholar, has forgotten that he is dealing with people who once lived and thought. We may learn from his pages where a man was at a certain date and the actual physical facts of what the man was doing. Those letters and papers which the biographer considers relevant he paraphrases or quotes. And, having done this, he claims to have gone as far as a biographer may go; these are the facts, anything else is fiction. Even if his books are not vivid, they are, he insists, completely impersonal and non-partisan, entirely accurate.

We may agree at once that such books are not vivid, but are they impersonally accurate? That is open to question. Although the author has quoted the documents he has used with rigid fidelity, keeping in every

* 'Biography as a Juggler's Art', *Saturday Review of Literature*, 9 October 1943, pp. 3–4, 19. Reprinted by permission of the author and the publisher.

misspelling and every omitted comma, the fact remains that he has made a selection among the many papers at his disposal. If he has written the life of a great character in history, we may be sure he has been able to quote only one document in five hundred, or a thousand. Of course, he has dwelt on the papers he considers most significant, but his judgement has depended on his own personal interpretation of his subject's career. Thus, if he considers his subject an honest man, he will regard suggestions of questionable practices in contemporary memoirs as undoubtedly inspired by jealousy and malice; it would distort the picture, he feels, to make much use of such irrelevant things. If, however, the biographer is convinced that his hero was an evil influence, these same evidences of wrong-doing will be given great weight. Admittedly this is an extreme example: the point is that no author can escape evaluating documents according to what remains, despite the most thorough scholarship, his own personal judgement.

Indeed it may be contended that biographies made up entirely of facts, dates, and quoted source material are in one way more misleading than those in which the author permits himself some leeway. When a writer draws his conclusions on paper instead of solely in his mind, we may recognize his point of view and take it into consideration as we read. But when an author keeps himself always in the background, we may only discover his prejudices by making a new study of the source material.

A purely factual biographer is forced by his method to present reality in an unnatural manner. Experience has trained every individual to evaluate the people he meets as living, active entities; he is not used to judging men from quoted documents. When we re-examine a packet of letters from an old friend we realize that much of the meaning lies not in the words written but between the lines. Probably factual biographers would admit this, but they would add that there is nothing to keep a reader from looking between the lines of the documents they have quoted. True, a reader can try; but he is in a much worse position to make an interpretation than is the biographer, who has studied five hundred or a thousand papers to the reader's one, and who has a much better background of knowledge of the period in which the subject lived.

Although a purely factual biography can present neither an entirely non-partisan interpretation nor a vivid picture of a living man, we must remember that the labour which goes into such a book is often extremely valuable in blazing new trails of knowledge. The expert documentarian is in his own way a worker of great ability, a Sherlock Holmes of the library shelf. Following clues as subtle as those employed by any detective of fiction, he undertakes an exciting search for the missing fact, the paper that has vanished. Back and forth across the world his magnifying glass moves; now he is rummaging in the attic of some descendant of his hero, now blowing the dust from documents in an historical society cellar. And often when he returns to the light of day at last, he is carrying carefully distilled on a packet of cards new data which may well revolutionize our understanding of his subject. Such a man has made an important contribution whatever the form of the biography he writes in the end. Indeed, the book is often a secondary matter, like the article in which a scientist reports his experiments. Whether the selection he publishes from the material he has found is broad or narrow makes little difference as long as he appends a full bibliography; other writers may now follow in his footsteps, and, whatever their achievement, it will be largely dependent on his labours. Purely documentary works are source books for biographies, not biographies in themselves.

At the opposite extreme are the several schools of biographers whose only interest is in creating brilliant pictures of human beings. Not aiming at sound scholarship, they use a technique which is much closer to romance than history. Some of the most successful go so far as to make accuracy secondary to the telling of a dramatic story. Not only do they improvise conversations, not only do they juggle chronology and make up events to fill gaps in their knowledge, but, should the development of their subjects' careers not accord with their ideas of suspense and climax, they do not hesitate to change fact in a way that they believe furthers fiction. Their books are not biographies at all, but novels.

Other biographers have a respect for accuracy, but fail to undertake the labour of examining the innumerable and scattered documents which are the source material in their field. They study the obvious printed sources, making great use of previously published lives, and from the material thus culled create a new interpretation. Many of the books thus prepared have definite virtues. A fresh point of view, brilliant writing, the vivid presentation of characters who walk and breathe, an easy readability that carries the eye from page to page;

these are on the credit side of the best of such works. On the debit side is a fundamental flaw in method.

As we have seen, even the most scholarly study represents in the way the material was selected a specific point of view. The romantic biographer uses several such interpretations to build up a separate interpretation, which may indeed represent an opposite approach from that which determined his source-books. Let us say that he is writing about a worthy who died at the height of the Victorian era. The original biographers of such a man, themselves Victorians, would report his life according to their ideals. But our modern biographer has discarded Victorianism, so he makes fun of his subject's smugness. Yet that subject may not have been smug at all; the biographer may be dealing not with the character under discussion at all, but with the character's previous biographers. He has no way of knowing unless he himself goes back to the original sources. This again is an extreme case, but the fact remains that the biographer who relies on rewriting previous lives can create nothing but an interpretation of interpretations.

However brilliant and comprehensive were the scholars who went before him, a writer who examines the original material in his field is likely to stumble on evidence that was unimportant from the point of view of his predecessors but which will open up to him new vistas of understanding. The more original and interpretative his approach, the more valuable he will find these personal discoveries.

Facts, dates, and documents then, all the seemingly uninspiring paraphernalia of the archivist, should be a biographer's inspiration. Both the usefulness and the authority of his book will be greatly increased if he employs notes to give the source of each of his statements. Although some publishers object to references on the ground that they may scare away readers, this attitude is extremely shortsighted, even from a strictly commercial point of view. The notes can easily be gathered in the back of the volume, designated by page and paragraph in such a manner that no numbers need appear in the text. Hardly noticed by the uninterested, these references will help the sale of the book in many ways. Serious works are often given to serious scholars for review, and the first thing a scholar does is to attempt an evaluation of source material. Furthermore, it is the experts who have a long-time interest in a field. Promotion aimed at the casual reader can keep a book in the public eye for six months or a year; after that the scholars have their innings. They push undocumented books into limbo, and keep the others alive indefinitely.

Once a biographer has mastered his original sources, his work has only begun. Now he must make a synthesis of his material similar to that a novelist makes from the observed facts of life. Before him lies the tangled record of a personality acting within a fixed period of years. He must weigh evidence and draw conclusions; he must interpret and explain. While recognizing that he cannot so far escape the limitations of the human mind as to write pure truth uninfluenced by ' is own personality and environment, he must none the less strive to do so. The broader his view-point, the closer he comes to a universal approach, the more valuable his book will be. There can be no possible excuse for his ever changing a fact, misquoting a document, or glossing over an event that the most non-partisan attitude of which he is capable tells him is significant. Complete intellectual honesty is perhaps the most important single attribute of the biographer.

Impartiality, however, need not imply lack of colour; the best biographies carry an overtone of excitement. There has long been a tendency among some intellectuals to regard the story-teller's art as a cheap trick which appeals only to common minds. A short story, we are told, is damaged by plot; a play is not art but 'box office' unless it is heavy and slow. Similarly a biography is regarded as a serious contribution in exact proportion to its dullness. This attitude represents a pointless limiting of the artist's opportunity by taking away one of his best tools.

Drama is natural to biography because it is natural to the human mind. Since most men who have shaped events have found their careers exciting, to drain off the excitement makes the picture untrue. Indeed, if a writer feels it necessary to alter events to create suspense and climax, it usually means he has failed to grasp the inherent possibilities of his subject. Facts are stranger than fiction; the imagination of nature is more audacious than that of man. What novelist could conceive of a career like Joan of Arc's, or Lincoln's?

Since all men live in time, chronology is the only natural thread on which the events of a man's life may be strung. This does not mean that the biographer must follow his subject methodically from birth to death. Like a novelist, he may anticipate major happenings and then work back through the years to the explanations, yet the basic rhythm of time which is the rhythm of life most never be obscured. Sometimes it is necessary for clarity to group like events together even if they happened in different years, but this is a dangerous expedient which should be resorted to as little as possible. No biographies are to my mind less vivid than those made up of essay chapters, each dealing with one aspect of the hero's career and headed 'The Statesman', 'The Poet', 'The Husband and Father'.

A basic problem facing every biographer is how to sketch in the historical background without violating the time element and impeding the narrative flow. On the one hand, the writer has a personality and a career to present; on the other, he is saddled with the cultural, economic, and political events of a period. Many biographers have been defeated by this seeming dualism. Some try to create pure character sketches, to separate a man's personality from his reaction to and his effect on his environment. Others have written erudite histories in which for chapter after chapter the hero is obscured from view by clouds of general data. Neither expedient, of course, can turn out a well-rounded book.

Whenever an artist becomes confused, perhaps the best plan is to return to the study of life. How, let us ask ourselves, does a man's environment actually impinge on his personality? Certainly not in a series of bursts which, like the explanatory chapters in a formal book, hit him from time to time with a great bulk of facts. A man's environment is an integral part of his life, a gradual revelation never separated from the subjective aspects of his personality.

Like the novelist, the biographer should keep his hero for ever in the foreground; he should see the world over his hero's shoulder. Historical events appear in the book at the time when they became of significance to the person under discussion, and this automatically keys them into the story. A biographer may, of course, include facts and analyses that were beyond his subject's experience, as long as he makes it plain that he is doing so, and always keeps clearly before his readers the reference of these matters to the career and personality with which he is dealing. A type of sleight-of-hand is required.

Indeed, a biographer must be a juggler, expert at keeping many bright balls circling in the air. Fact and imagination, sober scholarship and dramatic writing, character study and sound history, a sympathetic understanding of his hero and yet a judicial lack of special pleading, these are a few of the balls that must for ever fly around his head without colliding or dropping to the floor. But fortunately it is only in the rare moments when he masquerades as a critic that a practising biographer recognizes this analogy and realizes the enormous difficulties of his craft. When he is back in the greasy overalls of labour, he is again a simple craftsman, struggling with specific problems which he must handle as best he may. And if he sometimes wonders how his finished book will turn out, he can only hope it will be better than might be expected.

Mid-Twentieth Century

Sir Lewis Namier

* Human affairs being the subject matter of history, all human pursuits and disciplines in their social aspects enter into it. But as no human mind can master more than a fraction of what would be required for a wide and balanced understanding of human affairs, limitation and selection are essential in the historian's craft. Analytic insight into the tangle of human affairs coupled with a consciousness of his own limitations is the mark of the real historian, and maturity is attained perhaps later in his work than in any other discipline.

As history deals with concrete events fixed in time and space, narrative is its basic medium—but guided by analytic selection of what to narrate. The function of the historian is akin to that of the painter and not of the photographic camera: to discover and set forth, to single out and stress that which is of the nature of the thing, and not to reproduce indiscriminately all that meets the eye. To distinguish a tree you look at its shape, its bark and leaf; counting and measuring its branches would get you nowhere. Similarly what matters in history is the great outline and the significant detail; what must be avoided is the deadly morass of irrelevant narrative.

History is therefore necessarily subjective and individual, conditioned by the interest and vision of the historian. His interest if intense and sincere is contagious, and the test of his originality is whether

* From *History Today*, March 1952, pp. 161–2; reprinted in *Avenues of History* (1952), pp. 8–9. Included by permission of the author and Hamish Hamilton, publisher.

it is convincing; once stated, his discoveries should appear obvious. The discussion whether history is an art or a science seems futile: it is like medical diagnosis; a great deal of previous experience and knowledge, and the scientific approach of the trained mind, are required, yet the final conclusions (to be re-examined in the light of evidence) are intuitive: an art. The great historian is like the great artist or doctor: after he has done his work, others should not be able to practise within its sphere in the terms of the preceding era. Yet the great mass of the work even of the masters of the craft is devoted to studies of a preparatory character and primarily for the use of the profession. One must plough and sow before one can reap; and it is in such studies that the historian receives his training and keeps up his proficiency. The hackneyed witticism about 'dry-as-dust' historians who 'know more and more about less and less' comes mostly from people who write and read history without real thought or intellectual purpose—as a senseless ritual.

Biographies have become the ritualist form of English historiography; they predominate as much as portraits do in English oil-painting: both answer a custom and a demand, and pay homage to the importance ascribed to individuals; but they may also be due to fear of unbounded fields or to a lack of creative imagination. A biography has a beginning and an end, and a track to follow between the two points; and even great historians sometimes use its framework for studies of wider transactions and problems. But the typical political biography mixes up three different functions, and in that mixture finds an excuse for doing each badly. It uses the papers and correspondence of the biographee: an editor would have to annotate them carefully, collate them with other material, explain obscure transactions, and deal with problems on their own ground; the biographer can select whatever he chooses—'the human being' is his subject. But to deal with the human being would require knowledge of ancillary disciplines, foremost of psychology, both normal and pathological, and insight into the human mind and character; while most biographers if asked for their qualifications could only answer more or less like the girl who applied for the post of nurse to children: that she herself was once a child. Lastly, the 'background' can be compiled from elementary text-books—'after all', the biographer will protest, 'I do not claim to write an original history of the time'. Even 'and his Time' in the title is often treated as a mere excuse for sticking in anything, however irrelevant, found among the papers of the person concerned. True biography is a great and exacting art; but even biographies written on the assumption that this is the easiest form of history, find a much wider public than works of an impersonal character: they seem more human, and are therefore supposed to be 'easy reading'.

Marchette Chute

* This is a rather presumptuous title for a biographer to use, since truth is a very large word. In the sense that it means the reality about a human being it is probably impossible for a biographer to achieve. In the sense that it means a reasonable presentation of all the available facts it is more nearly possible, but even this limited goal is harder to reach than it appears to be. A biographer needs to be both humble and cautious when he remembers the nature of the material he is working with, for a historical fact is rather like the flamingo that Alice in Wonderland tried to use as a croquet mallet. As soon as she got its neck nicely straightened out and was ready to hit the ball, it would turn and look at her with a puzzled expression, and any biographer knows that what is called a 'fact' has a way of doing the same.

Here is a small example. When I was writing my forthcoming biography, 'Ben Jonson of Westminster', I wanted to give a paragraph or two to Sir Philip Sidney, who had a great influence on Jonson. No one thinks of Sidney without thinking of chivalry, and to underline the point I intended to use a story that Sir Fulke Greville told of him. Sidney died of gangrene, from a musket shot that shattered his thigh, and Greville says that Sidney failed to put on his leg armour while preparing for battle because the marshal of the camp was not wearing leg armour, and Sidney was unwilling to do anything that would give him a special advantage.

* From 'Getting at the Truth', *The Saturday Review*, 19 September 1953, pp. 11–12, 43–44. Reprinted by permission of the author and the publisher.

The story is so characteristic both of Sidney himself and of the misplaced high-mindedness of late Renaissance chivalry that I wanted to use it, and since Sir Fulke Greville was one of Sidney's closest friends the information seemed to be reliable enough. But it is always well to check each piece of information as thoroughly as possible and so I consulted another account of Sidney written by a contemporary, this time a doctor who knew the family fairly well. The doctor, Thomas Moffet, mentioned the episode but he said that Sidney left off his leg armour because he was in a hurry.

The information was beginning to twist in my hand and could no longer be trusted. So I consulted still another contemporary who had mentioned the episode, to see which of the two he agreed with. This was Sir John Smythe, a military expert who brought out his book a few years after Sidney's death. Sir John was an old-fashioned conservative who advocated the use of heavy armour even on horseback, and he deplored the current craze for leaving off leg protection, 'the imitating of which . . . cost that noble and worthy gentleman Sir Philip Sidney his life'.

So here I was with three entirely different reasons why Sidney left off his leg armour, all advanced by careful writers who were contemporaries of his. The flamingo had a legitimate reason for looking around with a puzzled expression.

The only thing to do in a case like this is to examine the point of view of the three men who are supplying the conflicting evidence. Sir Fulke Greville was trying to prove a thesis: that his beloved friend had an extremely chivalric nature. Sir John Smythe also was trying to prove a thesis: that the advocates of light arming followed a theory that could lead to disaster. Only the doctor, Thomas Moffet, was not trying to prove a thesis. He was not using his own explanation to reinforce some point he wanted to make. He did not want anything except to set down on paper what he believed to be the facts; and since we do not have Sidney's own explanation of why he did not put on leg armour, the chances are that Dr. Moffet is the safest man to trust.

For Moffet was without desire. Nothing can so quickly blur and distort the facts as desire—the wish to use the facts for some purpose of your own—and nothing can so surely destroy the truth. As soon as the witness wants to prove something he is no longer impartial and his evidence is no longer to be trusted.

The only safe way to study contemporary testimony is to bear constantly in mind this possibility of prejudice and to put almost as much attention on the writer himself as on what he has written. For instance, Sir Anthony Weldon's description of the Court of King James is lively enough and often used as source material; but a note from the publisher admits that the pamphlet was issued as a warning to anyone who wished to 'side with this bloody house' of Stuart. The publisher, at any rate, did not consider Weldon an impartial witness. At about the same time Arthur Wilson published his history of Great Britain, which contained an irresistibly vivid account of the agonized death of the Countess of Somerset. Wilson sounds reasonably impartial; but his patron was the Earl of Essex, who had good reason to hate that particular countess, and there is evidence that he invented the whole scene to gratify his patron.

Sometimes a writer will contradict what he has already written, and in that case the only thing to do is to investigate what has changed his point of view. For instance, in 1608 Captain John Smith issued a description of his capture by Powhatan, and he made it clear that the Indian chief had treated him with unwavering courtesy and hospitality. In 1624 the story was repeated in Smith's 'General History of Virginia', but the writer's circumstances had changed. Smith needed money, 'having a prince's mind imprisoned in a poor man's purse', and he wanted the book to be profitable. Powhatan's daughter, the princess Pocahontas, had recently been in the news, for her visit to England had aroused a great deal of interest among the sort of people that Smith hoped would buy his book. So Smith supplied a new version of the story, in which the once-hospitable Powhatan would have permitted the hero's brains to be dashed out if Pocahontas had not saved his life. It was the second story that achieved fame, and of course it may have been true. But it is impossible to trust it because the desire of the writer is so obviously involved; as Smith said in his prospectus, he needed money and hoped that the book would give 'satisfaction'.

It might seem that there was an easy way for a biographer to avoid the use of this kind of prejudiced testimony. All he has to do is to construct his biography from evidence that cannot be tampered with—from parish records, legal documents, bills, accounts, court records, and so on. Out of these solid grey blocks of impersonal evidence it should surely be possible to construct a road that will lead straight to the truth and that will never bend itself to the misleading curve of personal desire.

This might be so if the only problem involved were the reliability of the material. But there is another kind of desire that is much more subtle, much more pervasive, and much more dangerous than the occasional distortions of fact that contemporary writers may have permitted themselves to make; and this kind of desire can destroy the truth of a biography even if every individual fact in it is as solid and as uncompromising as rock. Even if the road is built of the best and most reliable materials it can still curve away from the truth because of this other desire that threatens it: the desire of the biographer himself.

A biographer is not a court record or a legal document. He is a human being, writing about another human being, and his own temperament, his own point of view, and his own frame of reference are unconsciously imposed upon the man he is writing about. Even if the biographer is free from Captain Smith's temptation—the need for making money—and wants to write nothing but the literal truth, he is still handicapped by the fact that there is no such thing as a completely objective human being. . . .

It might seem that the ideal biographical system, if it could be achieved, would be to go through the years of research without feeling any kind of emotion. The biographer would be a kind of fact-finding machine and then suddenly, after his years of research, a kind of total vision would fall upon him and he would transcribe it in his best and most persuasive English for a waiting public. But research is fortunately not done by machinery, nor are visions likely to descend in that helpful manner. They are the product not only of many facts but also of much thinking, and it is only when the biographer begins to get emotional in his thinking that he ought to beware.

It is easy enough to make good resolutions in advance, but a biographer cannot altogether control his sense of excitement when the climax of his years of research draws near and he begins to see the pieces fall into place. Almost without his volition, A, B, and D fit together and start to form a pattern, and it is almost impossible for the biographer not to start searching for C. Something turns up that looks remarkably like C, and with a little trimming of the edges and the ignoring of one very slight discrepancy it will fill the place allotted for C magnificently.

It is at this point that the biographer ought to take a deep breath and sit on his hands until he has had time to calm down. He has no real, fundamental reason to believe that his discovery is C, except for the fact that he wants it to be. He is like a man looking for a missing piece in a difficult jigsaw puzzle, who has found one so nearly the right shape that he cannot resist the desire to jam it into place.

If the biographer had refused to be tempted by his supposed discovery of C and had gone on with his research, he might have found not only the connecting, illuminating fact he needed but much more besides. He is not going to look for it now. Desire has blocked the way. And by so much his biography will fall short of what might have been the truth.

It would not be accurate to say that a biographer should be wholly lacking in desire. Curiosity is a form of desire. So is the final wish to get the material down on paper in a form that will be fair to the reader's interest and worthy of the subject. But a subconscious desire to push the facts around is one of the most dangerous things a biographer can encounter, and all the more dangerous because it is so difficult to know when he is encountering it.

The reason Alice had so much trouble with her flamingo is that the average flamingo does not wish to be used as a croquet mallet. It has other purposes in view. The same thing is true of a fact, which can be just as self-willed as a flamingo and has its own kind of stubborn integrity. To try to force a series of facts into a previously desired arrangement is a form of misuse to which no self-respecting fact will willingly submit itself. The best and only way to treat it is to leave it alone and be willing to follow where it leads, rather than to press your own wishes upon it.

To put the whole thing into a single sentence: you will never succeed in getting at the truth if you think you know, ahead of time, what the truth ought to be.

Philip Toynbee

* Nevertheless, the situation of the biographer whose material has already been collected—by himself or by someone else—is very like that of the novelist whose material has at last been chosen. For each, now, it is a matter of selecting this, rejecting that; putting this here, and then there instead. The pattern-making mind is now at work, creating a new order and a new truth. That the biographer is dealing with discovered material, the novelist with invented material, no longer matters to either of them. The biographer has begun to invent by the act of selection and arrangement; the novelist has begun to discover by the controlling logic of his previously invented material. Both are inventing their pattern; both, as they write, are writing out of their own experience and nobody else's. In fact, the more one uses those words 'discovery' and 'invention' the more interchangeable they seem to become.

But we are more often concerned with books than with the process of creating them, and when we examine the finished products, biography and novel, it seems that the initial distinction between them has become so remote as to be scarcely perceptible. Examine them first in the most literal way; look at them with the eyes and feel them with the hands. Each is within two covers; each consists of a certain number of pages, bound together; each has a beginning and an end. Imagine a savage who has never seen a book before, and imagine his reaction if he were told that this book, holding up a biography in a purple cover, is more 'like life' than that green-backed novel over there. He would

* From 'Novel and Memoir', *Nimbus*, II (Autumn 1954), 21–22. Reprinted by permission of the author.

spit, or laugh, and he would be quite right to do so. No book is like life at all, and it is only in a sense far more metaphorical than we usually recognize that one book can be said to *correspond* to real life more than another. It is worth remembering, from time to time, that *War and Peace* is much more 'like' a railway timetable than either are like life. In fact the printed numerals of the timetable are no more and no less like a real train than the printed words about Prince Andrew are like a real man.

Think for a moment, of the most renowned biography in our language—of Boswell's *Life of Johnson.* As we read that book we transmute what we are reading into the steadily solidifying image of a real man—but always into an image, never into a man. And an image is almost as unlike a man as is a book itself; in fact a book, the physical object, can at least be seen, felt, smelt and tasted like a man, while none of these things can be done to an image. For one thing Boswell's Johnson has a beginning and an end. There are many pages in between them, but even if there were a million more this figure would still be constricted as the real Johnson was never constricted. True the real Johnson was born and he died, but at every second of his life he was, as we all are, infinite, unseizable, imponderable. He had no edges.

And if we had no other references to Dr. Johnson, nothing would prevent us from supposing that Boswell had ingeniously *invented* his subject, out of thin air. Just as if Proust's Baron Charlus appeared constantly in contemporary memoirs and letters, we would have to accept that he had once lived. It is true that we react differently to a character in a book if we believe that some equivalent to him had once breathed and talked and suffered, but there is no real difference in kind between the subject of a biography and the hero of a novel. Both, by their artificial constriction, differ violently from the living people we know.

Whether he means to do so or not, Boswell implies that what he has written is all that there is of Johnson. We know otherwise: we have seen, for example, from Johnson's letters that there is a Johnson's Johnson who is very different from the hero of Boswell. He is no more 'like' the real Johnson, but to read about him reminds us that the real Johnson was not like anything at all which appears between the covers of a book.

What I am feeling here is that the act of writing about a real person, whether in a biography, in a memoir or in a work of history, instantly deprives him of many dimensions, instantly transforms him through print into a limited image. . . .

Sir Harold Nicolson

*[*The Oxford English Dictionary* defines Biography as 'the history of the lives of individual men, as a branch of literature'. This excellent definition contains within itself the three principles that any serious biographer should observe. A biography must be 'history', in the sense that it must be accurate and depict a person in relation to his times. It must describe an 'individual', with all the gradations of human character, and not merely present a type of virtue or of vice. And it must be composed as 'a branch of literature', in that it must be written in grammatical English and with an adequate feeling for style.

A biography combining all these three principles can be classed as a 'pure' biography: a biography that violates any one of these principles, or combines them in incorrect proportions, must be classed as an 'impure' biography. A pure biography is written with no purpose other than that of conveying to the reader an authentic portrait of the individual whose life is being narrated. A biography is rendered impure when some extraneous purpose intrudes to distort the accuracy of presentation.

Thus Voltaire's *Histoire de Charles XII*, although written and composed with consummate mastery, is not a 'pure' biography, in that it does not depict an individual character in relation to the background of the times. Carlyle's *Life of John Sterling*, although from the literary

* From 'The Practice of Biography', originally published in *The American Scholar*, Spring 1954, pp. 153–61; reprinted in *The English Sense of Humour* (1956), pp. 147–59. Included by permission of the author and publishers.

point of view his most attractive work is 'impure' biography, since it is not very precise, not a true portrait, and written with a purpose other than that of the direct delineation of an individual. Walton's *Lives* are without question masterpieces of English prose; but they sin against the principles of biography, since Walton is not describing human beings, but types of the particular form of quietism that he himself regards as desirable. Many biographies, on the other hand, are perfectly historical, really do paint, even if with clumsy strokes, the portrait of an individual, but are so badly written that they cannot for one instant qualify as literature. A biography therefore which does not combine all three of these fundamental principles must be defined as impure.

The development of the art throughout the ages shows us how ancient and how recurrent are these 'extraneous purposes' by which the purity of biography is infected. There is no better method of isolating the principles of pure biography than to trace the sources of these infections.

II

The original cause of all biography was the desire to commemorate the illustrious dead. A leader dies: his tribe or family feel that some strength has passed from them: they seek to perpetuate his magic by a monument. Cairns and monoliths arise; we have the regal sites of mighty pyramids; men scale the precipices and engrave a cenotaph upon the rocks of Bisitun; epics and sagas sing the legends of tribal heroes; the wrath of Achilles is rendered immortal and to this day men read with elation of the endurance and resource of Ithacan Odysseus; Balder and Beowulf come to swell the paean; the whole world echoes with the praise of famous men. With this epic strain there mingle elegies and laments. Widow-biographies are an early phenomenon; to the *Complaint of Deor* we add *The Wife's Complaint*. This commemorative instinct is bad for pure biography, since it leads the commemorator to concentrate solely upon the strength and virtue of his hero and to omit all weakness or shadow. Endemic, and sometimes epidemic, is this passion for commemoration; it has infected biography throughout the centuries.

The impulse is not primitive only; it operates to this day. It is but natural that when a great man dies his family should desire that his life should be written in such a manner as to emphasise his nobility and to hide his faults. Even the most enlightened survivors are inclined to entrust the biography of their dead chief, not to an outsider who may take too objective a view of his subject, but to some inexpert, but loyal, member of the family, who can be trusted to suppress all unfavourable truth. Occasionally the widow herself undertakes the task, sometimes with results as fantastic as those of Lady Burton's biography of her erratic but gifted husband. Even when an honest outsider is commissioned, he may be precluded from outspokenness by a laudable desire not to wound the susceptibilities of those to whom he is obliged. An even more curious and subtle effect of such family-inspired biographies is that the author may become influenced by the petty grievances or animosities cherished by the hero or his widow in their later years; instead of creating an impression of greatness he creates an impression of smallness. A classic instance of this unintentional diminution of a hero's character is provided by General Sir C. Callwell's *Life and Letters of Sir Henry Wilson*: there have been others since. The commemorative instinct assuredly operates in devious ways; but it is always perilous to pure biography.

A second extraneous purpose is the didactic purpose. People have always been tempted to take the lives of individual men as examples of virtue, or as cautionary tales indicative of the ill-effects of self-indulgence or ambition. Plutarch himself, the father of biography, admitted that he chose his characters as types of certain virtues and vices and as examples for emulation or avoidance by the young. Yet Plutarch happened to be a natural biographer, in that he was passionately interested in the way that individuals behaved; thus, although his lives of Anthony or Alcibiades, for instance, were intended to be cautionary tales, he soon forgot his didactic purpose in the fascination exercised upon his mind by the splendour of Anthony or the gaiety of Alcibiades. Flashes of admiration and delight illumine his pages, until both he and his readers forget entirely that an extraneous purpose of moral precept ever existed.

It is not so with other hagiographers. The lives of the saints and martyrs were not, it can be admitted, always intended to be historical accounts of individuals. Yet in more disguised form the didactic purpose continues to intrude upon biography; the desire to teach or preach, the desire to establish examples, the desire to illustrate some moral, theological, political, economic or social theory—all these irrelevant intentions infect biography with strong, and sometimes subtle, doses of impurity. The nineteenth-century biographers were most susceptible to the didactic temptation. 'The history of mankind', wrote Carlyle, 'is the history of its great men'. 'To find out these, clean the dirt from them, and to place them on their proper pedestal' appeared to him and his contemporaries a proper function of biography. This doctrine led to such impurities as *The Saintly Lives Series* in which, among other worthies, Lord Tennyson was portrayed, not as he was, but as the sort of Laureate that the author felt he ought to be. The reaction against the hagiography of the Victorians led to a development, valuable as a corrective, but, in its baser derivatives, damaging to the pure biographic stream. I refer to the introduction, by Froude and his successors and imitators, of the element of irony.

The satirical attitude of the biographer towards his subject may have come as a relief from the hagiography of the Victorians, but it can easily degenerate into false history and false psychology. Froude certainly provided a true picture of Mr. and Mrs. Carlyle; his portraits were condemned by his contemporaries as cynical, disloyal and in shocking bad taste. The influence of Samuel Butler came to transform Froude's attitude of negative scepticism into positive derision of conventional legends. Lytton Strachey, with his ironical titters, emerged as the deftest of iconoclasts; yet Strachey, who enjoyed paradox more than he respected precision, and who had little sense of history, exaggerated the lights and shadows of his portraits. His sketches were certainly vivid, personal and well written; but they were not 'history' in the sense that pure biography demands. In the hands of his imitators the manner of Strachey deteriorated so rapidly that it became an irritating habit of superciliousness. Philip Guedalla, with his trick of dramatic contrast, diminished the very real value of his writings by too great insistence on antithesis; his picture became distorted and out of focus.

Irony is, in any case, a dangerous tincture and one that should be applied only with a sable brush; when daubed by vigorous arms it becomes wearisome and even offensive. It is not merely that the reader is irritated by a biographer who implies in chapter after chapter that he is himself more enlightened, sensitive, or sincere than the hero whom he is describing. It is also that biography, if taken seriously, is an exacting task and not one that can be carried through with a sneer. The drudgery of collecting and checking material, the mechanical labour of completing a long book, require an effort more continuous than can be sustained by glimpses of self-satisfaction. The biographer must be constantly fortified by a fundamental respect, or affection, for the person whom he is describing; if all that he experiences is superficial contempt, his work will turn to ashes and his energy wilt and fail. No writer can persist for five hundred pages in being funny at the expense of someone who is dead.

There are other poisons, other temptations, to which this difficult art is liable. Biography is always a collaboration between the author and his subject; always there must be the reflection of one temperament in the mirror of another. The biographer should thus be careful not to permit his own personality to intrude too markedly upon the personality that he is describing; he should be wary of assigning his own opinions, prejudices or affections to the man or woman whose life he writes; he should take special pains to deal fairly with views which he does not share, or interests that bore him; his egoism should be muzzled and kept on a chain. He should constantly remind himself that it is not an autobiography that he is composing, but the life of someone else; the statue of Modesty should dominate his study, a finger on her lips.

A further temptation that may afflict the affable biographer is that of adding to his narrative the colours of fiction or romance. He may seek to convey reality by introducing imaginary conversations, or to brighten his pages by inserting really beautiful passages of scenic description:

'As their little cavalcade breasted the hill and emerged from the grove of umbrella pines (*pineus pinea*) that crowned its summit, the fair city lay before them, basking all amethyst in the fading light. The Palazzo Pubblico had already melted into the pink and azure shadows of the Piazza del Campo, but the Torre del Mangia soared upwards, straight as a tulip against the sunset sky. Galeazzo turned to his venerable companion. "Messir", he said . . ." '

Such passages fail to convince the attentive reader, who is aware that umbrella pines are but few at Siena and that the company at the moment were travelling west to east. The imagination, as well as the self-assertiveness, of the author must be held in check.

Such then are the instincts, poisons and temptations that render biography impure. An undue desire to commemorate, a too earnest endeavour to teach or preach, a tendency to portray types rather than individuals, the temptation to enhance self-esteem by indulging in irony, the inability to describe selflessly, and the urge to slide into fiction or to indulge in fine writing;—all these are the pests and parasites that gnaw the leaves of purity. Yet these are negative precepts, indicating the faults that should be eschewed. Are there any positive principles that can be recommended to the intending biographer?

III

It is self-evident that he should not select a subject outside the range of his sympathy or the area of his general knowledge. It would thus be a mistake for a man to embark upon a life of Pope if he were ill-attuned to the heroic couplet and disliked small stratagems. It would be a mistake to start writing a life of Anselm without some knowledge of Plato's doctrine of ideas, or to embark upon Erasmus when ignorant of the humanities. It would be foolish for an Englishman to venture on a biography of Calvin Coolidge, without having spent at least a year at Amherst and absorbed the indelible quality of that academy.

The ideal subject is one of which the author has direct personal experience and with which he can enter into sympathetic relationship. This raises the question whether it is in fact possible for any author—however skilled, courageous, or sincere—to write a 'pure' biography of a contemporary. It is clear that it will be of great advantage to him to have been personally acquainted with his hero and to have seen him, not only in his moments of public triumph or efficiency, but also in those interludes of lassitude, dyspepsia, or elation that reveal the character of a man. Important it is also to be able to visualize a person, not in the set postures of official busts or portraits, but in the more illuminating attitudes of ordinary life. It is valuable to be able to recall the manner in which he coughed or grunted, the exact shape of his smile or frown, the sound of his laughter, and above all the tone of his voice. We are all conscious that the personality of our acquaintances is conveyed to us, not merely by their physical appearance and expression, but also by their accent and intonation. It is illuminating to be told that Bismarck spoke with the piping notes of a schoolboy, that Napoleon, when angry, relapsed into the Corsican manner of speech, or that Tennyson when reciting his poems used the broad vowels of the Lincolnshire wold. It is valuable also for a biographer to be personally acquainted with the men and women who exercised an influence upon the life of his subject and to be able, by his own judgement, to assess their relative value. 'How strange', he will reflect, 'that my hero could ever for one moment have been taken in by such a charlatan as I know X to have been! How curious that he was never able to appreciate the shy wisdom, the fundamental integrity, of my dear friend Y!' This wider knowledge provides a system of triangulation, enabling the author to fix the position of his hero with greater accuracy than would ever be possible were he writing about people whom he had never personally known.

Such are the advantages—and they are immense—which the biographer enjoys when writing the life of a contemporary. The disadvantages are also apparent. He will be inhibited by his disinclination to offend the susceptibilities of survivors. It is not only that he will hesitate to wound the feelings of relations and friends; it is also that the enemies of his hero may still be living and will protest violently against any criticisms that may be made. To some extent he can evade this difficulty by refraining from expressing any personal opinion and relying solely upon the documents in the case. But the necessity of maintaining a certain level of taste, consideration, caution and kindliness, will certainly prevent him from revealing the truth in its most naked form.

Does this mean, I repeat, that it is impossible for an author to write a 'pure' biography of a contemporary? I do not think so. He will realize of course that, human nature being what it is, the reader of his book will pay more attention to those passages which reveal defects hitherto concealed, than to those which eulogize merits already familiar. The essential truth of any portrait depends upon the proper statement of relative values. A biographer should be aware that the 'startling revelation' is certain to startle, and will thus assume in the reader's mind and memory an importance out of proportion to the portrait as a whole. His revelations therefore should not be picked out in scarlet or orange but introduced in neutral tints. His aim should be, not to conceal defects or lamentable episodes, but to refer to them in such a manner as will indicate to the attentive reader that these shadows existed, without disconcerting the inattentive reader or wounding the legitimate feelings of surviving relations and friends. It is a question of tact and skill.

It has always interested me, when reading the biography of a person with whom I had been personally acquainted, to observe how the author deals with his faults. A device frequently adopted is to reveal the fault by denying its opposite. An extreme example of this method can be found in Sir Sidney Lee's biography of King Edward VII. Sir Sidney was an honest biographer, who desired to paint his portrait warts and all. I had often heard that King Edward was a voracious eater and that he was apt to pounce and gobble at the dishes placed before him. I wondered whether Sir Sidney would mention this genial characteristic and was impressed by the delicacy of his device. 'He had', wrote Sir Sidney, 'a splendid appetite at all times, and never toyed with his food'. It is by such ingenuity that the biographer is able to omit no detail and yet to cause no offence.

I should cite as an excellent example of the way in which an intelligent biographer can indicate defects without wounding feelings, Mr. Rupert Hart-Davis's biography of Sir Hugh Walpole. The attentive reader is made aware of all the lights and shadows in the character portrayed, whereas the inattentive reader is not for one moment startled or shocked. Every weakness of Walpole's character is abundantly illustrated, yet the resultant impression is that of a gifted and charming man. I recommend this work to all those who question whether it is possible to write a 'pure' biography of a contemporary figure. The artist has produced an authentic portrait owing to his sense of values; without such a sense, any biography is bound to be unconvincing.

IV

It is here that a natural gift of selection is so valuable. The aim is to convey the personality of some interesting individual to people or generations who never knew him when alive. It is not possible for a biographer, even if he take twenty years and volumes, to present the whole man to posterity. He can hope only, by intelligent and honest selection, to convey the impression of the aggregate of his hero's merits and defects. If he allows himself to deck his portrait with striking little snippets and tags, the unity of impression will be destroyed. His curiosity therefore must be moderated by selection and taste; he must preserve throughout a uniform tone; and he must try,—he must try very hard,—to arrange his facts in the right order.

'The value of every story', remarked Dr. Johnson, 'depends on its being true. A story is a picture, either of an individual, or of life in general. If it be false, it is a picture of nothing'. This precept should, I feel, be inscribed in lapidary letters on the fly-leaf of every biographer's note-book. A pure biography should furnish its readers with information, encouragement and comfort. It should provide, if I may again quote Dr. Johnson, 'the parallel circumstances and kindred images to which we readily conform our minds'. It should remind the reader that great men and women also have passed through phases of doubt, discouragement and self-abasement; that—perhaps on the very eve of their noblest achievements—they have been assailed with diffidence, or have resigned themselves to the fact that their vitality is ebbing, their zest has gone, their memory has become unreliable, and their will-power decayed. Without seeking for one moment to preach a lesson, a good biography encourages people to believe that man's mind is in truth unconquerable and that character can triumph over the most hostile circumstances, provided only that it remains true to itself. Amusing books can be written about ridiculous people; fiction and romance can be twined as honeysuckle around the silliest head; but I am convinced that a pure biography, if its effect is to be more than momentary, can only be written about a person whom the writer and the reader can fundamentally respect.

Does this imply a return to hagiography? No, it implies only that the intending biographer should be as cautious in his choice of subject as in the method he pursues.

Marchesa Iris Origo

* Most biographers of our own time, however—and certainly those dealing with public men—are more likely to complain of too much material than too little. Even Boswell, according to his diary, was so overwhelmed by the number of his notes, when he started to put them together, that he would sit in London coffee-houses with tears pouring down his cheeks; Virginia Woolf was hardly less dismayed by the number of Roger Fry's papers. And what must Franklin Roosevelt's biographer have felt, surveying the forty *tons* of documents at his disposal? We live in a historically-minded age, and I understand that a recent American statesman was even in the habit of having his telephone conversations recorded in large diaries.

Before such a plethora of material, even the most hardy biographer may well quail, especially if he ever realizes how many different ways there are in which his own subject, looking back, may himself have seen his story. 'A biography of B. B.', wrote Bernard Berenson only a few years before his death, 'could be written in many ways. The most fetching would be of the Horatio Alger type, the immigrant Jew boy from Poland who rises to influence and eminence. Fabulously exciting could be the recounting of the transition he witnessed from an almost neolithic civilization in Lithuania to the nuclear one of today. . . . The best and most rewarding account would be the story of his library, supplemented by the telling of how he acquired his works of art, how

* From 'Biography, True and False', *The Atlantic*, February 1959, pp. 38–42, as revised in *The Cornhill Magazine*, Centenary Number, Autumn 1960, pp. 379–94. Reprinted by permission of the author and the publishers.

he started his house and garden, and a psychological account of his marriage, his friends, his enemies, his enemy-friends'. And this list does not even mention the aspect which to many would seem the most significant—the passionate sightseer and art-historian who was, in the words of one of his admirers, 'the most sensitive precision-instrument that has ever been applied to the study of Italian art'.

Every biography, then, whether it admits it or not, is based on a process of selection—and here at once new problems arise. Is it possible to choose without becoming biased, to reject without falsifying? Most writers are familiar with the seductive tricks of the trade; the slight juggling with dates, the suppression of inconvenient letters or of remarks that are out of character or merely flat—the placing of a telling conversation or document where it is most effective, the smoothing out and the touching up. In the end a portrait is built up: slick, vivid, convincing—and false.

There are also, of course, the mistakes of sheer ignorance. I am thinking at the moment of one of my own, which was kindly pointed out to me in a letter from Rebecca West. I had mentioned, as an example of Mrs. Carlyle's touchiness, the disastrous Christmas party at The Grange at which Lady Ashburton presented her, from the Christmas tree, with a silk dress, after which Jane retired to her bedroom in tears. I thought she had made a good deal of unnecessary fuss—or, rather, that she had used this pretext to express a deeper resentment against her hostess. Rebecca West, however, pointed out my mistake. Her grand-aunt Isabella Campbell, who belonged to the Carlyle period, had often spoken of the episode, and had considered it 'a most extraordinary thing for Lady Ashburton to have done, as a silk dress was the recognized present for a housekeeper, and a friend of the family would have felt bewildered at receiving it. To wear a dress which one had not ordered from the start and had fitted according to one's own measures was a sign of social inferiority'. Plainly, therefore, on this occasion Jane was right to be offended, and I did not know what I was talking about. I still think, however, that Mrs. Carlyle was glad of so good an excuse to resent the behaviour of the woman whom her husband described as having 'the soul of a princess and a captainess', and whom he considered, which was worse, as witty as herself.

One way of guarding oneself against making too many such mistakes, is to write only about those times and places with which one feels an instinctive affinity. Most of us have some natural habitat in the past, and the failure, for instance, of Strachey's *Elizabeth and Essex* is probably due to the fact that he had strayed too far from his. In literature as in life, it is not profitable to force one's affections. Just as, in a conversation, there is sometimes an undercurrent of feeling, a secondary silent conversation, going on, in which the real exchange of feelings takes place, so in writing there should be a rich background of unstated knowledge, a tapestry that is never unrolled. We must know more, a great deal more, than what we tell. Two biographies, though extremely dissimilar, occur to me as instances: David Cecil's *Lord M.* and Sandburg's *Abraham Lincoln*. Both are good books, because both writers were well acquainted, long before they began to write, with the worlds that they describe: that of the families of 'the Great Whiggery', and that of the prairies of Knox County in Illinois. No amount of painstaking research can take the place of the sixth sense granted, even after a long lapse of time, to writers who have been at home in precisely the same world as their subject; it is only they who can distinguish a phrase subsequently invented from one really spoken, a likely gesture from an unlikely one. They know, long before being told, how their subject moved, spoke, ate; what their neighbours spoke about, and what they saw, on looking out of the window in the morning.

In this, indeed, the biographer somewhat resembles the translator, for a translation, too, is only possible where one is entirely familiar with the setting. I remember, for instance, once reading a rendering of Leopardi's *Sabato del Villaggio* in which the '*fascio d'erba*', the bundle of grass, which the girl in the poem is carrying, is translated as 'a truss of hay'. The image brought to mind is one of green hayfields and waggons and pitchforks and buxom country girls—an Austrian scene or an English. But there are no hayfields near Recanati. There are only steep, dun-coloured hills on which olive-trees grow, with wheat beneath them and perhaps a few vines, and by the edge of the road there are sometimes tufts of grass, of which town-dwellers cut an armful, to feed their rabbits. This was the bundle of grass brought home by Leopardi's '*donzelletta*'. A single misleading sentence—written not because the translator did not know Italian, but because he did not know Leopardi's birthplace—conjured up a whole non-existent world.

* * *

Three insidious temptations assail the biographer: to suppress, to invent, and to sit in judgement—and of these the earliest and most frequent is suppression. In the Middle Ages, indeed, it was rendered inevitable by the purpose which biography was intended to fulfil—to produce a noble example. The medieval view of history was that of a drama enacted within an established pattern—God's pattern for mankind. The lives of the men who came nearest to conforming with this pattern were related as an example to other, lesser men—and consequently a disproportionate number of early medieval biographies were concerned with the lives of saints, while others were about rulers or leaders rather larger than life-size. There was little attempt at psychological interpretation; the emphasis was on the saint's virtues or the prince's exploits. All that was unedifying was omitted. . . .

One of the most interesting examples of deliberate suppression appears in what, nevertheless, is still one of the great biographies in the English language, Mrs. Gaskell's *Life of Charlotte Brontë*. Mrs. Gaskell, who was herself a friend of Charlotte's (though not an intimate one) knew precisely what she intended to do. 'I weighed every line', she wrote, 'with my whole power and heart, so that every line should go to its great purpose of making her known and valued as one who had gone through such a terrible life with a brave and faithful heart'. In order, however, to achieve this admirable purpose, she did not hesitate to suppress, in Charlotte's letters, whatever revealed the intolerant, governessy element in her character, or the wild strain of passion in her youthful feelings for Ellen Nussey, in which her devotion to her friend was intensified by their shared religious aspirations. 'I am trembling all over with excitement', wrote Charlotte, 'after reading your note: . . . I have glimpses of Holy, inexpressible things'. And in another letter she played with the idea of living alone with Ellen in a cottage, 'where we could live and love until Death'.

These are the banked-down fires which burst into flame when Charlotte fell in love with the head of her school in Brussels, Constantin Héger—a Catholic and a married man. Without such passion we should not have had *Villette* or *Jane Eyre*. But four of Charlotte's letters to M. Héger—though Mrs. Gaskell undoubtedly saw them—were suppressed. 'Your last letter', Charlotte wrote to him, 'was stay and prop to me for half a year. When day by day I await a letter and when day by day disappointment comes . . . the fever takes me—I lose appetite and sleep and pine away.' But never does Mrs. Gaskell's *Life* suggest that M. Héger was anything more to Charlotte than a kind and stimulating teacher, nor that her increasing estrangement from Madame Héger was caused by anything but 'the English Protestant's dislike of Romanism'. And yet, nearly half a century after the publication of her book, Mrs. Gaskell wrote to a friend, 'I did so long to tell the truth, and I believe *now* that I hit as near to the truth as anyone *could*'. And she added, 'One comfort is that God knows the truth'. The strange thing is that, even now that we are aware of her suppressions and inexactitudes, we still feel that it *was* the truth that Mrs. Gaskell was seeking, and that her book comes nearer to the heart of the matter than the later works which show up its deficiencies.

There is, however, an even more serious temptation for the biographer than suppression, and that is sheer invention. An excellent instance is the one quoted by Professor Trevor-Roper in a somewhat merciless attack on Lytton Strachey: the length of Dr. Arnold's legs. Strachey had formed a very clear image of Dr. Arnold in his mind: he saw him as a noble, pompous figure, and—to introduce just the right additional touch of absurdity, of debunking—it was necessary that his legs should have been too short. Unfortunately, however, as Strachey himself once admitted to a friend, there is absolutely no evidence to show that Dr. Arnold's legs were shorter in proportion to his body than any other man's.

Now the danger of this kind of invention is that, once discovered, it shakes our capacity to believe anything that its inventor has said. 'Suppose we believe one half of what he tells', suggested Lord Mansfield to Boswell, about an acquaintance whose stories 'were unhappily found to be very fabulous'. 'Ay', Dr. Johnson later remarked, 'but we don't know *which* half to believe. By his lying we lose not only our reverence for him, but all comfort in his conversation'.

In the case of Lytton Strachey, we lose a good deal by losing this comfortable sense of faith. If Dr. Arnold's legs were not short, we say to ourselves, perhaps other diverting details were also false. Perhaps General Gordon did not retire into his tent with a Bible and a brandy bottle? (This indeed was a distortion of a passage in Chaillé-Long's Memoirs: Gordon merely took his prayer-book with him.) Perhaps Florence Nightingale did not, in childhood, put her dog's broken paw into a splint? Yet if, owing to our irritation about all this, we were not to read Strachey's *Queen Victoria*, we should miss a very good book.

Strachey himself stated that a biographer's equipment consists in three qualities—'a capacity for absorbing facts, a capacity for stating them, and a point of view'. The definition is a good one, for without a point of view no history can be written—but there is also a danger that it may not only shape, but distort the facts. The biographer who puts his wit above his subject will end by writing about one person only—himself. My personal complaint about *Eminent Victorians* would not be that it is inaccurate, but that it is thin, and that its thinness springs from condescension. If you wish to see a person, you must not start by seeing *through* him. Another instance of this occurs in the first sentence of a most interesting and conscientious biography—Harold Nicolson's *Tennyson*. 'We smile today at our Victorians', it begins, 'not confidently, as of old, but with a shade of hesitation: a note of perplexity, a note of anger sometimes, a note often of wistfulness, has come to mingle with our laughter'.

The fatal words are, of course, the first ones: 'We smile today'. The biographer has started by putting up a barrier—and even if, in the next few words, he suggests that it is beginning to crumble, he is still writing from the other side. He has, in short, succumbed to yet another of the biographer's temptations: the desire to sit in judgement. 'To penetrate', wrote the great French historian, Marc Bloch, 'into the unknown being of a man separated from us by a long stretch of generations, one must almost cast off one's own self. To tell him what one thinks of him, one need only remain oneself. The effort is undeniably less strenuous'.

Every work of art, of course, implies a previous process of assessment, and the judgement of character still remains the central problem of biography. But in so far as a biographer is also a historian, he should, I think, be very careful not to drown his subject's voice with his own. One peculiar function of biography is to show history as it was to the participant, to observe, for a moment, *das Gewordene als Werdendes*—what has come to pass, while it is occurring. Through the individual peephole of the man whose life we are describing, we can see history in the course of being lived. In one sense, all organized histories are unsatisfactory, because they are written with what in Italy is called *il senno del poi*, the wisdom of the future. But in individual lives we can seize, if nothing else, a most vivid sense of actuality: it is a pity to blur it.

Besides, our own judgements are surely not immune from change.

We will not, at the age of fifty, judge a man in the same way as we would have done at twenty-five. Two years before his death, Dr. Johnson asserted that he was 'ready now to call a man *a good man*', on much easier terms than formerly. With the passing of the years, the muscles of moral indignation sometimes begin to sag, the voice diminishes its harshness, and this is true even in the field of abstract thought. I remember asking Mr. Santayana, in his old age—when he was preparing an abridged edition of the great work of his youth, *The Life of Reason*—whether there were many things that he would now like to change. 'No', he gently replied, 'I feel I have much the same things to say—but I wish to say them in a different tone of voice.' . . .

To Virginia Woolf the central problem of biography was how to weld 'into one seamless whole' the 'granite-like solidity' of truth and 'the rainbow-like intangibility' of personality. It is, surely, impossible —but few writers have come closer to it than she did. The problem was one that fascinated her—not only in literature, but in life. 'Go on, this is enthralling', she would say, when her friends brought her an exciting piece of gossip. 'I feel as if a buried statue were being dug up piece by piece'. One of her friends once told me that, on a cold November evening, as he was making his way to her house, he came upon Virginia Woolf standing in the fog beside an apple-barrow, and asking the old apple-woman, in her deep, throaty, compelling voice: 'Tell me, what does it *feel* like to stand here in the fog on a dark evening selling apples?' I cannot vouch for the truth of this story, but certainly the question was one she often asked. 'What does it feel like', she would say to me, 'to wake up in the morning on a Tuscan farm?' And once I heard her say, perhaps not wholly without malice, to a disconcerted young peer: 'Tell me, what does it feel like to be a lord?'

Yet when, in her later years, she came to write a life of Roger Fry, who had been one of her closest friends, the book was curiously less vivid, more conventional, than the etchings in her essays. She found, indeed, the sheer effort of putting together the material for a full biography almost unbearably tedious. 'Donkey work', she recorded in *A Writer's Diary*, 'sober drudgery, appalling grind'. And when at last the book was finished, there was a most revealing final note: 'What a curious relation is mine with Roger at this moment—I who have given him a kind of shape after his death. Was he like that? I feel very much in his presence at the moment, as if I were intimately connected with him: as if we together had given birth to this vision of him;

a child born of us. Yet he had no power to alter it. And yet for some years it will represent him.'

* * *

Is biography, then, worth attempting at all? Where there are so many snares, would we do better to be silent? I think not. Many critics would deny to any biographical portrait the essential reality, the truth that is truer than truth, of the novelist's or dramatist's characters. Virginia Woolf herself did so, and more recently Olivia Manning, in an article on the future of the novel, has compared what she calls the flatness of Strachey's Queen Victoria with the rounded portrait of Madame Bovary. She scornfully attributes the present popularity of biography to 'a middlebrow snobbishness'—an extension of the prejudice against novels which already existed in Jane Austen's time—and considers its appeal to lie in precisely the limitations that it places on the writer's imagination.

I do not think that this is necessarily true. The biographer has, of course, a fixed pattern: he is, as Desmond MacCarthy once said, 'an artist upon oath'. But the calls upon his imagination and intuition are hardly less exacting. The novelist and dramatist, after all, do not create their characters in a void, but out of their experience or intuition. Shakespeare himself invented hardly any of his plots, but—having accepted a ready-made pattern for his characters' actions—was then free to give his whole attention to bringing them to life. And so surely, too, the biographer's true function—the transmission of personality—may also be, without its own pattern, an act of creation—giving shape, in Virginia Woolf's phrase, to a man after his death, and endowing him with what is, when we come to think of it, a very odd form of immortality. For of many great men of the past we know *only* what their biographers or portrait-painters saw. . . .

'The true history of the human race', wrote E. M. Forster in a recent article, 'is the story of human affections. In comparison with it all other histories—even economic history—are false.' He goes on to say that, owing to its reticent nature, it can never be written down completely, and this of course is true. Yet what little we do know of this aspect of history has come to us through biography or autobiography—what men have told us of themselves, or what others have set down about them.

The biographer who works with this material is dealing with what is both most complicated and most simple, most intense and yet most intermittent—the human heart. Every individual life is also the story of Everyman, and while it is the biographer's business to describe the passions, foibles and idiosyncrasies which make his subject a *person*, his work will be very thin if these individual traits are not also seen as part of a universal drama. 'A man's life of any worth', said Keats, 'is a continual allegory, and very few eyes can see the Mystery.'

Personally I do not think of truth as being made of granite, but rather as a note in music—a note which we instantly recognize as the right one, as soon as it is struck. Proust, who cultivated the art of memory as perhaps no one else has ever done, describes in a famous passage in *Du côté de chez Swann* how in later life he was sometimes able to hear again certain sounds which, he wrote, 'in reality had never stopped'; the sobs which had shaken him at a certain crucial moment of his childhood. 'It is only because life is now growing silent about me,' he wrote, 'that I hear them afresh, like convent bells which one might believe were not rung nowadays, because during the day they are drowned by the city hubbub, but which may be heard clearly enough in the stillness of the evening.'

The biographer who has acquired a similar sensitiveness to the continuity of emotion may realize at certain moments, when life is silent about him, that he has become aware of something about his subject for which he could not give chapter and verse, but which he knows to be true. For all genuine emotion leaves behind it an eternal reverberation. Whether it is always possible to hear or to reproduce it, is another matter, unless a writer has at his disposal such material as Keats' *Letters*—and even then, even then . . . But certainly even the faintest echo can only be heard by temporarily casting aside, as Bloch advised, one's own self and one's own opinions. For this reason I would say to the young biographer, who has upon his desk his first, intriguing file of papers, to examine them, if he can, with an almost blank mind: to let them produce their own effect. Later on, the time will come to compare, to sift and to draw conclusions; but first he should listen without interrupting. Sometimes then, as he deciphers the faded ink, a phrase will stand out which reveals the hand that wrote it. He may see, as suddenly as, at the turn of a passage, one comes upon one's own image in a mirror, a living face. Then, in this fleeting moment, he may perhaps reach a faint apprehension—as near to the truth as we are ever likely to get—of what another man was like.

C. V. Wedgwood

* The connexion between art and truth, that is the apprehension of truth and its communication by means of art, is the central problem of every writer and of every creative artist. All writers are confronted with it, and take their own ways to solve it with greater or lesser success. Many writers have committed themselves to opinions about it in private letters or public statements which in their turn become the subject of further analysis and discussion by ensuing generations of writers and critics. 'Art and Reality' was the subject chosen by Joyce Cary for his Clark lectures, the subject on which he concentrated his thoughts during his last illness, leaving behind him what is, at present, the last important statement to be made on this subject by an English writer. It will remain an important statement, though it will not long remain the last one, for the subject is inexhaustible. It presents questions which are of the utmost importance to the practising writer, and of scarcely less interest to the practising reader, that is the reader who takes his reading seriously and finds his pleasure enhanced by the sharpening of his critical faculties.

While it is true that the greatest art is to conceal art, and few admire writers who allow the mechanism behind their achievement to become visible, it is equally true that some appreciation of the technical skill of the artist deepens and enriches our pleasure. At the first impact of a beautiful poem or a great work of art we do not want to divert our

* From 'Art, Truth and History', *The London Magazine*, May 1959, pp. 37–39, 44–46; reprinted in *Truth and Opinion*. London: Collins, 1960. Included by permission of the author and William Collins Sons & Co. Ltd.

minds by considering the ingenuity of vocabulary, the sensibility of hearing, the subtlety in the association of ideas which have brought together certain effects of sound, and stimulated certain trains of thought to create in us a spontaneous reaction of delight; so with a great picture we do not want consciously to notice at the first instant the deliberate touches by which the balance and harmony of line and colour have been produced; but—there is no doubt—that at a second and third examination these things enhance our pleasure, because by recognizing the details of craftsmanship we make ourselves at second-hand partners in the act of creation whose results we admire. Moreover, apart from this subtle self-flattery in which all critical readers secretly indulge, the education of the ear, the mind, the eye to detect and value the finer points does actually enhance the initial impact that a work of art has on us, because we are enabled to react more quickly and more fully to the writer's or the painter's intention.

The subject is infinite. But I must ask you to turn away from its more exalted peaks, because my subject is not Art and Truth *alone*; here is History tagging on at the end. For the historian, the relationship of art to truth is a particularly exacting one; it may even seem rather a narrow one. What more is there to be said but that the historian has to tell the truth? At least that is ideally what he is supposed to do, and some would say that art does not come into it at all. But art *does* come into it, for within the limitations of our human condition, truth is not apprehensible without the help of art, since it cannot be communicated to another person without the help of art. To pass on any piece of information intelligibly requires a feat in the arrangement of words and ideas. Some have argued that art comes in at an earlier stage, before that of communication. Simply to apprehend a fact intelligently and intelligibly requires a degree of art.

Benedetto Croce has equated art with intuition and argued that we cannot *know* anything until we have given it a name, that is—formalized it in our minds, and that this formalization, or naming is essentially a creative art. His English disciple the philosopher and historian Collingwood said that an historic fact only has meaning for us, in so far as we can re-think the thought that created it. The historian, according to Collingwood, has to make the creative act himself in the first place in his own mind. On the intensity with which he can make it depends the depth of his understanding of it. That is the first move: the first creative act. Only afterwards comes the second creative act of communication. On the skill with which he can communicate his thought depends his power to convey the meaning to others. They are two separate things and there is art in both.

This is not really any different from the processes of thought of any writer dealing with reality. It is what happens with the novelist or at least with those who deal in life as it is: not of course with the writers whose quality is a heightened imaginative power, the allegorical or the romantic, who illuminate life by lifting it into another atmosphere. But the creative writer, the novelist who aims at giving us life as it is, faces the same problem as the historian—the problem of reading the meaning of an incident and conveying it to the reader. . . .

The historian has to do very much the same thing, with this difference: that the novelist is free to adapt and invent provided that the material is that of authentic and living experience. The historian, on the other hand, is dealing with events which once occurred independently of him and which he seeks to describe, or, if he is a pioneer, to re-establish accurately. But although everything about which the historian writes had at one time a separate existence in itself, it exists for him in the present only as he is able to re-think it. Thus the quality of our understanding of the past depends on the quality of understanding its interpreters have brought to it. . . .

The good historian whatever his theme must be an artist. Without art there may be accumulations of statements, there may be calendars or chronicles, but there is no history.

This then is what I want to emphasize about art and history: that any way of thinking about, or looking at, historical facts, which has any value at all, must be an exercise of the imaginative and discriminating faculties; History in any intelligible form *is art*.

But if history is *art*, in what way does the historian's attitude to art and truth differ from that of the essentially imaginative writers? The answer is, of course: very profoundly. It is the privilege and indeed the function of the creative artist to use—that is to manipulate and to intensify the truth about life as he sees it. The bare truth is not enough in itself. 'Realism by itself is fatal', said Turgenev, and, in another passage on the same subject 'Truth is the air without which we cannot breathe, but art is a plant, sometimes even a rather fantastic one, which grows and develops in this air.' It is self evident that these are two statements that no historian should make, or even think. Realism is fatal? but the historian laboriously strives after the whole unvarnished truth. 'Art is a plant, sometimes a fantastic one'—but the pedestrian historian cannot allow anything fantastic, except of course when the vagaries of human nature do really—as they sometimes do—produce a fantastic effect.

The letters and commonplace books of writers are full of indications of the way in which experiences and incidents from life can be and *must* be adapted, expounded, telescoped, or amalgamated to make novels and stories, to make *literature*. Henry James evolves a situation from a fragment of conversation overheard at a tea party; Joyce Cary describes the face of a woman seen on a boat-trip, a visual memory, which was later vitalized by the fragment of a half-heard anecdote and from which grew a story which was only very tenuously related to the chances which inspired it.

The work of creative imagination is *controlled* by experience; it has to spring from knowledge and understanding of life, but the writer is free to use and reject what he wants, to present a heightened or simplified picture; he is not subservient to the facts he has accumulated or the observations he has made. They are his material to be freely used as his art directs, and he can invent or discard as it suits him.

The historian cannot do so. He can only use what he has before him. He cannot invent and—this may be even more difficult—he cannot reject except within very cautious limits. The novelist—and this goes for the historical novelist too—can reject those parts of the material which for one reason or another seem to add nothing to what he wishes to project. Indeed selection of essentials is an important part of his art. The historian can only select in a much more limited manner; naturally he *does* select and reject because everything cannot be included in an intelligible book. There must be some theme or theory, and there must be some parts of the historical material which are adjudged not relevant. But over-selection, over-simplification are major causes of misrepresentation in history, and the historian cannot ask with the novelist: does this fact add anything to the pattern of my novel as I see it? to the projection of this character or this situation as I intend it? He has to ask: does this fact add anything to my knowledge and understanding of this incident, of this situation, of this epoch? And he must be very sure indeed that it adds nothing before he decides to pass it over.

The historian has to decide whether an apparently irrelevant fact is truly irrelevant. He also has to find a place for the awkward fact which does not fit with the pattern of development or the scheme of events as he had at first seen it. This is often a strain on his patience and his conscience. He has to find a place for new evidence which will make sense with the existing evidence whether or not it fits in with his own theories. If his theory is destroyed by new evidence, he must abandon it and start again. It is never safe and it is usually impossible to insert new material into the texture of an older theory. The attempt to do so produces a result like that picture of the Gerbier family which was begun by Rubens during his visit to England in 1630. Gerbier was an engraver, a go-between in the traffic in works of art, who was under the patronage of Charles I. He had a handsome wife and a family of pretty, plump children whom Rubens painted when he was staying in their house. But the lady was very fruitful, and had many more children later; so pieces were attached to the canvas at one side and additional little Gerbiers, not by Rubens, were introduced. The effect is very strange, not only because the picture has an extra foot or two that do not fit, but because the original fluid and beautifully placed composition by Rubens has been thrown out of balance.

New material, new evidence, additional historical facts are very like the little Gerbiers. They cannot just be added on. A new picture has to be painted, a new composition thought out, which will include all the children, or all the facts, in a newly thought-out relationship to each other. That is one reason why history is constantly being rewritten.

Hester W. Chapman

* Critics seldom differentiate between historical and literary biography. Yet the irregular and baffling limitations of the first and more difficult art—the sudden lack of material at some points, the embarrassing profusion of detail at others—set it apart, and call for a technique not required by the second, where gaps may be filled with extracts from or analyses of the subject's writings that sometimes result in new and valuable conclusions. The historical biographer has fewer outside resources; when his information fails he must manufacture stepping-stones for the reader, so that together they move from one aspect or climax to another, resuming the story as if no *lacunae* existed.

These stepping-stones are so hard to make that some historical biographers do not attempt to provide them, and force the reader to jump over the gaps; others fling down a shaky and conjectural interpolation on which he may not care to venture. 'Here', this kind of biographer says, 'the curtain falls. We know nothing of Armand de Tel-Quel until, in a smouldering dawn of July 1791, the tumbrils were rolling towards what is now known as the Place de la Concorde'. And if he is lazy and conceited enough, he will add guesses about his subject's thoughts and feelings, thus increasing the reader's discomfort. It is easy to mock the makeshifts to which a biographer may be reduced. Starting freely and well equipped, his position can become that of a prisoner in Little Ease. He wants, or has been urged, or is commissioned, to write the

* 'Notes on Historical Biography', *Times Literary Supplement*, 28 August 1959, p. 498. Reprinted by permission of the author.

life of a person about whom nothing is known during certain times. (He may not realize how much that lack of information will affect him until he reaches these particular points.) Is he to abandon his cherished subject altogether, or fall back on imaginative guess-work, or frankly confess his inability to proceed in a smooth and seemly manner? None of these solutions is attractive. There is, however, a fourth, one that might be described as the concealed bridge, across which the author conducts the reader so swiftly that the gulf is passed almost without awareness. It is set up by a short passage, in which the necessary dates are attached to some condensed background information which will be used again and which is personally relevant to the subject. (The reader must not be reminded that there is no information about the principal figure.) This short passage should merge with the paragraph in which the subject reappears. Thus the reader is given the impression of an active hero or heroine and of a continuous narrative. Not until the biography is finished, perhaps not even then, does he realize that a number of years has not been accounted for, and that he has been tactfully, and legitimately, deceived.

There are cases where darkness extends over such a long period—that of the subject's childhood is often without any material at all—that the biographer cannot construct a concealed bridge, because the gap is too wide. He is then obliged to lead the reader into the background, giving not a conjectural account of the principal figure but of the kind of existence such persons were accustomed to lead. In theory, this trick vexes and bores the reader; a skilled and cunning biographer may succeed with it, but he must not explain what he is doing. If he says, 'No doubt this was how the youthful Duchess spent her day', the reader will begin to mistrust him. 'Must have been', 'It is probable that' or—most dangerous of all—'we can imagine' are phrases that should be avoided.

It would be pedantic to follow these suggestions to their limits; if all biographers had done so, the lives of a great many remarkable people would never have been written—Sir Walter Raleigh's, for instance. It seems that there are no personal records, anecdotes or letters from or about him until he reached his twenties; the full flow of a vast quantity of material begins even later when, according to the standards of his own day, he was middle-aged. The result is that no satisfactory life of this arch-typal Elizabethan exists. They all have to start in the middle and are therefore mis-shapen: it cannot be otherwise.

Yet there may be a solution to this particular problem, and the biographer who discovers it will have done a great service to literature.

The handling of disproportionate material is not always as difficult as the control of voluminous and extensive information, which tends either to stun or to intoxicate the biographer, so that although he may produce an interesting and valuable book, the result is sometimes arbitrarily and capriciously selective, and sometimes heavy and monotonous; in the first case the danger is that the subject, darting in and out of the author's spotlights, will appear as a sketch or even as a caricature, instead of a portrait; in the second he or she may sink under the weight of the material.

The greatest difficulty of historical biography, one that has not yet been solved and perhaps never will be, is the relation of the background to the principal figure. The biographer has to decide, not once and for all but from moment to moment, how much knowledge he can assume on the part of the reader; and he may not even know what kind of biography he is writing until he has made some of these decisions. Thus a full-length, life-and-times biography can develop out of what began as a personal study, because the author has had to change his methods during the course of the work. The result may be interesting and important, but it is seldom symmetrical; and although this is not always a very serious fault, it does sometimes make the reader feel that he is being defrauded. 'I decided to read this book', he says, 'because I wanted to know about the private and personal life of the subject. Now I find myself involved in a series of events that don't interest me'.

The author should forestall this objection by making it clear at the outset that the subject's individuality will at some point be linked with public trends, and then the reader has been warned. While it is obvious that the lives of famous men and women cannot be made intelligible without some explanation of their religio-political backgrounds, these should, in the case of a personal biography, be insinuated, and not thrust upon the reader through an indigestible discourse in which the subject is only mentioned at the beginning. The heart sinks at the spectacle of a solid piece of prose opening with the ominous words, 'In order fully to understand . . .', and its insertion is in fact a form of literary laziness. The author has no right to polish off the background by breaking out of the framework of a personal biography in this way. The more acceptable method is to introduce the public situation through the private life. 'Shortly after her sixteenth birthday, X.Y.Z. realized that . . .' is a fairer and infinitely pleasanter way of inducing the reader to follow the author into areas he would otherwise have avoided; and there are many others.

Over-impersonal treatment also misleads and cheats through what seems to be the author's deliberate refusal to re-create the principal figure in private life; and with the end of the book comes the realization that this so-called biography has been used as a peg on which to hang a study of the period; this is quite as unprofessional as placing the subject in a vacuum. It may be that the subject, falling suddenly into obscurity, makes coordination difficult; but if the story has been properly handled up to that point, the transition from publicity to privacy is not only a welcome change but a chance for the author to use his technique in blending the two. Yet many throw away this opportunity by dismissing the obscure period with a daunting phrase. 'For the next ten years', they say, 'X.Y.Z.'s life was confined to family cares and trivial dissipations.' This method does not so much bridge a gulf as create a chasm. Worse than a trick, it is a heavy offence: one that was more often committed in the late nineteenth and early twentieth centuries, when historical biography was the prerogative of the scholar, who did not always concern himself with literary skill. Knowledge (rather of the period than of human nature) was his only trump card. Now, his tendency is to play all the aces up his sleeve, dazzling and bewildering the reader instead of enlightening him.

Setting aside the insoluble problem of the relation of the background to the principal figure, the sins that even the best biographer may be tempted into are so many that they must be roughly outlined under these headings: (1) dullness, (2) deliberate falsification and wilful misunderstanding, (3) falling in love with the subject, and (4) the application of modern standards to past customs and principles. From the literary court of law in which these faults are assessed and judged, two types of author must be excluded—the personal memoirist, and the 'official' biographer of a character whose relatives have commissioned and supervised his work. For obvious reasons, it is almost impossible to make the second kind of biography interesting. The value of strongly felt and expressed first-hand recollection is beyond price, however prejudiced and limited it may be.

Dullness. A dull historical biography can be valuable and important, especially if it falls into the life-and-times, definitive category, because it often provides the material the student needs, and from which other writers may draw their supplies. Some of the worst cases of dullness are mitigated by their bibliographies and notes; so the author's failure to bring his characters to life may be forgiven.

Falsification and wilful misunderstanding. These are generally the result of the author's determination to prove the innocence of a commonly censured principal figure. (In this connexion Richard III has recently been much in the public eye.) He wearies and irritates the reader by his protests, his massing of favourable evidence and his abuse of other biographers and historians. Those who know something of the period, fatigued by his omissions and caprices, will dismiss his pleas with a shrug or a smile. Such a biography conveys the impression that the author is primarily concerned with showing himself as a pioneer. Any fresh information he may have discovered thus becomes valueless. To whitewash is to obliterate. By the end of the book the principal figure has disappeared.

Falling in Love with the subject. This can result in an extremely readable biography. At first, the author's passion for the principal figure is infectious; then the reader, hitherto sympathetic, suddenly finds that he cannot go all the way; and he is nauseated by the author's masochistic grovelling before the subject's most unpleasant characteristics. Mary Queen of Scots is the prototype of what might now be described as the pin-up principal figure, making fools of her biographers (how *fascinating* that she shut her eyes to Darnley's murder, and plotted that of Queen Elizabeth!) just as she did of those who literally lost their heads for her in her own day. The obsession that produces this kind of biography is apt to create a violent and unfair antagonism to the subject: but perhaps that is preferable to the indifference and boredom caused by the authors in the second category.

Application of modern standards to past customs and principles. Oddly enough, the learned biographer is just as likely to fall into this sin as the inexperienced amateur. He knows his subject so well, and is so absorbed in it, that he slips easily into the past, unaware of any handicap, just as an absent-minded person may forget to take off his watch before having a bathe. Whether in defence or condemnation of past customs, he most often misleads over legal and sexual matters. Thus the reader, impressed by the author's knowledge and skill, is persuaded that in the sixteenth and seventeenth centuries every trial for high treason appeared as hideously farcical to the contemporary public as it does to himself. In questions of morality, he is invited either to yearn over or to shrink from, conduct that his forebears took for granted. The nineteenth-century biographer who condemned Charles II for 'flaunting' his mistresses was just as mistaken as his present-day counterpart, who invests that monarch's frequentation of seventeen rather dull and silly women with romance of his own making. The only defence of both writers is that their misconceptions may sometimes bring freshness to a too familiar period or character. It is better for the reader to picture himself in the milieu described than to look at it from far off, when it may become diminished and dulled by the author's detachment.

No historical biographer, however talented or conscientious, can expect to leave the court without a stain on his character; although he is bound to incur censure under one or more of the four headings, he may be able so to blend technique and knowledge as to produce a work that will be remembered and quoted with gratitude and delight. Writing biography is in fact a gamble, because at some point key material, hitherto unused or undiscovered, may suddenly turn up, and the author is faced with another decision—how can he use this information? If it does not fit in with his thesis, he is tempted to ignore it, and leave the tables. If he tries to enhance it by literary devices, he may lose his original stake.

The most agitating form of a winning discovery is that contained in a reported conversation. Here the over-cautious biographer avoids *oratio recta*, and the result is sometimes a sad bore. 'A. then informed B. that he knew him to be guilty, because he had seen him and C. together on the night in question. B. denied the charge, and a heated argument ensued.' Thus the reader is forced to look at the characters through the wrong end of a telescope; yet this is perhaps preferable to contemplating a dramatized version: ' "I saw you with C.", said A. B.'s eyes flashed, and his hand flew to his sword.' If the addendum is factual, it is better than the 'heated argument' phrase; but in that case the reader must know the exact circumstances of the conversation, and whether A. or anyone else observed B.'s actions.

So described and criticized, the historical biographer emerges as a pitiable and ludicrous figure, stumbling out of one quagmire into another. He may not deny this final accusation. He might add that he can be, and sometimes is, one of the happiest people in the world.

Leon Edel

* In a strange, pervasive and often subterranean way, the teachings of psycho-analysis have filtered into biography and criticism—and often in distorted form. Distorted because psycho-analysis itself has had to define and re-define its concepts; and because, as is usually the case, a certain amount of dilution, vulgarization and adulteration is likely to occur in the merging of two disciplines. Most literary scholars so far have not had a sufficient grasp of psycho-analytical ideas to apply them with accuracy. On their side, the psycho-analysts are for the most part rank amateurs when they come to the discussion of literature.

And yet students of literature, hitherto addicted to a hunt for 'sources' of the literary work, in seeking to understand the imaginative process, today indulge in another pursuit—an exuberant chase after symbol and myth, the 'inner' meaning of a work, the 'deeper' levels of imagination. This is, on the whole, a sign of health: it represents a more human, as distinct from *library*, view of the creative process. But what literary scholarship has not permitted itself to recognize, is the extent to which symbol-and-myth studies are related to, and indeed spring from, certain fundamental ideas stemming from Freud and Jung and those who have come after them. There are literary scholars in the Academy who understandably turn their backs on what they call 'mere psychologizing' only to involve themselves in a search

* 'The Biographer and Psycho-Analysis'; an abridged version of a lecture read at the Harvard Hitschmann Memorial Meeting, Boston Psycho-analytic Society and Institute, 23 March 1960; first printed in *New World Writing*, No. 18 (Winter 1961), pp. 50–64. Included by permission of the author.

for 'symbolic meaning', which is nothing if not a psychological search. Others have overtly accepted certain psycho-analytical concepts, but use them by rule of book and precept, as given laws; and apply labels with a free use of the psycho-analytical brush and quantities of jargonic paste. When a professor in an American college writes a paper, seriously published in the most authoritative of our scholarly journals, to prove the heroine of *To the Lighthouse* a bad mother, because she sides with her boy against the father and thereby (says the professor) reinforces his 'Oedipus complex', we have surely reached some new strange level of dogma. And when my students persist in asking me to discuss the 'sexual symbolism' in any novel we may be studying, whether it is relevant or not, I quietly wonder whether the humanists who gathered with Freud in Vienna are not stirring violently in their graves.

The problem is particularly striking in literary biography, where the biographer is now expected to know intimately the 'sex-life' of his subject (particularly whether he was hetero- or homosexual!) as if this were the essence of the matter. It is when I am cross-examined in this fashion about literary figures, or when I read documents of misapplied psycho-analysis, or when I am questioned out of ill-digested and misunderstood books (often written by psycho-analysts in response to some need to popularize their field) that I wonder whether the biographer-critic and the psycho-analyst should not declare eternal enmity between them rather than seek some meeting ground in their disciplines. For if literary essays using psycho-analysis are frequently misguided and distorted, psycho-analytic essays using literature can be no less hair-raising in their crudity and their strange simplifications.

But of course the two disciplines are not enemies. They are distinctly allies. Both deal in human experience and human behaviour; both are concerned with man's capacity to create and use symbol. Both are faced with common enemies—ignorance, vulgarization, intellectual laziness. Our task is not to increase this ignorance but to diminish it. And we can do this only by loyalty to our common problems: by perception, analysis, awareness, empathy—and candid discussion. As a biographer who has tried to use the psycho-analytic knowledge of our time, I should like here to discuss something of my theory and method: and how I believe biographers and psycho-analysts can achieve a closer understanding of what they do on their common ground. My remarks apply particularly to literary biography, but by extension much of what I say can be applied to other forms of biography as well.

The biographer seeking to write the life of a writer has, I would say, three principal areas which concern him above all others. The first is his relation to his subject, a situation in some ways like the psycho-analyst's relationship to his patient. The second is his relation to his material; that is his need to analyse the writings of his subject in a manner as concentrated and as close as the psycho-analyst's treatment of what he speaks of as the 'dream-work' of his patients; the biographer must establish a relationship between what has been written, and the historical data available to him: between what he knows of the life of the writer and what the writer has imagined in his work. And finally, the third area is that of the biographer's relation to his audience. I must undertake, since I work by the illumination of psychology and psycho-analysis, as well as in accordance with the traditions and conventions of my discipline, to translate into the discourse of that discipline—and of daily life—the special meanings I have read in my materials and the conclusions I have reached.

Now this is a different approach to biography from that of the traditional biographer, who often chooses his subject in happy unawareness that he may be selecting a paternal or maternal image, or that of some beloved, or hated, or ambivalently-regarded figure out of his past; and who then assembles his data by the light of his unconscious preconceptions, happily and innocently boasting that he is *objective*, and even 'scientific'. In the end, he arrives at a work that is an image *of an image* of himself, and of his identifications and distortions. Not all biographies are necessarily as bad as that: for there are biographers who are endowed with a firm grasp of reality and who achieve something better than what I describe, and in some instances have given us masterpieces of the biographical art. But such works are rare; and even these risk betraying, on close observation, certain failures in objectivity.

I

The biographer's relationship to his subject: Freud has admirably put the case in his essay on Leonardo where, in a paragraph's digression, he offers us a warning which too few biographers, and too few critics have heeded. He refers to the fact that certain biographers become 'fixated on their heroes in a very peculiar manner' and he continues: 'They frequently select the hero as the object of study, because for personal reasons of their own emotional life, they have a special affection for him from the very outset. They then devote themselves to a work of idealization, which strives to enroll the great man among their infantile models, and to revive through him, as it were, their infantile conception of the father. For the sake of this wish they wipe out the individual features in his physiognomy, they rub out the traces of his life's struggle with inner and outer resistances, and do not tolerate in him anything savouring of human weakness or imperfection; they then give us a cold strange ideal form instead of a man with whom we could feel distantly related. It is to be regretted that they do this, for they thereby sacrifice the truth to an illusion, and for the sake of their infantile phantasies they let slip the opportunity to penetrate into the most attractive secrets of human nature.'

The literary biographer, heeding Freud's counsel, must ponder deeply the relationship upon which he has embarked. He has focused upon a poet, a novelist, a man of letters. Certain qualities in that individual have arrested his attention. And why this one, and not another? This alone must give him food for thought. He must try to see, in so far as possible, what has prompted the choice. What is the force of the attraction? Yet how can he really know? The dangers of a kind of 'counter-transference' exist for him as they do for the psycho-analyst. I do not believe we can discover any single answer to this difficult question, nor set down a series of rules by which a biographer may disengage himself from his subject. It is a possibility that if he did disengage himself he might lose his desire to write the biography. There might be less motivation, less impulse to do so. There must be, I take it, a strong and compelling element in a biographer's attraction to his subject which pushes him on his difficult and often obsessive task, and it is mixed up in different degrees with all sorts of drives: a boundless curiosity, not unmixed I suppose with elements of *voyeurism*; a drive to power, common I suppose to most professions; a need for omniscience. And there is sometimes that other element—we have all encountered it—the impulse towards accumulation and ingestion of data. This can result in a very cluttered biography—if it ever gets itself written. We could, I suppose, say much about such concealed motivations in the biographer which are converted, when channelled, to constructive and artistic ends.

The best, I think, that the analytically-oriented biographer can do is to cultivate his awareness of such matters and to recognize the constant threat they represent to his objectivity. He thus may work a little less blindly and ignorantly. By searching for those 'attractive secrets of human nature' of which Freud spoke, by trying to uncover in his subject (and to observe in himself) the 'dynamic' of personality, the biographer may achieve a richer and certainly more sharply-focused biography than the biographer who works in the dark. He is able, in his speculative process, to recognize the existence of a series of possibilities rather than accept smugly the single answer to any given question projected by himself; and he can try to undermine systematically his own easy rationalizations. In a word, he indulges in fewer rigidities of thought and laxities of feeling derived from his own fantasies.

I am saying, in effect, that the biographer must try to know himself before he tries to know the life of another. Self-knowledge, however, is seldom fully attained. And yet his dilemma is that to write a good biography he must in some degree identify himself with his subject; how otherwise re-experience his feelings, his problems, his struggle? He must try to measure the world through the subject's eyes; moreover, he must penetrate into that world. Yet in becoming this other person, for the purpose of his biography, the biographer risks everything. He must, in every sense of the word, therefore seek to be that paradoxical figure which modern psycho-analysis calls the 'participant-observer'. He must be sympathetic, yet aloof, involved yet uninvolved. This is the very heart of his task.

II

As to the biographer's relation to his material: he must analyse it at every turn and with the same professional vigilance which the analyst exercises, making certain that he is *seeing* his material, not projecting figments of his own imagination into it. His responsibility to truth is as great as an analyst's, although his errors may perhaps not be as costly, since they do not reflect upon the living. To that extent he may be said to carry a less pressing burden in the pursuit of his task, but by the same token he is faced by certain larger difficulties.

His subjects neither talk, nor do they answer back. They are as inanimate as their pocket diaries and their cheque stubs, all the personal memorabilia which they have left as record of their passage on this earth —the butt-ends, as T. S. Eliot might say, of their days and ways—out of which, if you please, the biographer is asked to reconstitute their lives.

On the other hand, he does not have access to the first-hand information which the psycho-analyst can obtain; those confrontations which may prompt the subject to offer a conscious or unconscious validation. The subjects come to life most often in the works they left behind; but the story of their lives must be re-created out of these fragments by the biographer. The biographer, in other words, by the very nature of his task, is engaged in a work that is inductive and speculative; and even when his data is abundant, ultimate proof is far removed from him: the confirming voice, the subject's own revelation of his hidden self, is not as open to him and must be sought in more complex and difficult ways.

The biographer is concerned, as is the psycho-analyst, with the significance of the language used, with the imagery, and the nature of the fantasy; and the two stand squarely together on the common ground of their observation of man's rich and noble ability to create and utilize symbols; as well as his extraordinary capacity to indulge in a continual self-deception and to want to substitute for reality some other and pleasanter version of it. But where the conventional literary analyst and critic is concerned with form and substance, with the parts and their relation to the whole, the psycho-analytically oriented critic or biographer sees them constantly as images and symbols and words formed in the consciousness of his subject. In seeking the inner emotional content of a poem or of a novel I start with the analytic axiom, not always accepted by critics, that the poem is the poet's and no one else's, and not an impersonal thing; that the poem's character and nature issue from the poet's consciousness, and that its contents thus are always relevant and not fortuitous, significant in greater or lesser degree; that these contents are tissued out of memories of life or of reading which have become emotionally charged.

In saying this we reject the old and rather naïve concept of the happy artistic inspiration which just 'flew' into the poet's mind. The flight is outward from assimilated experience. We predicate in this process a series of choices open to the artist. Thus if Mr. Joyce chose to imagine a Dublin Jew named Leopold Bloom, or Mr. T. S. Eliot chose to create a character by the name of J. Alfred Prufrock, both of these artists engaged in an act of careful selection: why Prufrock and not Smith or Jones? Why necessarily Bloom? The creation of these characters, however mythical they may be, and however much they are fancies of their creators, reflects distinct states of mind and of feeling in Joyce and in Eliot at the time they are planning and writing these works. The works themselves should yield, on analysis, what this state of mind and of emotion was. Each work is a writer's signature. Poetry, said Thoreau, 'is a piece of very private history, which unostentatiously lets us into the secret of a man's life'. And Henry James was saying the same thing when he wrote that the artist is present 'in every page of every book from which he sought to eliminate himself'. This is the answer which students of literature, who venture upon psycho-analytic ground, can give to those who argue that the literary work is as impersonal as the artifact, that a poem is like a vase. To argue in this way is to attempt to strip a poem of all affect; to treat it as something rather mechanical, capable of being taken to pieces, like a watch; and to treat language as an absolute.

Those of us who work in the literary field are governed in textual study by the same laws of evidence and by the primary rules of logic which govern all analytic professions. The rest is a matter of the sharpened insight, the clinical eye and ear, the capacity to restore (with the greatest caution) some inflexion and tone to the inanimate words, and to arrive at that comprehension of the biographical subject which enables us to listen to him as with the proverbial 'third ear'. When that can be done, the biographer using psycho-analytic knowledge is ready for his final task. If he understands the motivations of his personage he can write his book. He can then even risk publishing a first volume while the second one is unwritten, and have the boldness to say that he is not afraid that new material will alter his fundamental insights. He has captured his man. New material may tell him more; but it will only further illustrate, in one way or another, that which he already knows.

III

The biographer's relation to his public is no less complex than his relation to his material. Having arrived at an understanding of his subject he must now recreate him in words, and as a palpable, living being, in language proper to himself and to those who will read of him. He cannot indulge in the language of the clinician. Clinical language is essentially a kind of verbal shorthand, in which psycho-analysts speak professionally to one another—and understand each other perfectly. Think how much they condense when they use the word 'oedipal'. Yet how many words are required to explain it! Nevertheless the adjective has been adopted in literary circles, and it is as outlandish and vague a way of describing an individual's problem as any in existence. It will doubtless do, in a professional paper; but what did it mean when the professor, mentioned earlier, used it to describe the allegedly terrible things the heroine of *To the Lighthouse* does to her son in shielding him from the rather gruff, and perhaps even hostile, remarks of his father? The word oedipal in that context was meaningless; and there is no one convenient label to describe the delicate relationships which Mrs. Woolf set on paper for us: the withdrawn father, his failure in empathy toward his son, the mother's desire to protect their child—and herself!—from her husband's failure to enter into the little boy's eagerness to go to the lighthouse: all this has to be described, not labelled, and we are, I'm afraid, rather over-labelled psycho-analytically these days. The main duty of the literary biographer, it seems to me, is to gain his insights, understand the motivations of his subject, and then cast aside this special language; bury completely the tools that have served him in attaining his ends. He must write indeed as if psycho-analysis never existed.

I feel, for instance, and I think it will illustrate what I am insisting upon, that Ernest Jones, in his biography of Freud, has written a work much more intelligible to the profession than to the lay public. A reader without psycho-analytic orientation is asked to take some rather bold leaps, to grasp ideas which appear strange and inconsistent—and indeed some of which are still subject to debate within the psycho-analytic disciplines. An example taken from the first chapter will illustrate what I mean. Dr. Jones describes the emotional problems which beset Freud, aged two, upon the impending birth of another child in the family:

> Darker problems arose when it dawned on him that some man was even more intimate with his mother than he was. Before he was two years old, for the second time, another baby was on the way, and soon visibly so. Jealousy of the intruder, and anger for whoever had seduced his mother into such an unfaithful proceeding, were inevitable. Discarding his knowledge of the sleeping conditions in the house, he rejected the unbearable thought that the nefarious person could be his beloved and perfect father.

Now this may have some meaning psycho-analytically, but is it acceptable biography? A moment's reflection on what we know about children would surely show that it never 'dawns' as consciously as this on a two-year-old that some man 'is even more intimate with his mother than he was'. If it did, he would be ready for the couch, and would not need play therapy, you may be sure. The passage is put by Dr. Jones too clearly in terms of adult sexual awareness and experience; it is, moreover, sheer guesswork. For what Jones is doing here is reading into the consciousness of the child material which, according to Freudian theory, exists in the unconscious. And this, I would argue, is not an appropriate way to write biography. Moreover, to plant words such as 'jealousy' and 'seduction' in the consciousness of a two-year-old—even if that child be Sigmund Freud—shows a failure in objectivity, and certainly in verisimilitude. A much more accurate way of expressing it would have been perhaps to say that Dr. Freud years later, in retrospect, felt that in his own infantile experience he had undergone a period of disturbance, or a sense of being set aside, at the advent of another child in the family. And although he had sensed, in that intuitive way in which children do, that somehow his father was involved in this event, he had concealed the thought that this parent, who seemed to him an ideal and wonderful figure, would thus deprive him of the place he thought he occupied in the very centre of his mother's life. I do this rather informally, not to rewrite Jones, but to translate him. Dr. Jones was much less concerned with translating his specialized concepts into the language of everyday life because he was talking a language that had become second nature to him. The literary biographer, when he borrows the shorthand of the psycho-analyst, must decipher it. It is not his language; it is not the language of the people; it is not the language of literature or literary criticism.

Psycho-analysts are, in the very nature of their work, deeply interested in the imagination and, in particular, the literary imagination. This derives in part from the humanism of Freud, and the example he set in certain of his brilliant papers in applied psycho-analysis; in his fascinating speculations on Shakespeare, or his essays on Ibsen and Dostoevsky or the essay on Leonardo. Anyone who is involved with the "dream-work" of man is likely to be fascinated by those who have brought to the creative "dream-work" a transcendent vision, fashioning with deliberate and conscious artistry poems and novels, or exercising the critical and analytical imaginations. Psycho-analysts again and again turn to literary figures to find illustrations for certain of their theoretical concepts. The writings of great men are, after all, splendid documents for analysis. They are among the finest statements of human observation, awareness, intuition and creative synthesis that mankind possesses.

To illustrate: I recently came upon a letter in which a writer of fiction was describing the nature of dreams. Here are some passages from this letter:

> I should say [says this writer] that the chances were a thousand to one against anybody's dreaming of the subject closely occupying the waking mind—and except—and this I wish particularly to suggest to you—in a sort of allegorical manner. For example, if I have been perplexed during the day in bringing out the incidents of a story as I wish, I find that I dream at night, never by any chance of the story itself, but perhaps of trying to shut a door that *will* fly open, or to screw something tight that *will* be loose, or to drive a horse on some very important journey, who unaccountably becomes a dog and can't be urged along, or to find my way out of a series of chambers that appears to have no end. I sometimes think that the origin of all fable and allegory, the very first conception of such fictions, may be referable to this class of dreams. . . . When dreams *can* be directly traced to any incidents of recent occurrence, it appears to me that the incidents are usually of the more insignificant character. . . . The obvious convenience and effect of making the dreams of heroes and heroines bear on the great themes of a story as illustrated by their late experiences, seem to me to have led the Poets away from the truth on this head. . . . Are dreams so various and different as you suppose? . . . We all fall off that Tower, we all skim above the ground at a great pace and can't keep on it, we all say 'this must be a dream, because I was in this strange, low-roofed, beam-constructed place once before, and it turned out to be a dream' . . . we all confound the living with the dead and all frequently have a knowledge or suspicion that we are doing it. . . .

There is much more in this letter. 'Old stuff', one might say, and one might add that this man has probably glanced at Freud on dreams! This is far from being the case. The letter was written more than a century ago, in 1851. It was written by a great novelist who was fascinated by dreams—written by him to a doctor, who had submitted an article on dreams to this novelist's magazine. The writer of that letter was not Dostoevsky, and not Henry James: it was Charles Dickens, and I would say that he captured certain essential aspects of dreams through that sense of reality, accuracy of observation, and capacity for introspection which such writers have. When I mention that Dickens was also interested in hypnotism and sought, (to be sure in a clumsy way) to cure a woman of her troubled nightmare-hallucinations by hypnotizing her, and this before Charcot, it will be recognized what a fine intuitive sense of 'dream-work' this novelist had.

So have they all had, these writers, and when we examine their writings we profit by their awarenesses. We can also seek out and speculate about the hidden impulses and unconscious motivations they in turn reveal. But there are occasions when psycho-analysts, writing about a man of talent or of genius, forget that he was an individual of great accomplishment and imagination, and seem to belittle him: as if to say, really he was after all rather a poor worm, because he was a narcissist; or they try to prove that he may have been a homosexual, as if this were a weakness in his art, or that his stories show a profound necrophilic impulse, etc., etc. Many papers and even books of this sort have been written and while they may be illuminating when they illustrate the primordial in the creator, they certainly can be described as *reductive* in method and in approach. Is this not in reality a little like saying that such and such a poet has a liver and kidneys and a heart: for when you reduce a man of genius to his unconscious drives that is all you are doing. To show that the liver is cirrhotic or that the heart is bad is merely to say that the individual has an illness. It is *what* these conditions make him do in his daily life that are the real matter for study and the essential part of his biography. The readers of a writer of genius are well aware that he was human, and fallible; that he possessed the human organs and suffered as men suffer; but they know him by that which was distinctive in him: and that which is distinctive in him for psycho-analysis in such instances, I would argue, is not merely the clinical picture of his unconscious, the dark primordial landscape of his Id.

Thus it is all very well to paint a picture of Robert Louis Stevenson as an 'oral' character; and it isn't hard to do so. The diary which his mother kept when he was an infant in which she recorded his feeding problems; those great feasts in Samoa where he held his own with the natives; the transformation potion which he had Dr. Jekyll drink when he turned into Mr. Hyde. We even know that this story was originally a nightmare in which Stevenson dreamed that he was being hotly pursued, and eluded his pursuers by swallowing something and changing into someone else. I remember reading a paper which made much of the orality of Stevenson, and drew a beautiful diagram of the Stevensonian unconscious, which could be splendidly documented, thanks to that early diary. These are enormously interesting and significant biographical facts; but they count for little unless we show that this individual who could write lovely verses for children, who married a woman older than himself and treated his step-children not as a father but as his playmates, and who hasn't a real heroine in any of his novels, nevertheless could spin a tale as marvellous and as pyschologically true as *Dr. Jekyll and Mr. Hyde*; and a tale that will be read always—wherever there are boys and wherever there is a dream of buried treasure. It isn't Robert Louis Stevenson, the helpless, tuberculous wanderer in distant places carrying his load of infantilisms who must be portrayed: that is his clinical history; it is Robert Louis Stevenson, who really wasn't helpless at all, save in the way we all are with our bodily ills: who, lying in bed, after lung haemorrhages could still pick up his pencil and scrawl his stories; who was capable of developing a high rich style that is among the most mature styles of our literature.

It would not be difficult to write a paper to show a Marcel Proust, suffering from allergies, asthmatic, high strung—oedipal—I will use that word since it would be used in such a paper. He could be called a narcissist; and we know much about his homosexuality. One might refer to his medical history; when he was born the doctors thought he was too weak to live. I suppose for diagnostic purposes this would have value. And these are again significant biographical facts. A psycho-analytic paper could do much with this data, and with the family history which we possess; do much with the material contained in Proust's own words, in his novel. To *confine* ourself to this data, as such papers do, is to portray the sickly weakling: which is not what Proust really was. The doctors thought him too weak to live, but he lived. He lived a life that was a direct consequence of all the terrible physical handicaps and the no less terrible mis-education of his emotions in childhood. In one sense he *was* mis-educated; in another, his emotions were educated to sensitivities far beyond those of persons less frail and less afraid of the particle of dust, the cold, the sounds that made necessary the cork-lined room. Even in his search for love Proust had to use indirection and subterfuge; he could not find an easy way for anything. How simple then to mock this figure—to call him 'sick, sick, sick', and to murmur 'neurotic art' and therefore sick art. But would this not be—has it not been—an enormous failure in perception? Proust the man was sick, Proust the artist was strong, healthy, assertive; he was more triumphant over veritably crushing forces and demonstrated a greater will for survival and a capacity for *life* than many of the living. I make no virtue of Proust's sufferings, but I celebrate man's incredible capacity to be creative in the very teeth of physical and psychological disaster. Remember that even as Proust was dying he was revising passages in his work dealing with the death of Bergotte. These are the victories of the human spirit over the forces of defeat.

Let me image what I have been saying: and I will use the familiar picture of the iceberg—of that small part which is above the water and that great invisible mass, the unconscious, submerged below the surface. When psycho-analysts write papers on literary subjects and describe the mass below the water-line, is it any wonder that most readers find it unbelievable and 'far-fetched'? The readers, after all, can see only that which is above the surface: and the submerged part is explicable only in relation to that which is visible. I do think that certain papers in applied psycho-analysis have lost much of their value because their authors have enjoyed their under-water snorkeling to such an extent that they never once looked up to see the great glittering exposed mass of the iceberg. In saying this I am not overlooking the admirable contributions to the psychology of the Ego of Ernest Kris or of Phyllis Greenacre. Psycho-analysts consider it wrong to look only at the top of the iceberg, but on occasion they reverse the mistake by looking only at what is below. To be sure, the submerged part determines the shape of what is above. Nevertheless it is the visible shape which confronts the world and the light of day, and it is the relationship between the submerged and the exposed which is all-important. The human structure cannot be fragmented and retain meaning.

Art springs usually from tension and passion, from a state of disequilibrium in the artist's being. The psycho-analyst reading the pattern of the artist's writings can attempt to tell us what this disequilibrium was. The biographer, reading the same pattern in the larger picture of the human condition, is bent upon showing how the negatives, when they were used to constructive ends, were converted to positives. I have already mentioned Proust and his allergies and his withdrawal from the pain of experience into the world of Combray, capturing in language the very essences which seem illusory and evanescent in man's consciousness. So Virginia Woolf, on the margin of her melancholia, which finally led her to take her life, sought to capture the feeling of the moment, to pin it in its fluttering butterfly state to the printed page. And James Joyce, human monster that he was, living in his totally alienated and dissociated world, sealing his eyes against it, saved himself by constructing in the teeth of his terrible existence, vast compulsive works, and in particular those word-salads that were this side of the madness of genius. These are all great victories of human endurance and of the creative imagination, victories indeed at times of literature over life. Before such men—even the most minor—it is necessary to maintain a certain humbleness of spirit; that fine sense of objective inquiry, which both the biographer and the psychoanalyst should—but do not always—cultivate; and the constant awareness that we sit not in judgement to tell people what they should have been or how they should have lived their lives, but to arrive at an understanding of them through empathy, perception, analysis, awareness. As a literary historian I know that whenever men have decided how others shall experience life—as the Inquisition did, as the witch-burners of Salem did, or the Hitlerians of our own time—this has meant a dead-end in human experience. Perhaps some day we will discover ultimate answers, and will be able to fold our hands in a kind of eternal placidity of 'adjustment'. But until such a time it is necessary to retain largeness of vision and a vast empathy. There is a short story of Henry James's which begins: 'Never say you know the last word about any human heart!' To the simplicity and wisdom of this we need add nothing. It is the quintessential statement for all who analyse the things of the human spirit with the tools of the mind.

APPENDIX

A SELECTIVE LIST OF ADDITIONAL TWENTIETH-CENTURY PUBLICATIONS CONTAINING CRITICISM OF BIOGRAPHY

[Does not include works represented in the main body of this collection]

FULL LENGTH STUDIES AND SEPARATE PAMPHLETS

Bowen, Catherine Drinker, *Adventures of a Biographer* (Boston: Atlantic-Little, Brown, 1959).

Britt, Albert, *The Great Biographers* (New York: McGraw-Hill, 1936).

Carver, George, *Alms for Oblivion* (Milwaukee, Wis.: Bruce, 1946).

Collins, Joseph, *The Doctor Looks at Biography* (New York: Doran, 1925).

Connely, Willard, *Adventures in Biography* (London: Laurie, 1956).

Dresden, Samuel, *De Structuur van de Biografie* (Den Haag: B. Bakker, 1956).

Dunn, Waldo H., *English Biography* (London: Dent; New York: Dutton, 1916).

Edel, Leon, *Literary Biography* (Univ. of Toronto Press; London: Hart-Davis, 1957); republished with considerable additions (New York: Doubleday Anchor Books, 1959).

Garraty, John A., *The Nature of Biography* (New York: Knopf; London: Cape, 1957).

Johnson, Edgar, *One Mighty Torrent: the Drama of Biography* (New York: Macmillan, 1937).

Johnston, James C., *Biography: the Literature of Personality* (New York: Century, 1927).

Longaker, John M., *English Biography in the Eighteenth Century* (Univ. of Pennsylvania Press, 1931).

Ludwig, Emil, *Die Kunst der Biographie* (Paris: Éditions du Phénix, 1936).

Maurois, André, *Aspects of Biography* [Translated from the French by S. C. Roberts] (Cambridge University Press; New York: Appleton & Co., 1929).

Nicolson, Harold, *The Development of English Biography* (London: Hogarth Press, 1927).

Pearson, Hesketh, *Ventilations: Being Biographical Asides* (Phila., Pa.: Lippincott, 1930).

Romein, Jan, *Die Biographie: Einführung in ihre Geschichte und ihre Problematik* [translated into German by Huber Noodt] (Bern: A. Francke, 1948). This was originally published in the Netherlands in 1946 as *De Biografie een Inleiding*.

Stauffer, Donald A., *The Art of Biography in Eighteenth-Century England* (Princeton Univ. Press, 1941).

– *English Biography before 1700* (Harvard Univ. Press, 1930).

Stuart, Duane R., *Epochs of Greek and Roman Biography* (Univ. of California Press, 1928).

Thayer, William R., *The Art of Biography* (New York: Scribners, 1920).

Trevelyan, G. M., *Biography: a Reader's Guide* (London: National Book League, 1947).

Valentine, Alan C., *Biography* [Oxford Reading Courses] (New York: Oxford Univ. Press, 1927).

ANTHOLOGIES WITH CRITICAL INTRODUCTIONS

Balch, Marston, ed. *Modern Short Biographies* (New York: Harcourt, Brace, 1935).

Durling, Dwight, and Watt, William, eds. *Biography: Varieties and Parallels* (New York: Dryden Press, 1941).

Hyde, Marietta A. ed., *Modern Biography* (New York: Harcourt, Brace, 1926, 1934).

Johnson, Edgar, ed., *A Treasury of Biography* (New York: Howell, Soskin, 1941).

Metcalf, John C., *The Stream of English Biography: Readings in Representative Biographies* (New York: Century, 1930).

Pinto, V. de S., ed., *English Biography in the Seventeenth Century* (London: Harrap, 1951).

SHORTER STUDIES

Adams, James Truslow, 'Biography as an Art', *The Tempo of Modern Life* (New York: A. and C. Boni, 1931), pp. 187–99. Also 'New Modes in Biography', pp. 171–86.

Adcock, St. John, 'The Gentle Art of Biography', *Bookman* [London], LXXV (October 1928), pp. 24–25.

Alexander, H. M. 'Wrong Ways to Write Biography', *The Writer's Handbook*, ed. A. S. Burack (Boston: The Writer, Inc., 1936), pp. 271–9.

Asquith, H. H., 'Biography' [an address delivered in 1901], *Occasional Addresses* (London: Macmillan, 1918), pp. 29–56.

Ausubel, Herman, 'Individuals in History', *Historians and Their Craft* (New York: Columbia Univ. Press, 1950), pp. 256–99.

Benson, A. C., 'The Art of the Biographer', *Essays by Divers Hands* (London: Royal Society of Literature, 1926), pp. 139–64.

Bidou, H., 'Biographies', *Journal des Debats*, XXXIX (30 September to 21 October 1932), pp. 554–6, 591–3, 633–4, 673–5.

Bowen, Catherine Drinker, 'On Being a Biographer', *Scripps College Bulletin*, February 1950. Other versions in 'The Business of the Biographer', *Atlantic*, CLXXXVII (May 1951), pp. 50–56; and as *The Writing of Biography* (Boston: The Writer, Inc., 1951).

– 'The Biographer Looks for News', *Scripps College Bulletin*, February 1958.

Bradford, Gamaliel, 'Biography and the Human Heart', *The Century*, CXX (Spring 1930), pp. 180–91. Reprinted in volume with the same title (Houghton Mifflin, 1932).

– 'The Art of Biography', *Saturday Review of Literature*, 23 May 1925, pp. 769–70.

– 'Confessions of a Biographer', *Wives* (New York: Harper and Bros., 1925), pp. 1–14.

– 'Psychography', *A Naturalist of Souls* (Boston: Houghton Mifflin, 1926), pp. 3–25.

Brooks, Van Wyck, 'Thoughts on Biography', *Sketches in Criticism* (New York: Dutton, 1932), pp. 105–16.

Bruce, Harold L., 'Biography', *Essays in Criticism by Members of the Department of English, University of California* (Univ. of California Press, 1929), pp. 77–87.

Bryant, Arthur, 'The Art of Biography', *London Mercury*, XXX (July 1934), pp. 236–43.

Burdett, Osbert, 'Experiment in Biography', *Tradition and Experiment in Present-Day Literature* (London: Oxford Univ. Press, 1929), pp. 161–78.

Chaumeix, André, 'Le goût des biographies', *Revue des Deux Mondes*, 7 per 42 (1 December 1927), pp. 698–708.

Clifford, James L., 'Biography: Craft or Art?', *Univ. of Toronto Quart.*, XXVIII (April 1959), pp. 301–9.

– 'Speaking of Books' [objectivity in biography] *New York Times Book Review*, 29 January 1956, p. 2.

Clive, John, 'More or Less Eminent Victorians: Some Trends in Recent Victorian Biography', *Victorian Studies*, II (September 1958), pp. 5–28.

Cook, Sir Edward T., 'The Art of Biography', *National Review*, LXIII (April 1914), pp. 266–84; reprinted in *Literary Recreations* (London: Macmillan, 1918), pp. 1–33.

Cranston, Maurice, 'Byways of Biography', *The Listener*, 24 October 1957, pp. 645–6.

Cross, Wilbur L., 'From Plutarch to Strachey', *Yale Review*, n.s. XI (October 1921), pp. 140–57.

Crothers, Samuel M., 'Satan among the Biographers', *The Cheerful Giver* (Boston: Houghton Mifflin, 1923), pp. 76–104.

Davies, Godfrey, 'Biography and History', *Modern Language Quarterly*, I (March 1940), pp. 79–94.

Dobrée, Bonamy, 'Modern Biography', *National Review*, XCIX (July 1932), pp. 121–9.

Drew, Elizabeth, 'Biography', *The Enjoyment of Literature* (New York: W. W. Norton, 1935), pp. 78–108.

Edel, Leon, 'That One May Say This Was a Man', *New York Times Book Review*, 24 June 1956, pp. 1, 12.

Ellis, Havelock, 'An Open Letter to Biographers' [originally written about 1896], *Views and Reviews* (London: D. Harmsworth, 1932), pp. 86–99.

Fuess, Claude M., 'The Biographer and His Victims', *Atlantic Monthly*, CXLIX (January 1932), pp. 62–73; and 'Debunkery and Biography', *Atlantic Monthly*, CLI (March 1933), pp. 347–56.

Garraty, John A., 'How Should You Tell a Man's Story?', *New York Times Book Review*, 5 July 1959, pp. 1, 10.

Gelber, Lionel M., 'History and the New Biography', *Queen's Quarterly*, XXXVII (January 1930), pp. 127–44.

Gordon, George, *The Lives of Authors* (London: Chatto and Windus, 1950), pp. 1–11.

Gosse, Edmund, 'Biography', *Encyclopaedia Britannica* [11th Edition] (Cambridge Univ. Press, 1910), III, pp. 952–4.

– 'The Custom of Biography', *Anglo-Saxon Review*, VIII (March 1901), pp. 195–208.

Graves, Frederick, 'The Rakers', *Westminster Review*, CLXXVI (December 1911), pp. 683–6.

Guedalla, Philip, 'The Method of Biography', *Journal of the Royal Society of Arts*, LXXXVII (21 July 1939), pp. 925–35.

Handlin, Oscar, 'History in Men's Lives', *Virginia Quarterly*, XXX (Summer 1954), pp. 534–41.

Harris, Frank, 'The Art of Biography', *Confessional* (New York: Panurge Press, 1930), pp. 168–76.

Hart, Albert B., 'The Modern Historical School for Scandal', *Current History*, XXXI (February 1930), pp. 968–70.

Hart, Francis R., 'Boswell and the Romantics: a Chapter in the History of Biographical Theory', *ELH*, XXVII (March 1960), pp. 44–65.

Hughes, Rupert, 'Pitfalls of the Biographer', *Pacific Historical Review*, II (March 1933), pp. 1–33; reprinted as pamphlet, Glendale, Calif.: A. H. Clark, 1933).

Johnson, Edgar, 'American Biography and the Modern World', *North American Review*, CCXLV (June 1938), pp. 364–80.

Johnston, George A., 'The New Biography', *Atlantic Monthly*, CXLIII (March 1929), pp. 333–42.

Jones, Howard Mumford, 'Methods in Contemporary Biography', *English Journal* [Chicago], XXI (January–February 1932), pp. 113–22.

Josephson, Matthew, 'Historians and Mythmakers', *Virginia Quarterly*, XVI (January 1940), pp. 92–109.

King, R. W., 'Biography and Curiosity', *Life and Letters*, X (August 1934), pp. 546–53.

Lee, Sidney, 'Principles of Biography' [1911], *Elizabethan and Other Essays* (Oxford: Clarendon, 1929), pp. 31–57; and 'The Perspective of Biography' [1918], pp. 58–82.

Lewis, Wilmarth S., 'The Difficult Art of Biography', *Yale Review*, XLIV (Autumn 1954), pp. 33–40.

Liddell Hart, B. H., 'Neo-Georgian Biography', *Cornhill Magazine*, CXLIX (February 1934), pp. 155–63.

Lynd, Robert, 'Fictitious Biography', *Books and Writers* (London: Dent, 1952), pp. 312–16.

– 'The Rights of the Dead', *New Statesman and Nation*, 24 January 1931, pp. 459–561.

Maitland, Frederick W., Introduction to *The Life and Letters of Leslie Stephen* (London: Duckworth, 1906).

Marcu, Valeriu, 'Biography and Biographers', *Men and Forces of Our Time* (London: Harrap, 1931), pp. 3–17.

Maurois, André, 'The Modern Biographer', *Yale Review*, XVII (January 1928), pp. 227–45.

– 'To Make a Man Come Alive Again', *New York Times Book Review*, 27 December 1953, p. 1.

Mumford, Lewis, 'The Task of Modern Biography', *English Journal* [Chicago], XXIII (January 1934), pp. 1–9.

Nevins, Allan, 'The Biographer and the Historian', *Humanities for Our Time*, ed. Walter R. Agard (Lawrence, Kansas: University of Kansas Press, 1949), pp. 45–66.

– 'Biography and History', *The Gateway to History* (New York: D. C. Heath, 1938), pp. 318–41.

– 'Is History Made by Heroes?' *Saturday Review of Literature*, 5 November 1955, pp. 9–10, 42–43.

Nicolson, Harold, 'How I Write Biography', *Saturday Review of Literature*, 26 May 1934, pp. 709–11.

Nock, Albert J., 'The Purpose of Biography', *Atlantic Monthly*, CLXV (March 1940), pp. 340–46.

Notestein, Wallace, 'History and the Biographer', *Yale Review*, XXII (March 1933), pp. 549–58.

Oman, Charles, 'On the Testing of Authorities', *On the Writing of History* (London: Methuen, 1939), pp. 56–75.

Partin, Robert, 'Biography as an Instrument of Moral Instruction', *American Quarterly*, VIII (Winter 1956), pp. 303–15.

Partington, Wilfred, 'Should a Biographer Tell?' *Atlantic Monthly*, CLXXX (August 1947), pp. 56–63.

Pearson, Hesketh, 'About Biography', *Essays by Divers Hands* (London: Royal Society of Literature, 1958), pp. 55–72.

– 'Warts and All', *Saturday Review of Literature*, 12 October 1946, pp. 13–14.

Pippett, Aileen, 'The Art of Leading a Double Life', *New York Times Book Review*, 28 August 1955, pp. 1, 20.

Plumb, J. H., 'The Interaction of History and Biography', *Times Literary Supplement*, 6 January 1956, Supplement, p. xxi.

Purcell, Mary, 'The Art of Biography', *Studies* (Dublin), XLVIII (Autumn 1959), pp. 305–17.

Raleigh, Walter, 'Early Lives of the Poets', *Six Essays on Johnson* (Oxford: Clarendon Press, 1910), pp. 98–127.

Schelling, Felix E., 'The Art of Biography', *Appraisements and Asperities* (Phila., Pa.: Lippincott, 1922). pp. 50–55.

Smith, Bradford, 'Biographer's Creed', *William and Mary Quarterly*, X (April 1953), pp. 190–5.

Smith, Samuel Stephenson, 'The Art of Framing Lies', *The Craft of the Critic* (New York: Thomas Y. Crowell, 1931), pp. 92–103; "The Criticism of Biography," pp. 104–19.

Stephen, Leslie, 'National Biography', *Studies of a Biographer* (London: Duckworth, 1898–1902), I, pp. 1–34.

Stern, Madeleine B., 'Approaches to Biography', *South Atlantic Quarterly*, XLV (July 1946), pp. 363–71.

Stewart, J. I. M., 'Biography', in *The Craft of Letters in England*, ed. John Lehmann (London: Cresset Press, 1956), pp. 6–25.

Sylvester, Richard S., 'Cavendish's *Life of Wolsey*: the Artistry of a Tudor Biographer', *Studies in Philology*, LVII (January 1960), pp. 44–71.

Symons, A. J. A., 'Tradition in Biography', *Tradition and Experiment in Present-Day Literature* (London: Oxford Univ. Press, 1929), pp. 149–60.

Tolles, Frederick B., 'The Biographer's Craft', *South Atlantic Quarterly*, LIII (October 1954), pp. 508–20.

Trueblood, Charles K., 'Biography', *Dial*, LXXXIII (August 1927), pp. 128–36.

Van Doren, Carl, 'Biography as a Literary Form', *Columbia University Quarterly*, XVII (March 1915), pp. 180–5.

Weedon, William S., 'Concerning Biography', *Humanistic Studies in Honour of J. C. Metcalf* (Charlottesville, Va.: University of Virginia, 1941), pp. 247–67.

West, Rebecca, 'Miss Gye', *Ending in Ernest* (New York: Doubleday, 1931), pp. 161–8.

Whibley, Charles, 'The Indiscretions of Biography', *English Review*, XXXIX (December 1924), pp. 769–72.

White, Neuman I., 'The Development, Use, and Abuse of Interpretation in Biography', *English Institute Annual, 1942* (New York: Columbia University Press, 1943), pp. 29–58.

Williams, Orlo, 'The Subject of Biography', *National Review*, C (May, 1933), pp. 693–702.

Wilson, Arthur M., 'The Humanistic Bases of Biographical Interpretation', *English Institute Annual, 1942* (New York: Columbia Univ. Press, 1943), pp. 59–73.

Wingfield-Stratford, Esmé, 'Biographers and Their Victims', *Fortnightly*, CXXXVII (April 1932), pp. 444–51.

SOME SPECIAL STUDIES OF LYTTON STRACHEY

Bacon, Leonard, 'An Eminent Post-Victorian', *Yale Review*, n.s. XXX (Winter 1941), pp. 310–24.

Beerbohm, Max, *Lytton Strachey* [the Rede Lecture, Cambridge, 1943] (Cambridge Univ. Press, 1943).

Boas, Guy, *Lytton Strachey* (English Ass'n Pamphlet, No. 93—November 1935).

Bower-Shore, Clifford, *Lytton Strachey: an Essay* (London: Fenland Press, 1933).

Dyson, A. E., 'The Technique of Debunking', *Twentieth Century*, CLVII (March 1955), pp. 244–56.

Gordon, George, 'The Art and Ethics of Modern Biography' [1932], *The Lives of Authors* (London: Chatto and Windus, 1950), pp. 12–22.

Kallich, Martin, 'Psycho-analysis, Sexuality, and Lytton Strachey's Theory of Biography', *American Imago*, XV (Winter 1958), pp. 331–70.

Lehman, B. H., 'The Art of Lytton Strachey', *University of California Publications in English* (1929), pp. 229–45.

MacCarthy, Desmond, 'Lytton Strachey as a Biographer', *Life and Letters*, VIII (March 1932), pp. 90–102; also in *Memories* (London: Oxford Univ. Press, 1953), pp. 31–49.

Nash, Rosalind, 'Florence Nightingale According to Mr. Strachey', *Nineteenth Century*, CIII (February 1928), pp. 258–65.

Raymond, John, 'Strachey's *Eminent Victorians*', *New Statesman and Nation*, 16 April 1955, pp. 545–6 [Cf. pp. 578, 616].

Russell, John, 'Lytton Strachey', *Horizon*, XV (February 1947), pp. 91–116.

Sanders, Charles Richard, *Lytton Strachey: His Mind and Art* (New Haven, Conn.: Yale Univ. Press, 1957).

Trevor-Roper, Hugh, 'Lytton Strachey as Historian', *Historical Essays* (London: Macmillan, 1957), pp. 279-84.

A FEW PSYCHOLOGICAL STUDIES

Allport, Gordon W., *Personality: a Psychological Interpretation* (New York: Holt, 1937).

Allport, Gordon W., *The Use of Personal Documents in Psychological Science* (New York: Social Science Research Council, 1942).

Baldwin, Alfred L., 'Personal Structure Analysis: a Statistical Method for Investigating the Single Personality', *Journal of Abnormal and Social Psychology*, XXXVII (April 1942), pp. 163–83.

Bühler, Charlotte, 'The Curve of Life as Studied in Biographies', *Journal of Applied Psychology*, XIX (August 1935), pp. 405–9.

Dollard, John J., and Mowrer, O. H., 'A Method of Measuring Tension in Written Documents', *Journal of Abnormal and Social Psychology*, XLII (January 1947), pp. 3–32.

Dooley, Lucile, 'Psycho-analytic Studies of Genius', *American Journal of Psychology*, XXVII (July 1916), pp. 363–416.

Frenkel, Else, 'Studies in Biographical Psychology', *Character and Personality*, V (1936), pp. 1–34.

Garraty, John A., 'The Interrelations of Psychology and Biography', *Psychological Bulletin*, LI (November 1954), pp. 569–82.

Gun, W. T. J., 'The Treatment of Ancestry in Modern Biographies', *Eugenics Review*, XXVI (April 1934), pp. 29–32.

Roman, Klara G., *Handwriting: a Key to Personality* (New York: Pantheon Books, 1952).

Schapiro, Meyer, 'Leonardo and Freud: an Art-Historical Study', *Journal of the History of Ideas*, XVII (April 1956), pp. 147–178.

Tozzer, Alfred M., 'Biography and Biology', *American Anthropologist*, n.s. XXXV (July-September 1933), pp. 418–32.

Index

GALAXY BOOKS

Aaron, Daniel	*Men of Good Hope*	GB58
Abrams, Meyer H., ed.	*English Romantic Poets*	GB35
Barker, Ernest, ed. & tr.	*The Politics of Aristotle*	GB69
ed.	*Social Contract: Essays by Locke, Hume, Rousseau*	GB68
	Reflections on Government	GB15
Bate, Walter Jackson	*The Achievement of Samuel Johnson*	GB53
Berlin, Isaiah	*Karl Marx: His Life and Environment*	GB25
Bowra, C. M.	*Ancient Greek Literature*	GB30
	The Romantic Imagination	GB54
Brower, Reuben A.	*The Fields of Light*	GB87
Bruun, Geoffrey	*Nineteenth Century European Civilization*	GB36
Clark, George	*Early Modern Europe*	GB37
	The Seventeenth Century	GB47
Clifford, James L.	*Biography as an Art*	GB70
ed.	*Eighteenth-Century English Literature*	GB23
Cochrane, Charles Norris	*Christianity and Classical Culture*	GB7
Collingwood, R. G.	*The Idea of History*	GB1
	The Idea of Nature	GB31
	The Principles of Art	GB11
Cruickshank, John	*Albert Camus and the Literature of Revolt*	GB43
Dean, Leonard, ed.	*Shakespeare*	GB46
Dixon, W. MacNeile	*The Human Situation*	GB12
Evans-Wentz, W. Y., ed.	*The Tibetan Book of the Dead*	GB39
Feidelson and Brodtkorb, eds.	*Interpretations of American Literature*	GB26
Gerould, Gordon Hall	*The Ballad of Tradition*	GB8
Gerth, H. H., and Mills, C. Wright, eds. & trs.	*From Max Weber: Essays in Sociology*	GB13
Gilby, Thomas, ed. & tr.	*St. Thomas Aquinas: Philosophical Texts*	GB29
Grierson, Herbert, ed.	*Metaphysical Lyrics and Poems of the Seventeenth Century*	GB19
Halsband, Robert	*The Life of Lady Mary Wortley Montagu*	GB44
Heiler, Friedrich	*Prayer,* translated by Samuel McComb	GB16
Herklots, H. G. G.	*How Our Bible Came to Us*	GB4
Highet, Gilbert	*The Classical Tradition*	GB5
	Juvenal the Satirist	GB48
Kaufmann, R. J., ed.	*Elizabethan Drama*	GB63
Knox, Ronald A.	*Enthusiasm*	GB59
Langer, Susanne K., ed	*Reflections on Art*	GB60
Lewis, C. S.	*The Allegory of Love*	GB17
	A Preface to Paradise Lost	GB57
Lindsay, A. D.	*The Modern Democratic State*	GB86
Lowrie, Walter, tr.	*Kierkegaard: Christian Discourses*	GB49
Livingstone, Richard, ed. & tr.	*Thucydides: The History of the Peloponnesian War*	GB33
MacNeice, Louis, tr.	*Goethe's Faust*	GB45

GALAXY BOOKS

Malinowski, Bronislaw	*A Scientific Theory of Culture*	GB40
Matthiessen, F. O.	*The Achievement of T. S. Eliot,* third edition	GB22
Matthiessen, F. O., and Murdock, Kenneth B., eds.	*The Notebooks of Henry James*	GB61
Mills, C. Wright	*The Power Elite*	GB20
	White Collar	GB3
Muller, Herbert J.	*The Uses of the Past*	GB9
Murray, Gilbert	*The Rise of the Greek Epic*	GB41
Otto, Rudolf	*The Idea of the Holy*	GB14
Peterson, Merrill D.	*The Jefferson Image in the American Mind*	GB71
Price, Don K.	*Government and Science*	GB72
Radhakrishnan, S.	*Eastern Religions and Western Thought*	GB27
Roberts, David E.	*Existentialism and Religious Belief,* edited by Roger Hazelton	GB28
Rostovtzeff, M.	*Rome*	GB42
Russell, Bertrand	*The Problems of Philosophy*	GB21
	Religion and Science	GB50
Schorer, Mark, ed.	*Modern British Fiction*	GB64
Schumpeter, Joseph A.	*The Theory of Economic Development,* translated by Redvers Opie	GB55
Shapiro, Harry L., ed.	*Man, Culture, and Society*	GB32
Shaw, T. E., tr.	*The Odyssey of Homer*	GB2
Sinclair, John D., ed. & tr.	*Dante's Inferno*	GB65
	Dante's Purgatorio	GB66
	Dante's Paradiso	GB67
Tillich, Paul	*Love, Power and Justice*	GB38
Toynbee, Arnold J.	*A Study of History, Volume 1*	GB74
	A Study of History, Volume 2	GB75
	A Study of History, Volume 3	GB76
Turberville, A. S.	*English Men and Manners in the Eighteenth Century*	GB10
Wagenknecht, Edward, ed.	*Chaucer*	GB24
Ward, John William	*Andrew Jackson: Symbol for an Age*	GB73
Wedgwood, C. V.	*Seventeenth-Century English Literature*	GB51
Whitehead, Alfred North	*An Introduction to Mathematics*	GB18
Woodward, C. Vann	*The Strange Career of Jim Crow*	GB6
Wright, Austin, ed.	*Victorian Literature*	GB52
Young, J. Z.	*Doubt and Certainty in Science*	GB34
Zaehner, R. C.	*Mysticism Sacred and Profane*	GB56
Zimmern, Alfred	*The Greek Commonwealth*	GB62

B&T 21-501